THE PIPER IN PEACE
AND WAR

GEORGE CLARK, THE PIPER OF VIMIERA.

From a print in the possession of Major Mackay-Scobie.

THE PIPER
IN PEACE AND WAR

BY
C.A. MALCOLM, M.A., Ph.D.

WITH THE ORIGINAL FOREWORD BY
THE DUKE OF ATHOLL, K.T., G.C.V.O.

PLUS

A NEW FOREWORD BY
PIPE MAJOR ANGUS MACDONALD, M.B.E.

WITH A NEW INTRODUCTION BY
PATRICK KING

LONDON
HARDWICKE PRESS
1993

Republished 1993 by Hardwicke Press
Impact House
20 Accommodation Road
London NW11 2EP
Great Britain

First published in 1927 by John Murray Limited, London

ISBN 0-9521580-0-0

Printed in the United States of America

INTRODUCTION

When Charles Malcolm wrote *The Piper in Peace and War* in 1927, the world was indeed a different place. The British Empire still existed, and we can assume that Malcolm like many others of the period, thought it would last forever. The public's attitude towards the army was also different in those days. Loyalty to a local regiment was not unlike the modern equivalent of supporting a local football or sports team. The Scots were fiercely proud of their regiments, especially the pipers, who represented the tradition and glory of their forefathers.

The Great War of 1914-18 had not long been finished, and the horrendous casualties of that conflict had also taken it's toll of the pipers, 500 had been killed and over 600 wounded. A staggering total when you consider how few pipers there were in the whole army.

Charles Malcolm was a quiet man, an academic who spent many years of his working life at the Signet Library in Edinburgh. He enjoyed nothing more than researching the history of his native land. He was very proud of being Scottish, like most of his race, and although not a piper himself he had a grasp of how important the instrument was to his nation's history. It is said that he was deeply affected by the horrors of the Great War and the casualties sustained by pipers, and this book is in part a tribute to their memory. The author painstakingly researched each regiment, talking to many veterans, listening to anecdotes and finally building the information into what has become a valuable historical document.

There is often a temptation to edit a book which is to be reprinted. More often it is to accommodate the language of a modern readership. Charles Malcolm's book was a labour of love and must remain intact, no benefit would be gained by changing his text. This reprint is therefore an exact copy of the original including footnotes, remarks, and black and white plates.

The author lived until 1961 and for reasons unknown, never chose to update the book, even after the Second World War. At the time of his death he could not have known, thankfully, how politicians were hell bent on slowly destroying the very regimental system that made the British Army not only the envy of the world but so successful in war.

What would the author have thought of the state of the Scottish Regiments today? One can only guess. The professionalism of the Scottish soldier still exists but their numbers have dropped considerably. When this book was originally penned there were two battalions of Scots Guards and twenty battalions of Scottish infantry of the line, each one with a pipe band. Today only one battalion of Scots Guards is expected to survive and only seven Scottish regiments remain. Even these numbers are doubtful at the time of writing this introduction.

During the past thirty years successive British governments have forced amalgamation or disbandment on so many regiments that their true identities have been lost. Some have been re-amalgamated so many times there hardly seems a point to it anymore. The reader, who will become familiar with the exploits of pipers and regiments in the book, may also wish to know their fate since the text was first written. The following part of this introduction will describe the changes and list those regiments who have now sadly disappeared.

The Scottish regiments and their pipers, in the years between the two world wars, were kept busy policing the Empire and other British interests. When the Irish Free State was created in 1922, the famous Irish regiments ceased to exist as part of the British Army. The Irish pipes however, continued to be represented by the three Ulster regiments.

Soon after the Second World War the Scottish infantry, except the Scots Guards, lost their second battalions. The surplus pipers were either absorbed into the remaining pipe bands or demobbed. After 1945 the end of empire was in sight, and the regimental mergers began. In Scotland the first changes occurred when the Royal Scots Fusiliers amalgamated with the Highland Light Infantry to become the Royal Highland Fusiliers. Then it was the turn of the Seaforth and Cameron Highlanders who merged as the Queen's Own Highlanders. Unfortunately, just thirty years later, the Queen's Own Highlanders were again earmarked for amalgamation, this time with the famous Gordon Highlanders. The threat to these two great piping regiments still exists at the time of writing, and this outrageous decision, made for political and not military reasons, is being fought rigorously.

The changes were not accepted by all, and in 1968 the Cameronians (The Scottish Rifles) chose disbandment rather than amalgamation. This famous regiment was just a few years short of its three hundredth birthday.

The Territorial Army fared no better, when in 1967 the

Scottish T.A. regiments were reduced to company strength of about one hundred and twenty men each and the pipe bands disbanded. These companies, each bearing their original regimental titles, were formed into two new regiments: the 51st Highland, and 52nd Lowland Volunteers. These new regiments, which took their names from the famous 51st and 52nd Divisions, immediately formed two new pipe bands.

Two famous regiments of Scottish exiles, the London Scottish and the Liverpool Scottish, both mentioned by Charles Malcolm, were also reduced to company strength and became part of the 51st Highland Volunteers. These Territorial Army regiments were fortunate enough to keep their identities and dress. The pipers and drummers of the London Scottish kept the distinctive Hodden Grey uniform and the Liverpool Scottish kept their Forbes tartan. Both regiments played a very important role in the 51st Highland Pipe Band. Since the Second World War four London Scottish pipe majors were appointed personal pipers to Her Majesty, The Queen Mother, a rare and special honour for a Territorial Army unit. In 1992 both the London and Liverpool Scottish companies were again reorganised in yet another bout of outrageous political cost cutting. The London Scottish became a company in the newly formed London Regiment, together with the London Irish Rifles, who also retained their pipers, and two English regiments, The Queens and Royal Fusiliers. The Liverpool Scottish became a company of the Kings Regiment (Liverpool and Manchester) T.A. and their pipe band lives on through the Regimental Association.

The Lovat Scouts were another unit that managed to survive, although only as a company, and are part of the

51st Highland Volunteers. The Scottish Horse and the Tyneside Scottish were less fortunate and have long since been disbanded.

There have been some improvements to army piping since Charles Malcolm wrote his book. In the 1950's the Ministry of Defence finally recognised the importance of piping in the army by creating a new post, currently titled Director of Army Bagpipe Music. The Director, the only commissioned officer piper in the British Army is in charge of the Army Piping School in historic Edinburgh Castle. He is also responsible for piping and drumming in the entire army.

The quality of pipers in the modern army is excellent and their role in the regiments are every bit as important today as they ever were. A new foreword has been written specially for this reprint by Pipe Major Angus MacDonald, M.B.E. of the Scots Guards. Angus MacDonald is one of the top pipers of this generation and is known throughout the piping world for his accomplished playing. Indeed, the quality of army pipers as musicians is probably better now than it has ever been.

When Charles Malcolm wrote his book the memories of the First World War, Boer War and the North West Frontier were still fresh in peoples minds. These were probably the last episodes in history when pipers were expected to lead an attack as a matter of course. Times have changed and the chances of pipers playing troops into action today are quite remote. Modern war does not allow such deeds, although there were eyewitness accounts of pipers in action during the Second World War.

Pipers of the Scottish regiments in the post-1945 world played their part in all the major hot spots including

Palestine, Korea, Kenya and Cyprus. In 1967, the pipe major of the Argyll and Sutherland Highlanders played the battalion back into the Crater district of Aden after several soldiers had been killed. In the continuing troubles of Northern Ireland the regimental pipe bands are deployed as infantry soldiers as well as musicians. During the Falklands War in 1982, pipers and drummers of the 2nd Battalion, Scots Guards, fought the Argentines with machine guns and sustained casualties. In 1991 during the Gulf War, the pipers and drummers of several Scottish battalions took their instruments to the deserts of the Middle East. The pipe band of the Royal Scots Dragoon Guards formed a tank squadron and fought their way into Iraq.

It can safely be said that as long as Scottish regiments remain part of the British Army there will be pipers. The piper is representative of the Scottish soldier, a warrior who has earned the respect of the world, both in peace and in war.

PATRICK KING
London, 1993.

A NEW FOREWORD
By PIPE MAJOR ANGUS MACDONALD, M.B.E.

I am honoured to be able to make my own small contribution to a book written about pipers. The author, Charles Malcolm, was a Scotsman who knew the importance of pipes to his country.

When I joined the Scots Guards as a young piper very little had changed in the way of pipers' duties as described in this book. Today though, now that the regiments have been cut down in size, pipers cover a wider range of activities from driving tanks to serving in the defence platoons and working in intelligence sections as well as being medical orderlies and stretcher bearers.

As a former piper in the army, I know what pipes mean to the troops in the regiment. Many a Guardsman has told me how much better he marched behind the pipes and drums as compared to the flute band or the regimental brass band. There is something exciting about the pipes that stirs every true Scot, and many other races too.

I have been fortunate to have travelled and played all over the world. In my experience the sight and sound of pipers from Scottish regiments have always been well received. They have been, and still are some of the best ambassadors this country has.

Once whilst on tour, in a country which shall remain anonymous, I was approached by a fellow who played in a pipe band. He asked me how I tuned the ban and I explained that the pipers blew individually for five minutes and then blew collectively for another five or ten minutes. I would then make minor adjustments to drones and chanters after which we would play again collectively, re-tuning once more before the performance.

"That sounds a complicated system of tuning to me" he said, so I asked him how his band tuned up—to which he replied, "We just congregate in the band hut and drink until it sounds good!"

Although written many years ago, this book is a good read and a tribute to those many generations of pipers who have served their country well.

ANGUS MACDONALD
May 1993.

FOREWORD

By THE DUKE OF ATHOLL, K.T., G.C.V.O., C.B.

MR CHARLES A. MALCOLM has asked me to write an introduction to his book *The Piper in Peace and War*. Every one who reads the book will admit that Mr Malcolm has taken an extraordinary amount of pains to collect his data, and that he has written a book which will be read with much interest by those who are fond of the pipes.

Tradition, unless set down on paper, is apt to become lost or inaccurate. It is well, therefore, that these traditions should be handed down in writing by those who are capable of doing so, and I think no one will deny Mr Malcolm's capability and zeal.

Probably there were never more pipers in existence than there were during the Great War, and never at any time were their services more appreciated. No good pipe band ever belonged to a bad regiment, and to those who understand the pipes it is a simple thing to judge of those who follow them. In times of peace the pipers keep the men together. Every individual man in the regiment takes a pride in the band because it is distinctive and of his own nation, proud and full of courage, but not aggressive, sometimes sad but always appealing.

The wide extension of pipe music in these days, when every mining village in the south of Scotland and every tourist resort in the north has its local pipe band, may have increased the number of pipers, but I doubt if it has improved their quality. But few of the modern airs have the special character or the distinction of the old music, and the old tunes, when played, have little difficulty in holding their own. While it is everything to have good band pipers in military units, the local bands are doing much to eliminate the old individual player, who was a musician first and a bandsman second. Some of the best pipers that I used to know in the old days—men with beautiful fingering and who put their whole soul into a piobaireachd— were indifferent players of marches. While the old airs are not being lost, for they are written down, very few of the modern pipers have a good repertory. Many of the best of them seem to have a sort of musical circle, like that on a roulette table. You can pick any number you like so long as it is shown on the wheel. These are their competition tunes, but outside that you must not and cannot go. Publishers, presumably for financial reasons, appear to be more interested in publishing the new tunes than the old ones, and in pushing their sale. The result is that

many young pipers do not know the grand old
tunes, but are experts at inferior modern ones,
and if, by chance, one strikes their fancy, we hear
that tune and no other till we are sick to death of
it. The old tunes, in their names and characters,
remind us of our hills and glens, of our history, of
brave men, of national sorrow and of times of
national joy. Can that be said of most of the
new ones?

While we have splendid pipe bands in the
Army, they are bound, for purposes of playing
together, to be stereotyped. One always feels
when they are playing that the pipers have
one eye on the Drum-Major in front and the
other on the Regimental Sergeant-Major behind.
I remember one young regimental piper, when
checked for indifferent playing, saying "My
thochts were on the counter march." Under such
conditions, it is difficult to have one's mind up in
the heavenly sphere of music.

We find the same thing in Highland dancing,
where large numbers are taught by the same
instructor at the same time. The boys at Scottish
Institute Schools dance beautifully. They all
skip at the same time in the same way and to the
same height. As a gymnastic or ballet display it
is fine. As Highland dancing the soul and joy is
gone out of it. When watching such displays or
competitions, I sometimes feel more joy in the
one that has strayed that in the ninety-nine that
have not.

In other words, the general extension of piping, while it may have done much to popularise the instrument, has not improved things from a musical point of view, and the efforts of those who love pipe music should be used towards maintaining standard and character rather than in increasing numbers. That Mr Malcolm should remind us, therefore, of the days that are gone is all to our advantage.

ATHOLL.

September 1927.

PREFACE

IT is not the purpose of the writer to treat of the various forms of bagpipe used in the past by the different nations of the world, but to trace as far as possible the work in peace and war of the skilful and intrepid masters of the "great war pipe of the north."

It may be noted, however, that the oldest memorial to a piper is not one to any distinguished Highlander or Borderer, to a M'Crimmon, a M'Intyre, a Mackay, a MacArthur, a Habbie Simpson, or a Hastie, but to an unknown Roman legionary, a member of the Roman Army of Occupation in Britain. His statue occupied a niche in the great Roman Wall from the Tyne to the Solway. Though Time has dealt gently with the effigies of this piper, it is to be regretted that it has not left his pipes in such a state as to enable us to trace the details of their construction. The bag is there, but not the drones. Yet here is evidence, though all the historians are silent on the point, that the legions of Cæsar marched to the strains of the pipes, and that the piper was a person of some consequence in the great armies of Rome. It is strange to reflect that, just as in later times the Scottish bagpipe has contributed to victory, so the armies of Imperial Rome seem to have been led to conquest by pipe music.

This attempt to rescue what might have been forgotten and to focus what has been stated in various regimental records, newspapers, and public speeches, imperfect as it is, would not have been possible but for the kindness of officers, non-commissioned officers, and men of H.M. Forces of Great Britain, Ireland, and the Dominions overseas, whose names are too numerous to mention; officials of the War Office, Public Record Office, and Canadian Headquarters. In particular I owe thanks to Colonel John Murray, D.S.O., for many helpful suggestions and reports; to Major Ian H. Mackay-Scobie who, besides revising proofs, lent prints and communicated numerous interesting facts; and to Mr Kennedy Stewart, M.A., and my brother Mr Peter Malcolm, M.A., for their labours in the revision and the correction of the typescript and of the proofs of this book.

CONTENTS

PART I

THE PIPER IN PEACE AND WAR

PART II

RECORDS OF THE PIPERS

CONTENTS

PART III

LIST OF ILLUSTRATIONS

PART I
THE PIPER IN PEACE AND WAR

CHAPTER I

(1) THE ARMY AND THE PIPER

EVERYBODY knows the piper; his dark green doublet, glossy black shoulder belt, and debonair bearing are familiar to all. Supplied with a uniform of finer material and better fit than that of the private soldier,[1] the piper is expected to set an example to the regiment. As a soldier he provides a standard of excellence in all the duties pertaining to the profession of arms. In the 2nd Battn. Cameron Highlanders just before the war every piper in the battalion was a marksman, and three of them were "best shot" in their respective companies. For it must be borne in mind that, though the pipers form a band, they are all members of some company in the battalion. They are relieved of certain duties which fall to the lot of the ordinary "duty" soldier, but in all regiments, with the exception of the Scots Guards, they have to perform certain fatigues. The Guards are provided with the most expensive instruments and dress, have no duties but to provide music, and enjoy the highest consideration of the officers of the regiment. With these advantages it is little wonder if they consider themselves the "best-off" soldiers in the Service.

[1] Except on ceremonial occasions pipers of all regiments, save the Scots Guards, now wear khaki tunics—a *post* war alteration.

Scottish regiments have had pipers as a rule from their formation, but for many years they were not recognised by the War Office.

(2) STATUS OF THE ARMY PIPER

The solitary piper remaining of the 36 pipers of Mackay's Highlanders, who blew, long and loudly, a note of welcome to Hepburn on the great war-pipe of the north, had to hide his noble instrument on all future inspection days as piper in The Royal Scots. The pipers were not dressed in the kilt but in the garb of the regiment. This is proved by a glance at the painting of some privates and pipers at Tangiers in 1684.

The officers of this, the oldest regiment in the world, were (and are) proud of their pipers, at one time (17th century) ranking the pipe-major as an officer; but they were compelled in 1769 by an edict of G.H.Q. to cancel the appointment of their pipe-major and drum-major. Protest on the part of two successive colonels of "The Royals," the Marquess of Lorne and Lord Adam Gordon, was quite in vain. To circumvent Headquarters, pipers were enlisted as pipers, but their names often appeared in the Rolls as "drummers." Thus pipers obtained the extra 1d. per day paid to these soldiers. In the Scottish Horse and the Lovat Scouts prior to 1914 pipers were "trumpeters." In the early Muster Rolls are officers, sergeants, and *drummers*. Thus disguised, a M'Crimmon appears in the original lists of the

Black Watch and in those of the 92nd, Cameron, Fassifern's favourite piper.

What would the old Highland Chiefs, who placed the piper fourth on the Roll of their hierarchy, have said on learning the clandestine nature of the gifted piper's army position?

The piper, who, in all clan battles, in all national conflicts, had led the van, found, at least on one occasion, his premier place denied by a drummer who insisted on leading. The piper then asked an officer: "Will a fellow that beats a sheepskin with two sticks gang in front o' me who am a museecian?"

The officer had to decide in favour of the drummer on the ground that he was officially recognised while the piper was not.

The earliest regimental pipe - major, whose name has come down to the present day, is Alexander Wallace, Pipe-Major of The Royal Scots in 1679. Adriel Duran who succeeded Wallace in "The Royals" has more resemblance to a Frenchman than a Scot, but both Wallace and he were "Officers."

Owing to the proscription of the highland dress and of most of the highland customs after Culloden, pipe playing declined, and pipers were so difficult to obtain that we find officers who raised regiments in the eighteenth century advertising for pipers. When Captain Duncan Campbell was getting in soldiers for the Duke of Argyll's Highlanders in 1794, he was concerned about the quota of pipers. "If you can meet with one or two good pipers," he wrote to a friend, "handsome fellows and steady, you might go as far as thirty guineas for each." This bounty, offered by a captain of the 3rd Foot (Scots) Guards at a time when men were flocking to the Colours for a "whack" at the French, suggests the scarcity of pipers.

The brilliant work of the pipers of the Fraser Highlanders at Quebec; of the 71st at Porto Novo and at Vimiera; of the 42nd, 79th, and 92nd at Waterloo—not to mention the numerous episodes in the Peninsula—had no meaning for Headquarters staff at Whitehall, whose sole query on seeing pipers with a regiment was: "Show me your authority for having pipers." The zeal of some of these officers in "demobilising" the pipers was amazing. In 1850 the 91st Argylls, who maintained an excellent pipe band, on being inspected prior to leaving for South Africa, were ordered by Major-General Browne, the inspecting officer, to leave their instruments behind—there being no authority for the regiment having pipers. That order was obeyed, but the officers, on landing at the Cape, sent home for a fresh outfit. In 1852 it was the turn of the 92nd (Gordons) to come under the inspector's eye. It was a most fortunate matter for Highland regiments as events proved. For the inspecting officer, Major-General J. E. C. Napier, on reporting the irregularity of the 92nd having pipers, received the following sharp reproof from the commander - in - chief, the Duke of Wellington : — " I am surprised that an officer who has seen, as you must have seen, the gallant deeds performed by the Highland regiments, in which their pipers played so important a part, should make such a report."

Probably it was due to this that a Horse Guards Order, dated 11th February 1854, was issued, intimating that: "The 42nd, 71st, 72nd, 74th, 78th, 79th, 92nd, and 93rd Highlanders have been allowed one pipe-major and five pipers each which are to be posted to the Service companies, when regiments are ordered to proceed abroad."

It will be noticed from the above that the 73rd (Perthshire) (now the 2nd Battn. Royal Highlanders), the 75th (Stirlingshire) (now the 1st Battn. the Gordon Highlanders), and the 91st (now the 1st Battn. Argyll and Sutherland Highlanders) are not included; these units were then Scottish only in name. Lowland units were ignored. The 90th, which was a light infantry regiment, probably deemed pipe music unsuitable to the short, smart step of light infantry, as it made no use of pipe music until 1882, when it was joined to the 26th (Cameronians) as the 2nd Battn. Scottish Rifles. In 1858 the 25th (King's Own Borderers) are taken to task, but on the colonel assuring Horse Guards that authority for pipers in the regiment was "lost in time," they were permitted to "carry on," but "on the footing that the pipers are classed as bandsmen—not drummers—and their expense borne by the regiment." It is odd to find the 26th being asked in 1863 for their authority to have pipers and being allowed three. (What would have been said if the officers who were questioned had shown the picture purporting to have been painted in 1713 of their regimental piper?)

The Scots Guards were also ordered in 1855 or 1856 to "drop" their pipers, but on their colonel — the Duke of Cambridge — protesting, they were permitted to remain as part of the establishment.

The Army Act of 1881 made no difference to Scots Lowland regiments in regard to their pipers. Highland regiments could always rely, since 1854, on having a complement of five pipers and a pipe-major maintained out of the public purse, but the officers of Lowland corps (except the Scots Guards) had to provide for these from their own pockets.

On 24th April 1882 the colonel of The Royal Scots tried to persuade the War Office to place all Scottish troops on the same footing regarding pipers as the Highland kilted corps, but failed, as the following letter shows :—

HORSE GUARDS, WAR OFFICE, S.W.,
23rd May 1882.

SIR,—I have the honour, by desire of the Field-Marshal Commanding-in-Chief, to acknowledge the receipt of your letter of the 24th ulto., submitting an application from the Officer Commanding the 1st Battalion, Lothian Regiment, for a Sergeant-Piper and Pipers to be borne on the establishment of that battalion, and to acquaint you that the Secrètary of State for War declines to sanction an increase to the establishment to the corps, but that H.R.H. will approve of a number of men not exceeding five being employed as pipers on the distinct understanding that no extra expense either for pay or clothing is thereby incurred to the public.—I have the honour to be, etc.,

R. H. HAWLEY, D.A.G.

The General Officer
  Commanding at Malta.

This Order, which continued the old inequality of treatment by refusing funds for pipers in Lowland regiments and permitting them for Highland was rescinded in 1918, and in consequence Scots and Irish regiments (except the Royal Ulster Rifles) have pipers on their establishment. Officers may have as many pipers as they please, but Highland regiments must pay for all above the number of six. The extra men are called " acting " pipers, and on field days and in time of war they return to the ranks as " duty " men.

It is not quite clear when exactly the pipers of Lowland regiments first adopted Highland dress. If the painting reproduced in Carter's *History* is genuine, the Cameronians had their pipers in Highland garb as far back as 1713.[1] The pipers of the Scots Guards alone wear blue coats with silver buttons arranged in two rows tapering in from the shoulders to the waist like those on the general's dress coat.

In the Highland regiments, which (with the notable exception of the Black Watch) were of later formation, the kilt was always worn by the pipers, unless ordered otherwise by the " Horse Guards." The green doublet only came into general use in 1856. Before that year the Cameron Highlanders alone had, since 1840, their pipers clothed with green doublets. According to Colonel Greenhill-Gardyne this colour was adopted by the Camerons because their uniforms had green

[1] From certain prints of the period it is clear that from 1840 the 21st (R.S.F.), the 25th (Borderers) and 26th (Cameronians) had their pipers in kilts ; those of the 21st and 25th having the Royal Stewart and the 26th the Douglas pattern.

facings, and the other Highland regiments copied the doublets of the Cameron pipers.   There, however, the Camerons were merely following the fashion of an older (disbanded) regiment— the Atholl Highlanders, raised by the fourth Duke of Atholl in 1777, the uniform of which corps was, for the rank and file, red jackets and "Universal" tartan kilt, and for the pipers and drummers green jackets with red stripes in the tartan kilt.   When the officers of the Sutherland Highlanders heard of the new style of doublet during the Crimean War, they remonstrated with their pipe-major on his want of "swagger," and assured him he would have to put on a good deal more with the new doublet.   A print of the year 1850 shows the piper of the 74th, now the 2nd Battn. Highland Light Infantry, wearing a dark green tartan doublet of the same pattern as his kilt.

Whatever pattern of dicing may embellish the bonnet of the regiment, the piper's bonnet is always plain; and only the pipers of the Black Watch now wear the high ostrich-feathered bonnet of the Highland regiments. This was not always the case, for until 1856 the piper's headdress was identical with that of the rank and file. Spats were first worn by Highland soldiers in 1856, each regiment having its own peculiar fashion.   The shoulder belt, on the other hand, goes back to the days when the trusty claymore was supported by this part of the soldier's equipment.   In 1855 all ranks, except the officers and pipers of Highland regiments, were ordered to wear waist belt alone, and to leave off the shoulder belt. The belts of the officers are white, those of the pipers black.

The piper of the present day in his kilt, green doublet, glengarry—with two blackcock feathers (worn when in review order), his tartan plaid, his patent-leather shoulder belt ornamented with silver, his jewelled dirk and sgian-dubh, is a very picturesque figure.

Admission to a regimental pipe band is not granted to every candidate. Many regimental pipers come from the Highlands,[1] and many from Falkirk and its neighbourhood, where there would seem to be special opportunities for learning to play the instrument. Certain schools, too, teach the bagpipe, and contribute a quota of pipers to the army. It often happens that a soldier enlists without any knowledge of the pipes, but having a taste for the instrument, applies for admission as a learner. If he shows aptitude, he is given the opportunity of daily practice, escaping all parades and guard duties. When he appears to the pipe-major to be sufficiently skilled to fill a place in the band he is brought before the colonel, or some officer entrusted by him with the duty of examining candidates, for the pipe-major is not usually vested with authority to admit aspirants to membership of the pipe band. The colonel, or his delegate, orders the piper to strike up certain tunes, and he is accepted or rejected, as a rule, according to the merit of his musical performance ; but not always. Some commanding officers have strong views on nationality. They consider Scottish

---

[1] In olden days Sutherland and Skye were the best recruiting grounds for army pipers.

birth as essential in a piper. A young London Scot, whose parents were both Scots, and who was himself an excellent piper, was denied a place in the pipe band of a battalion of the Camerons because his speech was pure Cockney. The South African Scottish had an Englishman in the ranks who was barred from the pipe band for purely racial reasons. Not all colonels, however, take this narrow view. One in command of a battalion of the Argyll and Sutherland Highlanders asked a young soldier piper to what part of Scotland he belonged. He received the answer, "Liverpool, sir," which delighted him so much that he at once admitted the friendly "alien."

A great change has taken place in recent years in the attitude of the Scot towards English pipers, and there are at the present time some excellent pipers from south of the Tweed in the army. All that the men in the ranks care about is whether the piper can play. They often have no preference for music specially intended for the pipes, and a piper who can adapt a music hall melody to his instrument is frequently approved of by the soldiers. The Gordon Highlanders once had such a piper. His name was, let us say, Smith, and he had enlisted as a private in that distinguished Highland regiment, although he was of English birth and upbringing. He had fallen in love with the pipes, and, having learned in barracks to play, he became a member of the pipe band. Very soon his faculty for rendering popular tunes and pantomime songs on the pipes made him a favourite with the men of the regiment, so that small parties on the march with only one piper

always wanted Smith for that piper. Now the
other pipers regarded such a use of the bagpipe
as desecration, and the lot of Smith as a member
of the pipe band became a hard one. The judg-
ment of the men, however, was endorsed at many
Highland gatherings and piping competitions
where Smith invariably carried off the principal
prizes for marches, strathspeys, and pibrochs.
But this did not tend to ameliorate his situation
in relation to the other pipers. From the pipe-
major down they showed a most unsportsmanlike
spirit towards their English comrade. So intoler-
able did their persecution become, that in the
end Smith deserted from the regiment in Ireland.

Many years afterwards the Gordons moved
into a hill station in India where they had for
neighbours a battalion of the Cameron Highlanders.
The customary hospitality was extended to the
newcomers. The sergeants of the Camerons
entertained the sergeants of the Gordons, and
there, one of the senior sergeants of the Gordons
recognised in Pipe-Major MacGregor of the
Camerons the long-lost Piper Smith. Explana-
tions followed, and the sergeant promised to say
nothing about his discovery, at the same time
assuring the pipe-major that there was little
chance of his being recognised, as there were
very few men left in the regiment who had known
him.

On the very next evening, however, the
officers of the Camerons had the officers of the
Gordons to dinner. There the sole remaining
officer of Piper Smith's period, Major " Black,"
recognised the pipe-major as he marched round

the table playing and when he drank the customary glass. Next morning the major called on the sergeant to discuss the situation, and concluded the conversation with " No, we'll say nothing to anyone." " Did you speak to Smith, sir ? " asked the sergeant. " Oh, no ; he seemed to be doing very well, and I was very glad to see it ; but it is better not to *know* that he is a deserter."

Before a piper can become a pipe-major— " sergeant-piper " is the official rank — he must satisfy the authorities of his ability as a composer, and a player of pibrochs, marches, and strathspeys. According to the reports of competent judges, good pibroch players are very rare. The "pibroch" may be called the classical form of bagpipe music, and the piper who studies the pibroch often despises the march and strathspey as inferior branches of the piper's art, although he admits that, to the unsophisticated crowd and private soldier, they are perhaps more pleasing. Pipe-Major W. Ross, 2nd Scots Guards, one of the most distinguished pipers of recent times, is the official authority on army pipe music. Pipe-Major Ross is in charge of the Army Piping School, to which pipers who wish to become pipe-majors usually go for instruction and examination.

The Army pipe-major has a grievance : his status is far from satisfactory, inasmuch as he must always remain a sergeant in the battalion, while the bandmaster ranks as a warrant officer, and the drum-major takes charge of the brass band and the pipe band on parade. There are no grades of pipe-majors. He can never become a warrant officer like the bandmaster ;

yet the brass band is dropped in time of war,
while the pipers go where the battalion goes and
are a part of the organisation for victory.

This "subjection" of the pipe-major has prevented many an excellent piper from accepting
appointment as "sergeant-piper" and is thus a
handicap in many instances on a battalion pipe
band.

CHAPTER II

THE PIPER IN BARRACKS AND CAMP

DAY in day out, from morning to night, the soldier is dependent on the piper. Not only does the piper provide musical entertainment in the intervals of relaxation, but he rouses the soldier from bed in the morning, calls him to his meals during the day, and sends him to sleep at night. The soldier opens his eyes in the morning to the strains of, "Hey, Johnnie Cope, are ye waukin' yet!" Other appropriate tunes, such as "Brose and Butter," or, "Bannocks o' Barley" call him to breakfast and dinner. "O, Jock, are ye glad ye listed," or, "Bundle and Go" may be the summons to tea.

"Highland Laddie" warns the Royal Scot to dress for parade. In another regiment it may be "Pibroch o' Donuil Dubh," or, "Bonnie Dundee," that conveys the same message. On the parade ground the "Assembly" of the clan to which the regiment belongs, musters the men to their places. The Seaforths, being Mackenzies, fall in to the strains of "The Mackenzie Highlanders," the Argyll and Sutherland Highlanders to "The Campbells are Comin'," the Camerons and others to "Pibroch o' Donuil Dubh."

At six o'clock or half-past six in the evening, once or twice a week, the full pipe band in spring

16

and summer plays "Retreat." Pipers and drummers march up and down the barrack square for half-an-hour playing for the entertainment of the men. The tunes usually selected at this time are those which are most popular with the rank and file, and the custom is the occasion of daily delight to many soldiers.

The piper's work is by no means over yet. The piper on duty warns the officers to dress for mess. Then while they dine he provides music, and at the wine stage the colonel sends for the piper, who has hitherto been marching up and down outside, to enter. Round and round the mess table goes the piper playing a march, which, merging into a strathspey, finishes off with a reel.

If the colonel is an enthusiast and knows the piper to be competent for such a difficult perform-ance, he may ask for a pibroch, but that will be *caviare* to most of the guests. In the 2nd Battn. Argyll and Sutherland Highlanders the officers, continuing a pious custom of their predecessors, the 93rd (Sutherland) Highlanders, have a lament played for Fallen Comrades. With eyes down-cast and head supported on hand, the lament is listened to in perfect silence. This ceremony never fails to impress the guest who happens to witness it for the first time.

A glass of whisky or of wine is handed to the piper as guerdon by the colonel at the end of the performance. The piper salutes, says "Slainte" (Health), and drains the glass.

On "Guest" nights, the pipe-major and three or four selected pipers are present. The programme

B

usually consists of three "sets"—each set containing a march, strathspey and reel. Between two sets the pipe-major plays a pibroch, then gets a *cuaich* of wine or whisky, which he drinks to the health of all present. Usually each captain has his coat-of-arms emblazoned on the banner of his company piper, the reverse side bearing the regimental crest and Battle Honours. At the end of the musical entertainment the pipers depart.

"First Post" is sounded at 9.30, and "Last Post" at 10, but once or oftener a week there is a turn-out for "Tattoo" at 9.30 o'clock. As the word implies, this is a signal given by drum-beat to warn all soldiers to repair to their quarters. While the pipes play the warning each man in the regiment, not on duty or on leave, is parading for the Roll Call by the sergeants on duty.

Finally at 10.15 the pipes convey the order "Lights Out." Sharp to the minute the pipers' benediction, "Sleep, Dearie, Sleep,"[1] wails out on the night. The men of the Scots regiments have named the tune "Soldier, lie down on your wee pickle strae." Although this is the most popular air for "Lights Out," the Black Watch and the Scots Guards[2] have "Donal Blue," and some others "Fingall's Weeping."

The piper's duties are not exactly the same in all regiments, some having a longer and some a shorter programme than that indicated.

The "Prisoners' Call" is given in The Royal Scots and in the 1st Battn. Gordon Highlanders by the pipers striking up "A Man's a Man for a'

---

[1] An old Gaelic air : "Caidel mo ghaol"—"Sleep my Love."
[2] Scots Guardsmen call it : "Oh ! good Lord ! my rifle's rusty."

that,"[1] to which immortal sentiment the soldier has
added "Though he get fifty days' C.B."   In other
regiments this tune is strictly forbidden, as is also
"Lochaber No More," the "Lights Out" tune
of The Royal Scots alone.   In other regiments
than The Royal Scots this fine old tune is only
used at funerals, its appropriateness for these sad
occasions explaining why it is barred at all other
times.

The idea, common among civilians, that
Highland regiments are the most enthusiastic
supporters of the bagpipe, and that all the best
pipers are to be found in their bands, is not quite
correct.   The regiment to which most good pipers
would like to go is probably the Scots Guards.
There they have nothing to do but play their
pipes and be idolised by the Londoners, whereas
in Scots regiments of the line they have certain
"fatigues" to perform.   Moreover, the officers
of the Guards make much more of their pipers
than do the officers of Highland regiments.   Even
the officers of Lowland regiments are said to be
more lavish in their provision for the pipe band
than their comrades of the Highland regiments.

Much depends on the taste of the officers in
pipe music.   Where the officers are not much
interested, the pipe-major, or "pipie" as he is
familiarly styled, will lay down the law as to the
programme of music; and the men may be regaled
with Scots airs not recognised as pipe tunes,
and even by pantomime songs neatly turned
to the use of the expressive pipe!   Such pipers
are regarded by many soldiers as first class.

[1] An old Gaelic melody : "The Black Lad, my darling."

Where, on the other hand, the officers have a knowledge of pipe music, such liberties are never permitted. More than one O.C., for example, has banned "Annie Laurie," and, notwithstanding its place in the repertoire of the oldest regiment of the line, "A Man's a Man for a' that" is forbidden in certain other regiments. In times past the Camerons did not allow their pipers to play "The Campbells are Comin'," nor would the Seaforths reciprocally permit theirs to play "The March of the Cameron Men."

Progressive pipe-majors in pre-war days did not welcome the presence among the officers of the sons of former officers, because they invariably demanded the tunes which their fathers had listened to, whereas "pipie" was anxious to introduce new airs. One cannot help sympathising with the officer who was conserving the traditions of the regiment; but time brings changes no matter what efforts may be made to prevent them.

In the eighteenth and first half of the nineteenth century pipers played without any drum accompaniment. In some corps each company marched or doubled past the saluting base to the marching or the charging tune of the battalion played by the piper of the company. Later this was altered, so that the pipers of all the companies, with the drummers, stationed opposite the saluting base, act as one band while the companies march or double past.

The charging tune to which a regiment doubles past on parade, and to which they double into action, is a matter of regimental taste. While some are satisfied with any strathspey, others tenaciously hold to one, as, for example, the Seaforth Highlanders, whose "Cabar Feidh" (Deer's Horns) is famous. The Camerons have "Because he was a Bonnie Lad," and the Gordons "The Haughs of Cromdale." The "Monymusk" of The Royal Scots is an old favourite pipe tune, and the Royal Scots Fusiliers' "Cutty's Wedding" was popular with the French villagers, and with a certain British General during the war.

Every Scots regiment marches into barracks or camp to a tune which never varies, "Scotland the Brave," "The Campbells are Comin'," "Pibroch o' Donuil Dubh" being favourites.

The most extraordinary of all is the "Black Bear" played by the pipes and drums of the 1st Battn. Cameronians. When the bass drum sounds a double beat there is a pause and the battalion breaks into a cheer, after which the pipe band continues.

CHAPTER III

THE BAGPIPE IN BATTLE

THE earliest Scottish record of pipers accompanying troops into battle occurs in the archives of the Chiefs of Menzies. Mention is made there of the hereditary pipers of the clan . . . the M'Intyres, some of whom accompanied the Clan Menzies to the Battle of Bannockburn. One of the most highly prized heirlooms of the clan is a bagpipe played by one of their pipers on that great day. The evidence for the presence of pipers at Bannockburn is entirely traditional. Robert Burns, an admirer of pipe music, wrote the immortal "Scots Wha Hae" to the tune of "Hey Tutti Taiti," which, tradition says, was the tune played at Bannockburn. Neither Barbour in *The Bruce*, nor Buchanan in his *History*, alludes to the instrument although others are mentioned. This negative evidence does not, however, carry very much weight, as the greatest animosity existed in Barbour's and in Buchanan's days between Highlander and Lowlander. Only their common danger had brought the two races together in the time of Robert the Bruce. The Lowland historian would not deign to notice the barbarous equipment of the Highlander, and the Highlander was not in the habit of committing his annals to writing. Tradition was served in the Highlands by recitation of the deeds of one generation by the next, and by all succeeding.

Nearly a hundred years later than Bannock-burn, in 1411, Donald of the Isles, with 10,000 men, was defeated at Harlaw by Alexander Stewart, "The Wolf of Badenoch," in what has been described by a high authority as "the bloodiest battle ever fought in Scotland." Of the presence of pipers at this battle there is again no documentary evidence, but one of the oldest pipe tunes, "The Battle of Harlaw," if not coeval with the battle, was probably composed not long after. Almost all, if not all, the martial music of the pipes commemorating an event in the history of the people has been produced by a musician under the influence of the excitement aroused by the event.

Sir Walter Scott's description of the battle on the North Inch of Perth in 1396 may here be recalled. At a certain stage of the fight the pipers, who had been stimulating the clans to feats of desperate valour and endurance, threw aside their instruments, and rushing at one another with their daggers, "the piper of Clan Quhele was almost instantly slain, and he of Clan Chattan mortally wounded. The latter, nevertheless, again grasped his instrument, and the pibroch of the clan yet poured its expiring notes over the Clan Chattan, while the dying minstrel had breath to inspire it." Scott further states that the Feadan Dubh, or Black Chanter, which the piper of Clan Chattan used, is in the possession of Cluny MacPherson, the chief of his clan.

The demand for pipers by officers commanding

Scottish battalions in 1914 had its counterpart as early as 1641, when the Earl of Lothian in a letter to his father, the Earl of Ancrum, after reporting the progress made in recruiting, proceeds, " We are well provyded with pypers. I have one for every company in my regiment, and I think they are as good as drummers" (*Ancrum and Lothian Correspondence*, quoted by A. W. Inglis). When Alexander MacNaughton raised his two hundred Highland bowmen for service against the French in 1627, the chronicler was careful to note the names of the two pipers, " Allester Caddell " and " William Steel " (*Highland Papers*, vol. ii., *Scot. Hist. Soc.*, 2nd ser., vol. v., p. 115).

Long before that year Highland and Lowland pipers were serving in France, Germany, Holland, and Norway. The regiments of the Scots Brigade which served on the Continent from 1582 to 1782 had pipers in plenty. One of their pipe tunes, "The Lowlands of Holland," attained a wide popularity, but the music has unfortunately been lost. More famous still was the " Scots March," which, played over all France and Germany, is said to have struck terror to the hearts of the enemy wherever it was heard. Now known as " Dumbarton's Drums," it is the regimental tune of The Royal Scots, the modern representatives of the Scots Brigade.

In Grant's *Memorials of Sir J. Hepburn*, p. 231, an account is given of the transference of the Scots Brigade, which had fought under Gustavus, to the service of France : " After the battle of Nordlingen (1634) the remnants of the Scottish regiments were placed under the

command of Duke Bernard of Saxe Weimar. . . .
When the agreement had been arranged between
Sweden and France, it was decided that Duke
Bernard's troops should be taken into French pay ;
and shortly afterwards a junction was formed at
Landau between the Duke's forces and the French
troops which were under the command of Marshal
de la Force and Sir John Hepburn.

" The foot consisted almost entirely of Scotsmen, and were all that remained of the thirteen
gallant regiments which had served so long and so
bravely under Gustavus. Among these veterans
were the remnants of Hepburn's own old regiment and the *one remaining company* of Mackay's
Highlanders.

"All greeted their old commander with ac-
clamation and joy, by beating the 'Scottish
March' as he approached, while a deafening
cheer rang along their sunburnt lines, and the
last solitary piper of Mackay's Highlanders blew
long and loudly a note of welcome on the great
war-pipe of the north. And as they all wished
to take service under him (Hepburn) in France,
the whole were incorporated into one corps, to
be styled in future ' *Le Régiment d'Hébron.*' " [1]

Later Hepburn's regiment became known as
the Douglas Regiment, and Dumbarton's, the
Earl of Dumbarton being the brother of Douglas,
the former colonel. From him the regimental
march-past tune got its name " Dumbarton's
Drums," and it is significant of the importance
of the pipe band that the name of this tune
was sometimes applied to the regiment.

[1] So called owing to the difficulty of Scottish pronunciation.

A minor incident in the wars of Gustavus
Adolphus was the destruction of a small force
of Caithness and Sutherland men on their march
through Norway to join the Swedish commander.
Of this ill-fated expedition there remains a side
drum in the Museum of Uppsala, and a piece
of music still famous in Norway, entitled the
"Sinclair March." This was the tune played
by the pipers who led the unfortunate little
company of three hundred Scots.

The pipers of Mackay's Highlanders received
in pay twelve Rex dollars a month, a sum equal
to £3, 0s. 9d. in 1630, to £10, 12s. 6d. in 1880,
and surely something like £300 a year at the
present *post-bellum* rates. It is hardly likely
that the rate was so high in the Douglas Regiment, and The Royal Scots certainly did not
enjoy such a munificent scale of remuneration.

Pipers were, as a matter of course, attached
to the army of the Marquess of Montrose. Their
best known tunes were named "Montrose's
March" and "The Highlanders' March." The
opposing Lowlanders had also their pipers, whose
principal marching air was named in compliment
to their leader, "Leslie's March." At the battle
of Philiphaugh, it is said that one of Montrose's
pipers, while playing close to the banks of the
Ettrick, was shot by the foe. His body rolled
down the bank into the river at a spot still
known as "The Piper's Pool." A similar story
is told by James Hogg of a piper in the army
of Claverhouse at Bothwell Brig. As the Ettrick
Shepherd supplies a somewhat detailed account
of the incident he may be quoted here: "The

piper to Clavers' own troop stood on the brink
of the Clyde playing ' Awa', Whigs, Awa' '
with great glee; but being struck by a bullet,
either by chance or in consequence of an aim
taken, he rolled down the bank in the agonies
of death; and always as he rolled over the bank,
so intent was he on this old party tune, that
with determined firmness of fingering he made
the pipes to yell out two or three notes more
of it till at last he plunged into the river and
was carried peaceably down the stream among
a great number of floating Whigs." (Hogg's
Jacobite Relics, vol. i. p. 259; quoted in Dalyell's
Musical Memoirs of Scotland, p. 26.)

Royalist and Cromwellian seem to march
through the seventeenth century to the notes
of pipe and drum. The muster of Monk's men
at Coldstream and other places, and their march
to London, were accompanied by pipe and drum.
" General Monk's Right March," or the " Highlanders' March," is the name of one of the tunes
of this period, preserved in John Playford's
Dancing Master, published in 1651. (A. W. Inglis.)

One of the most striking features of the bright
pageant produced at Stirling in 1651 in honour of
Charles II. after his coronation at Scone was the
band of eighty pipers under John M'Crimmon,
" to whom all the pipers in the army gave the van
and acknowledged him to be their chief." Charles
having expressed a wish to be introduced to the
" Prince of Pipers," M'Crimmon acknowledged
the royal compliment by composing the celebrated
tune, " Fhuair mi pog do laimh an Righ " (I got a
kiss of the King's hand). In September of the same

year M'Crimmon was taken prisoner at the battle
of Worcester, a misfortune which he deplored in
a pibroch composed during his captivity.

A dull poet who was present at Killiecrankie
described the rally to the standard of James II. :

> Hic belli buccina signum
> dira dedit, Martemque ciens rauco ore pithaules
> inflarat plenis marsupia turgida buccis.[1]

From Killiecrankie dates "The Killiecrankie
March," a beautiful bagpipe melody, and that
most famous of all pipe tunes, "Up and waur
them a', Willie." Printers, ignorant of Scots,
have been known to give the name of this tune
as "Up and warn them a', Willie," in a praise-
worthy effort to make the title intelligible to
English readers.

It was at this period that the Edinburgh
Regiment, now the King's Own Scottish Borderers,
was raised, and for some years recruiting went on
briskly for various regiments serving abroad. In
Musselburgh a goodly body of recruits had been
assembled. They were led to their home depot
by Alexander Waugh, the town piper of Musselburgh, who rendered this public service to the
young soldiers from purely patriotic motives and
love of his calling; but the officer in command
of the recruits wished to include him among the
newly-enlisted men. It was only by invoking the
aid of the law that Waugh regained his liberty.
(Chambers's *Dom. Ann.* vol. ii., p. 194.)

All the performers on the bag and chanter

---

[1] Here the dread trumpet gave the signal for battle, and the
piper, calling to war with hoarse note, blew up the swelling bags
with inflated cheeks.

were not on William's side at the Battle of the
Boyne. The pipers of the Irish Dragoons and
the Infantry played as vigorously as did the Scots
pipers with the Government troops. "The Battle
of the Boyne" was a popular tune with the
Orangemen, who also knew it by the name of
"Down, Croppies, Down," and it was correspond-
ingly irritating to the Catholics. More than a
century after the date of the battle mischief-loving
pipers of the Highland Regiments stationed in
Ireland were occasionally in trouble for rendering
the tune to inappropriate and unsympathetic
audiences.

Two years before the battle of the Boyne, in
1690, was fought the battle of Cromdale, at which
the Jacobites were defeated. On the day of the
battle a Jacobite piper climbed to the highest
point of the Haughs of Cromdale and there he
continued to play until he fell and died. Whether
the noble air, "The Haughs of Cromdale," was
composed in memory of this or of an earlier
episode at Cromdale, where two battles had
previously been fought, is not certain, though
the probability is that it refers to the engagement
of 1690. The Piper's Stone (*Clach a phiobair*)
is still pointed out as the spot at which the piper
of 1690 fell (*Flood*, p. 137).

The stirring strains of the bagpipe were again
heard in the rising of 1715. The indecisive issue
of the battle of Sheriffmuir was no fault of the
pipers on either side, we may be sure. The
rousing "Sheriffmuir March" is a memorial of
the event, which eclipses the "calculated" music
of the Hanoverian troops. This "calculated"

music was played by three companies of Argyll's Highlanders on their entry into Perth and later into Dundee. The first company marched in, their pipers playing "The Campbells are Comin', Oho, Oho." [1] The second company entered to the tune, " Wilt thou play me fair, Highland Laddie ? " and the third derisively piped out " Stay and take the Breiks with thee." While several Jacobites in these cities had their hopes raised on hearing the first air, deeming it to be from the Earl of Mar's men, there lingered no further doubt on their part when numbers two and three were heard (*Dalyell*, p. 23).

Thirty years later the Irish war-pipes opposed the Scottish on the field of Fontenoy, where the Irish Brigade helped the French to victory over the British, among whom were the Black Watch in their baptism of fire. The Irish pipers on that occasion played "St Patrick's Day in the Morning " and " White Cockade."

In the same year, 1745, the last effort of the Stewarts to regain the throne of Britain took place, and before Prince Charles had finally left these islands Scotland's greatest piper, Patrick M'Crimmon, was killed at the head of a party of M'Leod of Dunvegan's men attempting to capture the Prince, then a guest at Moy Hall. M'Crimmon, who was a Jacobite at heart, had a presentiment that he was to die, and it is to this melancholy circumstance that we owe "M'Crimmon's Lament."

From the gathering of the clans in Glenfinnan, to the swan song of M'Crimmon, the skirl of the pipes seems to dominate this rebellion of the '45.

[1] The proper title is " Baile Inneraora "—Town of Inveraray.

Prince Charlie was himself a piper, and his triumphal entry into Edinburgh was headed by a hundred pipers. Again he crossed the Eden with a hundred pipers, if we may believe all the reporters of these historic events. A set of pipes which had belonged to the Prince was sold among the Cardinal York's effects in 1824, and another set was in the possession of Mr James Skene of Rubislaw. So closely was the bagpipe identified with the Pretender's cause that it was in danger of being regarded as an instrument of sedition. It is on record that it was decided in an English Court of Law to be an instrument of war.

James Reid was tried at York as a soldier in the rebel army. Reid's defence was that he was a piper ; but the judge arguing that as no Highland regiment ever marched to battle without its pipers, the bagpipe must be regarded as an instrument of war. Reid was accordingly sentenced to death and duly executed for being a piper.

At the battle of the Heights of Abraham, for the capture of Quebec, the pipers of the Fraser Highlanders were encouraging the regiment with their most stirring airs and the men were fighting like heroes, when a staff officer, not holding the same opinion of the bagpipe as the judge in Reid's case, ordered the pipers to cease playing. The result was that the Highlanders began to weaken in their attack and even to give way. The tide of victory appeared to have turned, and our forces were being driven back. The staff officer became frantic, and sharply blamed the officer in command of the Fraser Highlanders. His reply was, " Well, sir, it's your fault in stopping the pipers from playing. Even now they would be of use." "Let them play then," was the answer. Play the pipers did, and to such purpose that the regiment responded as one man, shook off their lethargy, and poured over the enemy like a mountain torrent. Their renewed dash and energy astounded the enemy, who fled before them beaten and broken. Thus the pipers saved the day, and helped to gain the Dominion of Canada for the British Crown.

Similarly a piper of the Black Watch was the pilot to victory at the capture of Fort Washington in 1877. First to scale the heights he played till he fell, mortally wounded, while his comrades, animated by his stirring air, thrust forward and captured the position.

How the piper of the 71st (now 1st Highland Light Infantry) at Porto Novo, in the opinion of the commander-in-chief, Sir Eyre Coote, helped to win the battle, and how another piper of the same regiment set the example followed later by Findlater, Laidlaw, Stewart, Richardson, and many more regimental pipers, will be told in the separate summaries of their respective regiments.

CHAPTER IV

THE PIPES IN STRANGE PLACES

THE " great war-pipe of the North " has been heard in every region where the Great War was waged— on the plains of France and Flanders, in Macedonia, Gallipoli, Egypt, Palestine, Mesopotamia, East and South-West Africa, India, on every sea over which the White Ensign has flown, and in the remotest corners of Russia.

In *The Times* of 21st September 1918, Mr Edmund Candler describes how a Russian colonel of Scottish descent was strangely affected by the sound of the bagpipe. " Colonel Leslie spoke no word of English and only a word or two of French. He had been an ' exile' for over three hundred years. An ancestor came over in Queen Mary's time to train Ivan's cavalry, and his family had been in Russia ever since. There was no outward trace of the Scot in him, and he did not wear his nationality on his sleeve. I think my orderly, a man of the Seaforths, was the first Highlander he had met. He had read of the pipes, he told me, in his family records, but it was at Mendali, on the inhospitable shores of Luristan, that he heard the music of them for the first time, and it was a Punjabi piper who piped the Cossacks in. . . . The Partizanski (a tribe of Cossacks, whose flag bears the Scottish Thistle, the English Rose, and the Russian Bear,

C

and the motto in Russian, *Nemo me impune lacessit*)
rode in singing their Russian part-songs, a deep-
toned chant, the sergeant-major of each sotnia
conducting with his whip.   They were greeted by
the 'Hurrahs!' of the British soldiers and the
Mahommedan sepoys, and the war-cries of the
Jats and Sikhs ; when the Sikhs broke in with their
'Wah Guru ji ka khalsa!   Wah guru ji ki fatteh!'[1]
the Cossacks broke off their song and cheered.

"As the infantry filed into camp with their
long bayonets fixed in Russian fashion, the piper
of the Punjabi battalion, a pupil of the pipe-
major of the Black Watch, strode backwards and
forwards playing each company in to the tune
of the 'Campbells are Comin',' 'Scotland the
Brave,' and the regimental slogan, 'Hot Punch.'
And the Russian colonel, Leslie, hearing his
native pipes for the first time, nearly wept.

"After dark," the writer continues, "the
Cossack and Indian troops had amusements.
First the Cossacks danced ; then the Bangaish
sepoys of the Punjabi battalion gave us the wild
Khattak dance of the North-West Frontier,
swinging swords and leaping dervish fashion.
The Cossacks cried, 'Musik! musik!' and the
Punjabi piper came in with 'The De'il's in the
Kitchen,' which started them off dancing again."

The bagpipe is, of course, no strange instrument
to the Sikhs, Gurkhas, Pathans, and Dogras, each
regiment of which has its own pipe band.   The
keenness and enthusiasm of these dusky warriors
for pipe music was sometimes a joy, sometimes a

---

[1] Success to the followers of the holy Guru!   Victory to the
holy Guru!

penance, to the Scottish pipe-majors detailed for their instruction. Before the instructor was out of bed, a knocking at the door would announce an Indian novice anxious to obtain a special lesson in order that he might outstrip his comrades. In the pre-war days of a certain Indian Army mess, it was the nightly entertainment, which custom never staled, to watch the pipe-major's acceptance of the customary drink from the colonel after the piping. All eyes were fixed on the piper as he drained the glass, reversed it, and returned it. Then he raised the right elbow, wiped his mouth with the back of his hand, and gave the final salute. All this, unremarked in the Scottish piper, was droll when rendered by an apt pupil from the Himalayas, who copied his model "to the finger-tips."

Some Stornoway gunners, hearing well-known Highland airs played in the Egyptian desert, hurried in the direction of the sound, and were mightily astonished to find that they were being rendered by a Sikh pipe band and by the 21st Indian Mountain Battery. Well pleased were the performers in finding a critical but appreciative audience in the Highland artillerymen. These men of the Ross Mountain Battery, pipers every one, considered the skill of the Indian soldier pipers "not at all bad." The Indians, recognising the "piper look" on the Scotsmen's faces, passed their pipes to the Scots, who in their turn played for the delectation of the Indians. Then to complete the parallel, perhaps, the Indians gave a demonstration of Highland hospitality by entertaining the strangers to *chapati*.

CHAPTER V

THE INFLUENCE OF THE PIPES

BEFORE the Great War the skirl of the pipes
was heard in every corner of the world, as well
as on the hills and lochs of Scotland. The
power of the piper to stir the emotions was
recognised by tourists in the Highlands who
might chance to hear the strains of the instrument borne across the water from a piper pacing
the slope of a distant hill. Even the listener
who failed to distinguish the melody as one
known to him would often fall into Words-
worth's mood as expressed in "The Reaper,"
and experience the sensation of hearing a tale
of "old, unhappy, far-off things, and battles
long ago." To the soldier fighting his country's
battles on foreign soil the appeal is vivid and
direct. The breath of the piper can call forth
tears or laughter, it can inspire contempt of
danger, arouse the pride of race, and evoke
readiness for self-sacrifice. Who that has heard
it can ever forget the sound of the pipes at a
soldier's funeral ?

The French people acknowledged the charm
of the music dispensed by the military pipers
for the delectation in the first place of the
Scottish soldiers. Villagers and *poilus* showed
everywhere the liveliest interest in the music

of the pipes, and the keenest appreciation of the entertainment provided wherever " Retreat " was played. An example of this occurred at Soissons where the extreme right of the British line touched the French left. There the piper played " Retreat " when in " Rest," and each evening he was immediately surrounded by the entire French battalion nearest to the British line, so that he had to stand instead of marching as he played. Over and over again he had to respond to the demands of his audience to have the music repeated. The piper was as amazed as he was gratified to receive encores from his foreign audience.

The French understand pipe music. They had a small form of the instrument themselves at one time, called the " Musette," and they must have gone to battle sometimes to the strains of such an instrument, for a French piper was taken prisoner at Salamanca ! But it is not for marching troops.

When the pipers of the Scots Guards were travelling through France they were astonished to find that a Maître d'Hôtel, who had asked them to repeat a certain tune, had taken the whole piece down correctly after the second rendering. Their astonishment was increased at Paris when a French gentleman handed the pipe - major a hastily-written score of a long and intricate march and strathspey immediately after hearing it once, with the request that he might be so good as look over it and say whether it had been taken down correctly ; and it was. The pipers still marvel at this phenomenon.

A curious example of the effect of pipe music

on the French occurred at the siege of Pondicherry
in 1793.   The 72nd (now the 1st Battn. Seaforth
Highlanders) "were on duty in the trenches,
exposed to a burning sun and a severe cannonade
from the fortress.   Colonel Campbell, field officer
of the trenches, sent his orderly to Lieut. Campbell
of the Grenadiers, requesting that the piper of
the Grenadiers might play some pibrochs.   This
was considered a strange request to be made at
so unsuitable a time; it was, however, immediately complied with; but we were a good deal
surprised to perceive that the moment the piper
began, the fire from the enemy slackened, and
soon after entirely ceased.   The French all got
upon the works and seemed more astonished
at hearing the bagpipe than we with Colonel
Campbell's request" (Lieut. Campbell's Journal,
quoted in Cannon's *Historical Records of the
72nd Regiment*, 1848, p. 32, footnote).

The Italians, excellent in music above all
other nations, delighted in the music of the
pipes, and the King and Queen of Italy on
several occasions had the pipers of the 2nd Royal
Scots Fusiliers, the 2nd Gordon Highlanders, and
the 6th Argyll and Sutherland Highlanders to
play to them by special request.   At Bucharest
the Royal Family of Roumania listened with
evident delight to the pipe music of Piper
Thomson of the 11th Battn. Scottish Rifles,
whom they afterwards entertained to dinner.

But the pipes are not carried to entertain the
foreigner.   It is for their influence on our own
men of the British armies that they are prized.
In the confusion and depression of the retreat

from Mons, when our regiments had become
hopelessly mixed at one place, and were marching
wearily, the units of one regiment mingled with
those of another, a field officer, observing the
pipe-major of the 2nd K.O.S.B. tramping along
with his pipes mute under his arm, called to a
battalion officer to get the piper to play. "Play
up, pipe-major," said the officer. "Sorry, sir, I
can't; my bag is too dry." When this explana-
tion was reported the field officer inquired: "Is
it the piper or the pipe that's too dry?"—a
sarcasm which put the Borderer pipe-major on
his mettle. With some difficulty he managed
to get a very small supply of water from almost
empty water-bottles, "soused" the bag and struck
up. Only two drones responded, but the effect
was magical. New life seemed to enter the
exhausted and despondent ranks. They got into
step and made much better progress.

British soldiers looked for pipers when going
up the line or coming from the trenches. On one
occasion an English battalion, worn out by a long
spell in the trenches, felt unable to get back to
billets; an officer then obtained the services of
some pipers, and no sooner had these begun to play
than the English soldiers stepped out like men
inspired.

In the *Scotsman* of 30th July 1917, the Rev.
George Dodds described a situation similar to the
lady's in Tennyson's lyric, "Home they brought
her warrior dead." The wife of a soldier who had
been severely wounded found her husband dead
when she got to France. She sat stricken and
tearless till the funeral party started to take the

soldier to his last resting-place.   In the same
condition she followed him to the grave; but on
the way a party of pipers, returning from the
cemetery, met the procession, and, turning to pay
their tribute of respect to an unknown comrade,
led the way, playing "Lochaber No More."
The plaintive music stirred the dormant, stunned
emotions of the young widow as nothing else
could; her apathy departed, and, sobbing quietly,
she took her place beside the grave.

The "brave music" of the 110 pipes and
70 drums on the Square in Arras on 25th May
1917 will never be forgotten by anyone who was
there.   But it does not need many pipers to
produce an effect on the most unlikely of audiences.
Mr Robert Blatchford when on a visit to the
Front with other pressmen, felt depressed by the
sadness of the scenes through which he was
passing, "when we caught a whiff of sound that
made us all start. 'The pipes! the pipes!' It
was a company of Highlanders on the march,
the pipers at their head. I—well, I took my
hat off. It was the only thing to do, and my
companions did the same, and in silence and
with beating hearts we moved slowly past the
line.   Oh the good Scots faces, grim or gay,
the wild elation of the pipers!

"I could have shouted, or danced, or cried, or
—anything. But being British I did nothing.
But it was some thrill."

"JOCK IN THE THICK OF IT: COMING AWAY FROM THE TRENCHES."

From a drawing by Georges Scott.

[*The Graphic*

[40

CHAPTER VI

PIPE MUSIC

(1) *Battle Music.*

To the average, uninitiated ear the bagpipe seems
at first to play but one tune, and that one by no
means tuneful. Salute, march, strathspey, reel,
and pibroch, with all their subtle shades of musical
expressions, their doublings and treblings of grace
notes, fall on undiscriminating ears, if not dis-
cordantly, at best as a medley of sound, a tartan
clamour. But to the true Highlander and to the
lover of the pipes every note has its meaning.
All the emotions of the human heart—joy or
sorrow, love or hate, admiration or scorn, anger
or fear—all are within the range of the instrument
in the hands of a master. Now he is sarcastic,
now he breathes vengeance, then he is despondent,
and anon he lifts his audience on the wings of
elation. He revels in description; the clash of
arms, the tumult of battle, victory and defeat
hanging uncertain in the balance, the pæan of
triumph, the soft croonings of peace and rest,
and the tripping lilt of days of merry-making
follow one another on his magic pipe.

In war the piper is the direct representative
of the ancient bards,[1] whose part it was to rouse

---

[1] Following the harpers.

their clansmen to deeds of heroism by reciting the glorious achievements of old-time warriors. So the piper has inherited a stock of music handed down from ancient days, music in which the famous battles of the past are celebrated for the encouragement of the soldiers of the present day. Of these "Cogadh no Sith" (War or Peace?) is one of the oldest and best known. All the clans have played it for centuries when preparing for battle. It was played at Waterloo when the 79th (Cameron) Highlanders, formed in hollow square, were awaiting the enemy's attack. The situation was doubtful, every nerve was tense, and then Piper Kenneth M'Kay,[1] true to his calling, calmly paraded around the outside of the square playing this appropriate tune. There were no misgivings as to the result after that.

Bagpipe tunes form a musical record of the battles in which Highland regiments, or clans, with their pipers have taken part. A piper who was there composes a commemorative piece. If his rendering is received with approval (and masters of the pipe are severely critical) the music is added to the long list of similar pieces for repetition when the appropriate occasion offers. If it fails to reach the standard of excellence it drops in favour of older or stronger compositions. Thus the "Battle of Harlaw" has rung through five centuries, and shares immortality with such later pieces as the "Battle of Sheriffmuir," "Battle of Waterloo," and others. Piper William Ross of the 42nd produced such a memorial of the Crimean War in his "The Alma," which is still popular.

[1] A native of Tongue, Sutherland.

It is too soon yet to attempt to appraise the output of the pipers of the Great European War. Moreover, that war was so unlike any former war that traditional treatment had to be modified. Then again so many pipers have been killed in the Great War that many masterpieces may have been lost. But there is already something to be recorded. The *doyen* of army pipers, Pipe-Major Robert Meldrum, has produced "The Highland Brigade at Mons," and Pipe-Major William Lawrie of the 8th Argyll and Sutherland Highlanders, the "Battle of the Somme." This gifted piper, reckoned one of the finest of his day, succumbed in 1916 to the hardships of trench life in France. In the opinion of many good judges this piece, one of many by the same composer, is likely to have its niche in the pipers' temple of fame.

The "Battle of Arras," by Pipe-Major M'Lean, 5th Cameron Highlanders, is a stirring battle tune and has already become popular with not a few battalions.

Piper Simon Fraser, 6th Cameron Highlanders, has to his credit several pretty pieces arising out of his experiences in the war, of which perhaps the best known are "Eyes Front" and "Delicia Chisholm," a "Salute" in honour of the Inverness-shire poetess who devoted so much of her talent to the service of her county regiment.

On the Macedonian Front, where British troops had not only to contend with an untiring foe, but with insidious disease, Piper Gillon of the 2nd Cameron Highlanders was able to portray in pleasing manner some of his memories in a melody entitled "The Balkan Hills."

Sergeant-Piper Purgavie, 1st Battn. King's Own Scottish Borderers, who, as one of the immortal 29th Division, participated in all the hard fighting on Gallipoli, before enduring that of the Western Front, signalised the battalion's departure from Flanders in a neatly turned melody "The 25th's Farewell to Marcoing."

Lastly, it was reserved for an officer of the Seaforth Highlanders to describe his battalion's entry into Baghdad in 1917 in a pipe tune quickstep, which the composer—Major Ian H. Mackay Scobie—has entitled "The 72nd's Entry into Baghdad."

From these, and others yet to come, will doubtless emerge a few that will endure like those earlier melodies: "The Alma," by Piper Ross; "The 25th's Farewell to Meerut," by Pipe-Major Balloch; "The March to Coomassie," by Pipe-Major John Macdonald, 42nd (the Black Watch); the "Barren Rocks of Aden," by Pipe-Major M'Kellar, 78th (Ross-shire Buffs), now 2nd Seaforth Highlanders; "The 79th's Farewell to Gibraltar," by Pipe-Major Macdonald.

(2) *Regimental Marching-Past Tunes.*

Everyone who has witnessed a regimental inspection may have noticed that the companies march past the saluting base to the music of the band. The music played on these occasions is not chosen in haphazard fashion but is the same year after year, and is in fact the regiment's marching-past tune. Every regiment has one; Scottish battalions have generally one played by the brass band and another played by the pipe band.

Curiously, the most popular air with the pipers is "Highland Laddie," used, though with different accent, by the Scots Guards, Royal Scots Fusiliers, 2nd Battn. the Black Watch, 2nd Battn. Highland Light Infantry, the Gordon Highlanders, and by the 2nd Battn. Argyll and Sutherland Highlanders.

The oldest marching-past tune belongs to the oldest regiment, The Royal Scots, whose seventeenth-century predecessors made it reverberate throughout France, Germany, and Holland. The sound of the old Scots march is said to have been so potent as to ensure success straightaway for the Scots, a fact observed by the crafty German whose drummers learned and practised the tune in order that they too might derive the like happy results, but there the charm failed. It was for the Scots alone; and no enemy could be deceived by a stranger intermeddling therewith.

Much has been written upon this old tune and its variations; it is generally accepted as the same as that of the old song, "I serve a Worthie Ladie O"; the lady of the song being then Princess of Bohemia, daughter of James VI. and I. A romantic Royal Scot, or one of his admirers of a later day, set the tune to other words, beginning, "Dumbarton's Drums beat bonny O, they mind me of my Nannie O"— which makes quite a nice accompaniment—and "Dumbarton's Drums" is the name it has gone by since 1678-99 when the Earl of Dumbarton was colonel of the regiment.

The King's Own Scottish Borderers have the stirring tune, "Blue Bonnets over the Border"; and

"Kenmure's on and awa', Willie," also Jacobite,
serves the anti-Jacobite Cameronians—old 26th
Regiment .The 42nd (the Black Watch), Seaforth
and the Queen's Own Cameron Highlanders have
"Pibroch Donuil Dubh," a very old tune which
originally commemorated the victory in 1431 of
the Islesmen, the Macdonalds, over the forces of
the Earls of Mar and Caithness. It was natural
that the successors of these Macdonalds, many of
whom were in the 42nd and many more in the
original regiment of the 79th Camerons, should
adopt it, and having been used, that " Pibroch
Donuil Dubh " should remain in these regiments.
The 2nd Battn. Scottish Rifles—old 90th Perthshire Light Infantry—have " Atholl Highlanders,"
a tune written for and used by the Atholl Highlanders from 1777 to 1783, when that regiment
was disbanded. But an extraordinary departure
from the normal was made by the old 71st,
now 1st Battn. Highland Light Infantry, in
their choice of " Whistle o'er the lave o't," an
air attributed to John Bruce, a Dumfries fiddler
of 1720, and also claimed by Ireland. " The
Campbells are Comin' " appropriately serves the.
1st Bn. A. and S. Highlanders, who, as the 91st
Argyllshire Hdrs., were raised by the Duke of
Argyll—a Campbell ; but it does seem out of place
in the Seaforth Highlanders where it is played
before entering barracks—until one learns that the
name of one of their most venerated colonels-in-
chief was Lieut.-Gen. Sir Colin Campbell, and
that it was this tune which was said to have been
played by the 2nd Bn. (78th) in their advance on
Lucknow in 1857 when " The Campbells are

Comin'" sounded the sweetest of all music to the imprisoned residents.

> Oh! they listened dumb and breathless,
> And they caught the sound at last;
> Faint and far beyond the Goomtee
> Rose and fell the pipers' blast.

Why, it has been asked, do the Gordon Highlanders have "Highland Laddie" and not "Where Gadie rins," which they play for "Fall In"? The answer is found in the origin of the regiment —the old 92nd—which, raised by the Marquess of Huntly and his mother, the Duchess of Gordon, was composed of men not so much from the territory of the Gadie but the confines of Inverness, from the Macdonalds and Camerons who knew not the Gadie nor Bennachie.

With territorial battalions "Scotland the Brave" is the most popular. The Scottish Horse, however, have the "Scottish Horse March," composed in South Africa by the Duchess of Atholl; the Lovat Scouts rely on "Lord Lovat's Strathspey," the London Scottish cling to "Highland Laddie," the Liverpool Scottish to "Glendaruel Highlanders," and the Tyneside Scottish — a wartime force of four battalions of the Northumberland Fusiliers—preferred the "Nut-Brown Maid."

(3) *Charging Tunes.*

In the old Clan fighting days the rival pipers kept up the spirits and the fighting energies of their comrades by means of the liveliest airs. The practice was continued by their descendants

who enlisted in the regiments of the King and
these strathspeys and reels they played when the
battalion was at the "double" and also when
in action.

In the Great War the Seaforths' "Cabar
Feidh" was over and over again heard amidst
the din of artillery, though not so clearly as
in the older days of battle. "Cabar Feidh"
shares with the Gordon Highlanders' "Haughs
of Cromdale," or "On wi' the Tartan," the distinction of being the most famous charging tune
in the whole army. "Cabar Feidh," however,
has a long history and an illustrious, while the
Gordons are largely indebted to Piper Findlater
for the fame of the "Cock o' the North." Any
strathspey is good enough in a tight corner
for most battalions, but The Royal Scots would
appear to stipulate for "Monymusk" and the
Royal Scots Fusiliers for "Cutty's Wedding."
The "Cameronian Rant" was adopted by the
Cameronians and "Because he was a Bonnie
Laddie" by the Camerons.

The piper declares the tune, however, and
from accounts given me by pipers in the various
battalions there was a surprising variety. Piper
Laidlaw, V.C., of the 7th Battn. K.O.S.B., after
parading the bullet-swept parapet to the tune
of "Blue Bonnets," trotted with his fellows,
playing "Standard on the Braes o' Mar." On
the Balkan Front, Piper—later Pipe-Major—
Clancy of The Royal Scots deliberately selected
a tune not intended for the *Piob Mhor*, but one
decidedly appropriate, in view of the enemy
village at the time on fire: "Keep the Home

"THE PIPING TIMES OF PEACE."
From a picture by Fred Roe, R.I.

Fires Burning." The composer of this once topical song surely never dreamed that his tune would be adopted by an army piper for such an occasion, or that it would encourage the bayonets of The Royal Scots to drive the Bulgars from a position in Salonica.

PART II
RECORDS OF THE PIPERS

PIPERS OF THE SCOTS GUARDS

THE history of the Scots Guards prior to the year 1914 has yet to be written. Mr Andrew Ross, who was commissioned to undertake the duty, died unfortunately before accomplishing half the work. Nevertheless he discovered many important facts relating to the early career of the regiment which, by the way, commenced in 1641—not 1661 as hitherto supposed. Mr Ross has also the credit of tracing to the Scots Guards several companies of Highlanders which in time became merged in the main battalion. These Highland companies were, towards the close of the seventeenth century, stationed in various parts of the Highlands and, along with some Lowland companies, assisted the Black Watch to maintain good order.

There is no reference to any pipers which the Lowland companies may have had — no record of any pipe music played by the pipers of the Scots Guards on the march to Bothwell Bridge or elsewhere; but there is proof of the piper's presence in the Highland companies of the regiment. These companies had been reduced in number in December 1704, when one of their officers, Lieut.-Colonel Duncan Mackenzie, was ordered to command the company which was to proceed to London for the purpose of being added to the main body of Scots Guards. That

Highland company entered the city arrayed in the "proper Caledonian dress," with broadswords and targets, and preceded by their piper.

Londoners must have gazed with astonishment on the strange spectacle of Highlanders in tartan kilt and plaid, of which they may have heard, but which they had never till then beheld : and they must have marvelled to hear the strains of the bagpipe, an instrument that was equally foreign to their ears.

These Highland soldiers were probably soon afterwards breeched and gaitered and made uniform in appearance with their comrades of the Lowland, but it is unlikely that the piper was "dropped" or that he was forced to exchange his kilt for trousers or breeches; the average Englishman of the period manifested much interest in kilted men and pipers who found their way to England. There was one Scots piper who was captured in the battle of Worcester, 1651, who discovered to his amazement that he was regarded by his captors as an object of wonder and admiration; he was encouraged to play his pipes and a post was given him in Bath, where he prospered.

Though the first Highland piper of the Scots Guards fared well it is doubtful whether he had many successors. The Guards appear to have had pipers towards the end of the eighteenth century. They were without them in the first half of the nineteenth century ; Colonel Greenhill-Gardyne recollects the re-introduction of pipers in the Scots Guards about the year 1853, when he was a subaltern in the Coldstreams, and of the early pipe-majors he has some interesting stories to relate. The first pipe-major of the 2nd Battalion was pipe-corporal Murdoch Macpherson of the 42nd, who continued to wear his Black Watch uniform for some time after he had joined the Guards. To the 1st Battalion went Ewen Henderson, a Grenadier piper of the 92nd, for whom the Guards had to exchange a private of theirs. Ewen, who accompanied the Guards to the Crimea, was a well-known personage in the regiment and had the honour of playing before the Royal Family on many occasions. There in Buckingham Palace he was paid many a compliment, but the greatest interest for Ewen was his performance before H.R.H. the Princess of Wales, later H.M. Queen Alexandra. That performance was often recalled, and the kind words which Her Royal Highness addressed and the golden napoleon which she graciously bestowed on the pipe-major. That token of royal esteem Ewen greatly treasured and showed to particular friends. An officer teased him by offering £5 for the coin, and had the satisfaction of hearing the loyal Highlander's indignant "No, sir! nor £500!"

Among the rank and file the pipers of the mid-nineteenth century were very popular, one private, Roderick Ross, who hailed from Inverness, being the most ardent auditor. Roderick was a strapping Guardsman of six feet four, and with an enormous chest and muscles; all tunes were pleasant to his ears—all except that of "Lochaber No More." As soon as the opening notes had sounded Roderick's chest would heave and all the other marks of suppressed emotion would be revealed to all around. The pipers used to take an unkind delight in witnessing the distress of Private Ross, who used to remark: " I canna' stand 'Lochaber No More,' it aye gars me think o' deserting."

The pipers, who had been unofficially introduced and made part of the Scots Guards establishment, learned soon after their return from the Crimea that the inspecting officer having discovered that they were not " officially authorised " they would be sent off packing. The news was like a bolt from the blue, but the officers were determined to keep the pipers, and, fortunate in having the Duke of Cambridge as colonel, made a successful appeal against the edict. In the correspondence that followed, the adjutant-general agreed to allow the pipers, in view of the " regiment being Scotch, it is considered that pipers will facilitate recruiting "; in another letter he " deems it especially necessary (to have pipers) on account of the duties of the Guards about the Court."

The pipers were then placed on a better footing, and one which not only made them part of the establishment but eased the officers of their maintenance, for, by an Army Order of 1856, each of the two battalions of the Scots Fusilier Guards—as they were styled from 1831 to 1877 — was to have a pipe-major and five pipers, free of cost to the officers, the pipe-major to be paid 2s. a day, and each piper 1s. 2d. a day with an additional penny a day to each as " beer money."

The pipers of the Guards are not permitted

to play their companies into action, nor can they show the varied records of other regiments in regard to foreign service; for the Guards never serve abroad except in time of war, when they are placed in the " tightest " corners.   The pipers are then either ammunition carriers or stretcher-bearers; they were in the Egyptian War, 1882-4, and in the South African War, 1899-1902, where their gallantry in fetching the ammunition to the front was the subject of praise.   Two young pipers of the Guards who performed these duties in the Boer War were in the Great War, one Pipe-Major William Ross and the other Pipe-Sergeant Alexander Martin, both of the 2nd Battalion.   The 1st Battalion with its eight pipers landed in France in August 1914, and took part in the retreat from Mons.   On that depressing forced march, when everyone trudged along weary and despondent, the pipe-major, Alexander Ross, brother of the pipe-major of the 2nd Battalion, set his pipes to a lively tune. The men at once " changed step," pushed back their shoulders and tried their hardest to march erect; the piper's tune was an unexpected comfort and inspiration; then they noticed that the pipe-major limped as he played, and, looking at his shoes, saw blood oozing and were amazed at his pluck and unselfishness.

In the first battle of Ypres, where the battalion was heavily engaged, Piper Mackenzie was employed as ammunition carrier.   Carrying one bandolier of ammunition to front-line trenches several times in an engagement is a trying occupation, yet Mackenzie carried more than one over

each shoulder—and he ran! Only a strong man
and a fearless could manage that for any length
of time. The men in the trenches—themselves in
peril—trembled to see the piper on his frequent,
trotting journeys, expecting each minute to see
him fall. Still he carried on all day—but not
quite. Before night had gone the brave Mackenzie
had fallen, mortally wounded. The war had taken
heavy toll of the eight pipers of this battalion, only
two of the eight surviving at the close of 1914.

The 2nd battalion, which had reached France
on 2nd October 1914, with sixteen pipers, were
left with but six pipers at the end of 1914; their
casualties had been sustained while the pipers
served in the trenches or as stretcher-bearers.
One of the most deplored of these casualties was
Pipe-Sergeant Alexander Martin, who, after using
his rifle in the trenches, was placed in charge of
the stretcher-bearers and there he showed unvary-
ing gallantry and devotion to the wounded. The
regiment was gratified when they learned that the
popular piper sergeant had been awarded the
D.C.M. and that the *Gazette* notice of the award
made mention of his "conspicuous gallantry and
resource throughout the campaign when in charge
of stretcher-bearers" and of his having "on many
occasions picked up wounded men and carried
messages under heavy fire."

Martin was further marked out for a staff
appointment or for a cadetship as an officer and
got his "marching orders" while in the trenches.
Congratulated by his comrades, he had said the
last of farewells and departed. "Lucky beggar,"
they said as he left, but alas! he had not proceeded

far on his road to the base when he was hit on the forehead by a stray bullet and died instantaneously—on the very day on which he had completed twenty-one years' service.

For a regiment that does not generally overestimate the merits of its members, it speaks volumes for the valour and the mental abilities of the pipers of the Scots Guards that so many of them were considered worthy of holding commissions. The two brothers Ross, pipe-majors of the 1st and 2nd Battalions respectively, were recommended, but both declined. Piper Bruce Hobson and Piper Archie M'Phedran availed themselves of their recommendation, Hobson going to the Royal Berks Regiment, and M'Phedran to a Yorks battalion. Both survived the war, though M'Phedran was badly wounded while leading his platoon into action.

The losses to the pipers by deaths, wounds, and promotions led to the drawing up of a new scheme by the officers of both battalions for the better preservation of their pipers. The 1st Battalion pipers were put on transport lines; while those of the 2nd Battalion, besides their duties there, had to play the battalion up the line to a point decided on by the O.C., from which they played the battalion back after their spell in the trenches.

PIPERS OF THE ROYAL SCOTS

THE oldest regiment in the world, The Royal Scots may also claim priority over all other existing regiments in the use of the bagpipe. When, in 1634, Sir John Hepburn arrived in Germany to resume command of his old corps he found the remnants of other Scots units waiting to be absorbed by his regiment, and among them some of the Mackay Highlanders, whose last surviving piper of a band of thirty-six "blew his notes of welcome" in honour of Hepburn.

Probably he was the first piper of the regiment, as one year later (1635) the establishment is stated to consist of 8316 officers and men, of whom *one* was a piper. That piper was doubtless a Mackay of the great piping family of the Mackays in Reay on the borders of Sutherland and Caithness, with an extensive repertory of pipe tunes with which to regale The Royal Scots on the line of march and in action, one of the favourite melodies of his old regiment having been the "Strathnaver Highlanders." When he retired the regiment replaced him by a Lowlander named Alexander Wallace who appears on the Roll of 1679 as "Pipe-Major," and he in turn was succeeded in 1704 by Adriel Duran. The pipers then did not wear the kilt but their stirring tunes on the march in foreign lands attracted considerable attention and the pipers themselves were deemed worthy of a prominent place in the painting of an eminent painter of battle scenes, J. P. Stoop, whose "Destruction of the Mole of Tangier, 1684" shows four red-coated, white-breeched pipers of "The Royals" in the foreground. "Dumbarton's Drums" were famous even then, and Adriel Duran, pipe-major, a person of distinction for he appears on the "Roll of Officers entitled to a bounty of £3."

Apart from these facts the records of the seventeenth and eighteenth centuries do not mention pipers until 1769 when the officers were in danger of losing them. In that year the authorities at Horse Guards took exception to the pipe-major and the drum-major being on the strength of the corps. The hint conveyed to the commanding officer to get rid of them brought forth a protest from the colonel, the Marquess of Lorne, later 5th Duke of Argyll, whose plea to have the drum-major and pipe-major retained, merely met with a polite note from the inspecting officer, who reminded the colonel that one battalion of the Royal Regiment had never had either of these officials, and he did not see the necessity for a regiment having either. Still the Marquess argued, but with the same result, the English inspecting officer closing the correspondence with the remarks that he "should be sorry The Royals should be deprived of any honorary distinction belonging to it; but no person whom I have consulted is of opinion that a drum-major and a piper can add to or take from the honour of that most respectable corps."

Orders like that were understood to apply to occasions when the regiment was on inspection parades, but not otherwise, and thus the vexing business was overcome. The entries in the official records of the regiment in the later years of the eighteenth century on inspection days note that "Drum-Major and Piper (are) absent from inspection with the Duke of Argyll's leave," and, later, in 1787 and 1788, with "Lord Adam Gordon's leave" (Inglis, in Leask and M'Cance's *Records of The Royal Scots*).

The fact that these entries mention only *piper* and not *pipers* suggests that the term referred to the only professional piper (or pipe-major) and that the other pipers necessary for a battalion were in the ranks on inspection days—that they were "acting pipers" like those of to-day—which probably accounts for the paucity of records relating to the pipers in the battles fought by The Royal Scots. At all events the pipers were players of merit, as the Prize Lists of the Highland Society of Scotland amply prove. In their annual competition held in 1793 Donald M'Kerchar, "Piper to the Scots Royal," won fourth prize; in 1796 he was second, and in 1798 gained the premier place. The pipe-major, Hugh M'Gregor, who competed in 1799, obtained third prize.

Unfortunately, the Records are entirely blank in the matter of pipers thereafter until 1882, when the colonel, H. G. White, obtained official sanction for a pipe band, the expenses of which were to be met by the officers, an arrangement that was maintained until after the close of the Great War when, thanks to the representations of the Lowland Association, the Government undertook payment of the pipe band consisting of a pipe-major and five pipers.

If the pipers had no chances of gaining distinction in the wars of previous centuries they were afforded many opportunities in the Great War, opportunities of which they availed themselves. The pipers of the 1st Battalion were in the trenches in France, and later in Macedonia. Piper Robertson, who was promoted duty sergeant, and Piper Armour, advanced to the rank of coy.-sergeant-major, were both awarded the D.C.M. and M.M. Piper Macmillan won fame and favour as a scout, his daring exploits, accurate reports and map sketches being singled out for special mention, which resulted in the award of a D.C.M. In 1919 he was appointed pipe-major of a battalion of the Gordon Highlanders.

The 15th—1st City of Edinburgh—Battalion, to which had been given the bagpipe that had been played by Gilbert Kerr in the Antarctic regions when the *Scotia* was there in 1911, took part in the 1916 Battle of the Somme. Pipe-Major David Anderson, who carried these pipes, had been ordered to stay behind with the pipers. That was an order not to the taste of the strapping pipe-major, who had all the old-time piper's zeal for being in the forefront of battle; he implored his O.C. to be permitted to play his comrades in the Advance, and was allowed. Striking up "Dumbarton's Drums" he marched on, but was hit and brought to the ground. Still he played, though unable to move, continuing his tune, like Clark at Vimiera, and Findlater at Dargai, until he lost consciousness. How Anderson escaped alive must ever remain a mystery; he was found and carried off by the stretcher bearers, who did not trouble themselves about the pipes, which, unfortunately, were lost in consequence. The pipe-major had struck the imagination of the soldier of all regiments there, and when the announcement was made that a *Croix de Guerre* would be awarded to the officer, N.C.O., or man who was, in the opinion of the whole Division, the most conspicuously gallant figure in the day's fighting, the Division unanimously voted Pipe-Major David Anderson *the* man. The other battalions were equally proud of their pipers. Of the pipers of the 8th (Territorial) Battalion the most outstanding in his duties on the field, tending and bearing off the wounded, was Pipe-Major J. M. M'Dougall, an ex-piper of the Black Watch, who, for his great gallantry at Festubert, where he lost an eye, was awarded the D.C.M. The 9th (Territorial) Battalion, one of the Edinburgh contingents, had a gallant soldier in Albert Forsyth, who was killed in action soon after winning an M.M.

In the earlier stages of the war posthumous honours were not conferred, otherwise the relatives of Pipe-Sergeant Andrew Buchan, an ex-Gordon Highlander, would have had either the V.C. or the D.C.M., in recognition of Buchan's extraordinary valour in the action of 27th June 1915, on Gallipoli, where his prowess as a combatant was the common topic of the 1/4th Battalion, and of other units. Two battalions were signally unfortunate in losing several pipers before reaching the battle-field—the 7th (Territorial) Battalion by the railway collision at Gretna in May 1915, which caused the deaths of Pipe-Major Gair and four pipers; and the 10th (Territorial) Battalion, whose pipers, along with half the battalion, were transferred to the Royal Warwickshire Regiment, in which, though their music was much appreciated on the march and in rest billets, was not utilised in battle.

After all, there were few, if any, opportunities on the Western Front for displaying the various qualities of the Scottish bagpipe. The French and the Belgians were quickly accustomed to the habits of Scots regiments with their pipers; but on the Macedonian Front it was quite different. There the all-conquering Scots' bagpipe had rivals —of a kind—in the pipes played by the Greek shepherds, and the still different pipes played by Serbs and Bulgars. It was a novelty—each of these—to the Scots pipers, who liked none of them. In this connection there may be mentioned an entertainment given by the officers of a Greek regiment to the officers of The Royal Scots, in return for the hospitality of "The Royals" to them. On the earlier occasion the pipers of The Royal Scots had played the classic airs of their "ain countrie" for the benefit of the unenlightened Greek. When the return dinner was in progress the officers of The Royal Scots found that their hosts were equally mindful in the matter of a musical "treat." For, round and round the table marched ten Greek pipers with their pipes—long

E

bags with chanters, but no drones — playing Hellenic "tit-bits," which the Scots, not at all liking, had to endure in polite silence, and as politely applaud when the strange music ceased.

The capabilities of the Scots bagpipe for all kinds of music were more leisurely examined on that Front than on any other. It was there that Pipe-Major George S. Allan composed "Lothian Lads" and "The Royal Scots' March thro' Salonica," both deemed by competent judges very good works, and there, too, Piper Clancy paid tribute to his friend Pipe-Cpl. M'Nab, appointed pipe-major of the 3rd Battn. Royal Scots Fusiliers, in a neat tune which he entitled "M'Nab's Farewell to The Royal Scots." Clancy was a humorist and a good piper. It was he who, while trotting on the flank of his company in an attack on a village, part of which was then in flames, tuned his pipes to suit the occasion in the popular song of the war period, "Keep the Home Fires Burning," to the vast enjoyment of the troops.

It is rather singular to find the pipe history of The Royal Scots in 1918 and 1919 following precedents set in former centuries. "The Scots March," which the Royal Scots had hummed or whistled as their pipers played before them three centuries back—through Flanders, France, Germany, Austria-Hungary, Bavaria and Sweden, was succeeded in 1918 by other Scots marches, including "Dumbarton's Drums," "Scotland the Brave," and "Blue Bonnets over the Border," played by the pipers of "The Royals" and other Scots units as they marched into Germany, crossing the edge of Waterloo where, in 1815, their predecessors had also played "Dumbarton's Drums" while The Royal Scots had fought. Never, however, until 1918 had Scottish troops marched into Germany with massed pipe bands playing "Blue Bonnets over the Border," charming the youth of that country in a manner reminiscent of the pied piper of Hamelin City described by Browning.

Far off from them one solitary piper of another battalion of The Royal Scots—J. Smart—was doing his best to lighten the wearisome journey to Russia, where British troops were sent to assist the loyalists of Russia against the Bolsheviki. They were "sidetracked"; the centre of attraction was Germany, where the massed pipe bands of the Scottish regiments paraded and played through the streets and where Scottish Colours were presented to several units—surely the first occasion in history when Colours were presented on enemy soil.

Another parallel with the seventeenth century pipers of The Royal Scots may be found in a notable pipe melody composed by one of the pipers of the regiment. In 1634 a piper had played a "Salute" in honour of Colonel Sir John Hepburn, and in 1919 Pipe-Major Chas. Dunbar paid a similar compliment to the colonel-in-chief, Her Royal Highness the Princess Mary, in his "Princess Mary's March."

PIPERS OF THE ROYAL SCOTS FUSILIERS

THE officers of the second oldest Scottish regiment
of the line have not been prone to exaggerate the
importance of their pipers as an aid or bulwark
or tonic to the troops. Yet they had three
pipers from the very start of the regiment in
1678, and these three pipers doubtless played
their fellows on the march to Bothwell Bridge
and other centres of Covenanting activities before
finding more congenial fighting in the Netherlands and Flanders. There was no room in the
regimental chronicle for the pipers at Steenkerk,
Landen, Blenheim, Ramillies, Oudenarde, Mal-
plaquet and Dettingen, in each of which engagements the pipers must have been heard. Nor is
there any record of their presence at Sheriffmuir,
whither the Fusiliers were sent on their return
to Scotland and where pipers on both Jacobite
and Hanoverian sides were conspicuous.

A similar reserve characterised the battle of
Culloden, where the regiment and its pipers
were present, though an amusing incident which
occurred on the eve of that fight is told of the
colonel, Sir Andrew Agnew, and one of the
pipers. The Scots Fusiliers were then in occupation of Blair Castle, and the colonel, standing
by an open window, saw in the distance the
Duke of Cumberland approaching. Outside and

in front of the Castle a piper was lounging along with some other soldiers, quite indifferent to royalty and commanders-in-chief. The colonel, on the other hand, deeming the occasion worthy of a salute on the pipes shouted to the idle piper, " Blaw! blaw, ye scoundrel, dinna ye see the King's ain bairn ? "

The resultant "blaw" of that Fusilier piper in his perfunctory salute to an uncomprehending German prince was a waste of energy, the anti-thesis of the pipe-playing of the opposing handful of Jacobites. Lord George Murray, their com-mander, was aware of the meditated attack by Sir Andrew Agnew and his Fusilier regiment, and having at the time no men sufficient to meet the attack, had recourse to stratagem. His twenty pipers and parcel of fighting men he scattered behind a peat dyke at Dalnaspidal with orders to the pipers to play, while the claymores of the Highlanders were to be brandished. All this was done, and Sir Andrew, falling into the intended deception, beat a retreat, imagining that the widely scattered pipers indicated a large body of fighting men.

The pipers of the Scots Fusiliers were not trained in these arts, nor are they mentioned in any of the engagements in which the regiment was prominent, from Laffeldt to Saratoga, from Martinique to the Napoleonic Wars—except that of Waterloo. One might almost have imagined that the pipers had ceased to be borne by the Fusiliers were it not for the Muster Rolls which attest their establishment and the two eighteenth-century pipe tunes of the regiment—" The Scots

Fusiliers," which was their marching tune, and a "quickstep" known as the "March of the 21st Regiment of Foot."

The piper himself emerges in 1830 in a painting which shows him smartly attired in Royal Stewart tartan trews, Kilmarnock bonnet with red "toorie" and red and white dicing; and immaculate red, tailed coat with high collar and with two brass grenades on the points of the "tails." The piper has his black waist belt and black shoulder belt, from which depends his sword—all which proves that particular attention was paid to him by the officers. Colonel Groves, who has a reproduction of the piper in his history, quotes an earlier historian for the statement that two pipers only were in the regiment about that time, and that "for some reason they were abolished in 1850, but in 1870 they were again introduced and their number increased to ten." May the reason be found in the person of Sir De Lacy Evans who was colonel from 1850 to 1870? As a Welshman he probably had an antipathy to the bagpipe. Matters were still further settled in 1876 when an Order was issued permitting the regiment to have a pipe-major and three pipers for each battalion, the additional pipers being "acting" pipers.

Three years later the 2nd Battalion, which had been raised at Paisley in 1858, set out for the South African War with the pipers at their head. After an exciting voyage in the steamship *City of Paris*, which struck a rock just as it was steaming into Simon's Bay, the troops were safely disembarked and, with pipers playing, entered

Durban, where the music of the pipes created considerable excitement among the residents. The battalion marched into Pietermaritzburg on 5th April 1879, and there again the pipers were the main attraction. The Scots Fusiliers were then part of the British Force which took the field against Cetewayo whose warriors numbered 20,000 and whose fighting attracted many correspondents of English newspapers. These spectators were apparently more impressed by the appearance of the kilted pipers of the Royal Scots Fusiliers at the head of the long column of troops than with any other detail of the soldiers. That was "the first bit of music of any kind I have yet heard in the Division," wrote the correspondent of the *Daily News;* and, in the fierce fighting that soon followed, that correspondent could not forget the sensation caused by the Fusiliers' pipers who "filled the air with the breath of battle . . . sending out skirls that sounded far above the fusilade and the screams and yells of the combatants."

In the Boer War of 1880-1, where the 2nd Battalion were also engaged, the pipers were not specially noted, nor in their next campaign, that in Burmah, where from 1885 to 1887 they had Burmese to "tackle," are the pipers' services made the subject of remark. They were relied upon to supply the music on all their marches and in the South African War of 1899-1902, where Pipe-Major Muir was shot while playing a company across the veldt, the pipers were in the forefront of all the marches. They led the 2nd Battalion, after the Relief of Ladysmith, into the Transvaal

—the first British regiment to enter; and they
were part of every party that went to the various
townships in that province for the ceremony of
hoisting the Union Jack. The pipers had done
well, but the chief honours were with the battalion
generally, who were, in recognition of their many
great services, given the white hackle for their
sealskin headdress, which ornament had been taken
from them in 1837.

The Great War which saw the Royal Scots
Fusiliers increased to eight battalions, of which
two were Territorial and four "New Army"
battalions, did not lead the officers to make any
great alteration in the duties of their pipers.
They did not play in action but carried rations
from transport lines to the trenches under cover
of night and often under intense gunfire. When
two battalions were changed into Labour units
the pipers did duty like the rest.

The ration-carrying pipers and drummers were
highly popular with all ranks for they never failed
to deliver supplies. Indeed the colonel of one
battalion had a special parade of his battalion at
the close of the war for the purpose of express-
ing his thanks to the pipers and drummers for
"the splendid services which they had rendered
throughout the war."

There was one piper of the 1st Battalion who,
more than all the others, was in great favour with
his fellows. He was Lance-Corporal Wallace,
known from of old as "Dodger" Wallace on
account of miraculous escapes from all kinds of
trouble. He had served eighteen years with the
Colours and had passed through the Great War

without wound and without illness—the only piper of his unit with that record. At one period he was the only piper left in the battalion. And his comrades, in virtue of these facts, considered that his pre-war nickname of "Dodger" had been well justified.

PIPERS OF THE KING'S OWN SCOTTISH BORDERERS

THE "Edinburgh" regiment, which was raised in 1689—in the record time of four hours—for the defence of the city of Edinburgh against the attacks of the active supporters of the deposed king, James VII. and II., had some pipers to thank for the feat. They were probably not unmindful, for, two years later, when stationed in Holland, they sent home another recruiting party which engaged the services of the town piper of Musselburgh. That was an unfortunate step which led to a lawsuit brought by the piper on finding that he was held as an enlisted soldier, no longer free to return to his comfortable duties in the burgh. The piper won his action and the fresh draft had to sail without him.

The early records of the regiment being imperfect, the adventures of the pipers in the campaigns in Ireland, Spain, and Flanders are long forgotten. How they survived the vicissitudes of the regiment seems extraordinary; in 1736 the whole unit—with the exception of the officers and non-commissioned officers — was disbanded, or rather transferred to Oglethorpe's regiment, and a fresh start made by recruitment in Ireland. Yet the pipers must also have been excepted from that transfer. They were conspicuous at Culloden, where they played the 25th or "Edinburgh" off the field, just as they or their predecessors had played their companies off Sheriffmuir in 1715 —perhaps to the very tune to which Lord Balmerino had listened when, as an officer of the regiment at Sheriffmuir, he had decided to quit the Hanoverian for the Jacobite cause. But the captured Balmerino of Culloden can have had no further interest in the pipers of his old regiment as he was marched off to his doom. Unfortunate, gallant Balmerino!

No feature in the strange history of the regiment is so extraordinary as the constancy with which the officers of all periods of the regiment clung to their pipers. Though Sterne does not mention them in *Tristram Shandy*, nor the chronicler of the various battles of Fontenoy, Roucoux, Val, Minden, Warburg, Campen, Fellinghausen and Wilhelmstal, they were at each and all of these. The pipers were even permitted to continue when, in 1782, the regiment which had been so long known as the " Edinburgh," or 25th, were compelled to assume the name and style of " The Sussex Regiment." That unpopular title, which annoyed everyone in the regiment from the colonel to the drummer boy, had to be endured until 1805, when the king honoured them by entitling the regiment the " King's Own Borderers." And yet, during the period of their English name, the pipers had composed some marches, one of which they named, in honour of their O.C., " Lord George Lennox's March " — tunes which were discovered by Mr A. Wood Inglis.

The promotion of the regiment to the " royal " name meant, besides the alteration to royal blue

in the yellow facings of uniforms and Colours, a
new dress for the pipers. Thenceforth they wore,
in virtue of their title, the tartan of the Royal
Stewarts, against whom their predecessors had
fought.

It would almost seem as though the " Borderers "
had, like Balmerino, changed their views, for their
pipers chose for their marching-past tune the
Jacobite " Blue Bonnets over the Border," quite
regardless of the fact that their regiment had gone,
not to the aid of " Bonnie Dundee " but to his
overthrow ; and with the same disregard of history,
they adopted as their charging tune "The Standard
on the Braes o' Mar," which the old members of
the regiment had tried to capture.

That the pipers have all along been well cared
for by the officers is attested by several facts.
Highlanders with a reputation as pipers were
wont to choose the 25th as the best unit for their
genius. Even Highland youths sought places in
its band, and Alex. Sutherland, a boy piper of
the regiment in 1811, was so skilful a player as
to win a prize in the Highland Society's competition, and some years later had the honour of
being appointed Pipe-Major of the 79th Cameron
Highlanders. Promotion to that rank in the 25th
was slow, for their pipe-majors had a habit of
remaining long in the regiment. There was Pipe-
Major John Mackay, whose name is treasured by
the Clan Mackay as a piper of renown, though
his record in the 25th is shadowy—unlike that of
his son, also Pipe-Major John Mackay, who was
long in office in the Argyll and Sutherland Highlanders, and afterwards in the Liverpool Scottish.

Then there was Pipe-Major Donald Mackenzie, son of the celebrated John Ban Mackenzie, the last "king of pipers," whose preference for the 25th in the fifties of the nineteenth century was a source of sorrow to his fond parent, who had wished him to join the 92nd; and it was looked upon by the officers of that Highland regiment as an insult to them to have a Lowland regiment in possession of one of the best players in the country. What they could not manage by appeal to the officers of the 25th, they tried to accomplish by other avenues—strategy which the 25th strongly resented. The 92nd found that they would have to desist, if civil war were not to ensue; and so the Lowlanders were left in peace to enjoy the pibrochs, marches, and reels, which their pipe-major artistically played. Not many years after that episode a worse fate seemed in store. It was the time when zealous inspecting officers had their eye on regiments with pipers, as unwarranted intruders. In 1858 the inspecting officer inquired for the authority of the 25th's pipers. The O.C., unaware of the royal warrant of 1805, adduced the evidence of some active veterans of more than thirty years' service, who averred that they remembered seeing and hearing pipers in the regiment since they were boys. That was considered satisfactory and the Deputy-Adjutant-General allowed the 25th to have their pipers, whose association with the regiment "appeared to be lost in time," but on condition that the public were put to no expense and that the pipers were to be placed on the footing of bandsmen and not of drummers.

That meant no change in the arrangements

of the regiment; the pipe band continued to be
provided with the best of instruments purchased
by the officers, but the pipers were not placed
in the forefront of battle when the regiment went
into action.

That was not surprising, for, notwithstanding
the presence of pipers, the 25th was too often
regarded as an English unit—their title of "King's
Own Borderers," which they bore from 1805 to
1887, having been no index to their Scottish
character. That was made evident in 1881, when
the War Office proposed to alter the title to "The
York Regiment King's Own Borderers" and their
depot to be at York—a proposal which was
dropped only after much public protest had been
made. It was not until 1887 that the present
title of "King's Own Scottish Borderers" was
given, the depot established at Berwick, and the
territorial area extended to the southern counties
of Scotland.

Through all these earlier vagaries the regiment
might have lost its Scottish identity had it not
been for the pipers who remained unchanged. The
regiment they remembered in their pipe tunes: the
"Badge of Scotland," the popular work of Pipe-
Major Mackay,[1] referring to the regimental badge—
the crowned Castle and St Andrew's Cross; the
"25th's Farewell to Meerut" of Pipe-Major John
Balloch, one of the most favoured tunes of recent
times. Balloch, who in 1886 transferred from the
Cameron Highlanders to the Borderers and took
part in the Tirah campaign, was one of the many
veterans who rejoined his old regiment on the

[1] A. and S. Hdrs.; a son of the Pipe-Major of the K.O.S.B.

outbreak of the Great War in 1914, when he was posted pipe-major of the 8th (New Army) Battalion serving in France until the close and so making a total of thirty-two years' service with the regiment.

The obscurity which attended the pipers of the K.O.S.B. in earlier wars was removed in the various theatres of the Great War in which the regiment was engaged. Mention has been made of Pipe - Major M'Intyre in the Retreat from Mons, where the 2nd Battalion had its share of hardship; the 1st Battalion was later to find itself at the Dardanelles as part of the immortal 29th Division. There the pipers had their rifles, bayonets, and other equipment and were in the ranks, their pipes were with them, strapped to their kit, and only removed and played when their companies were on the march or in rest billets. They were excellent soldiers. Piper John Maitland distinguished himself in action and was awarded the Military Medal; Higginson —a Scot, in spite of his name—was mentioned in despatches for valour in a bayonet charge. His comrades fully expected the D.C.M. for which he had been recommended, but his fall in action made that impossible. Posthumous medals were not then awarded. Of the eleven pipers who had landed with the battalion on "Y" Beach on 25th April 1915, only three endured the entire period of occupation of the peninsula, namely, Pipe-Major William Mackenzie, who was awarded the Military Medal, Piper Thomas Turnbull and Pipe - Sergeant James Purgavie. One grievous disappointment Purgavie experienced. After having captured a Turkish

trench, the Borderers rested; Purgavie, having
found a comfortable corner in the first line
trenches, went to sleep.   He slept until a counter
attack awoke him; he looked round, saw none
of his friends, for they had all fled, and shots
fell fast and furious in his direction.   No time,
he knew, was to be lost if he were to escape.
Yet there were his valuable pipes lying in the
vacated corner along with his kit.   The kit was
as nothing compared with his bagpipe, one of
the finest—a thirty-six guinea set, gifted by the
officers—and he could not afford to lose that.
One moment he hesitated and then, startlingly
reminded by the rain of shots of the yelling
Turks, he dashed for cover, leaving his much-
prized pipes to the Turks.   When Purgavie was
given another set of pipes for use in France he
was in the habit of making unfavourable remarks
on their quality, though they were really very
good and assisted him to produce his "Farewell
to Marcoing."

Of the pipers of the New Army battalions of
the Borderers who brought much credit to the
regiment, it is astonishing to find how many
were old members of the regular battalions—
pipers who had been drawing their long service
pensions for many years prior to the eve of the
Great War.   Besides Pipe-Major Balloch, there
were Robert Mackenzie, a veteran of fifty-nine,
with long service, good conduct medal, and war
medals for Cemazah, 1888, Chitral, 1895, and
Atbara, 1898—one of the coolest and most gallant
soldiers in the field.   Mackenzie always played
his company into action to the admiration of his

[*Illustrated London News*

PIPER LAIDLAW OUTSIDE THE BRITISH TRENCH PLAYING "BLUE BONNETS OVER THE BORDER."

From a picture by S. Begg.

company; his officers had obtained for him the D.C.M., but unfortunately he did not live to wear it as he fell in action at Loos. Thomas Richardson, who succeeded Mackenzie as pipe-major, was also a veteran piper of the regiment, whose years numbered 58.

The battle of Loos, which accounted for the loss of so many pipers as well as of other combatants, enabled Piper Daniel Laidlaw, a veteran serving with the 7th Battalion, to distinguish himself by doing that which so many heroic pipers have done in all wars—playing such airs as would inspirit his comrades to victory. The men, crouching in their trench, stupefied by gas, saw Piper Laidlaw walking up and down the parapet of the trench, heard the invigorating strains of " Blue Bonnets over the Border," and, hearing them, forgot all but the instant desire to be up and at the enemy. Over the top and off at the double, they heard parts of the "Standard on the Braes o' Mar," though, by then, Laidlaw had been wounded.

The startling effect of the piper's playing was fully appreciated by the British authorities, who rewarded Laidlaw by making him a " King's Corporal" and bestowing on him the coveted distinction of V.C., which the French staff duplicated by their award of the *Croix de Guerre.*

Nor were the pipers of the territorial battalions one whit less heroic. Before entering France they had served in the Dardanelles and in the Egyptian and Palestine campaigns. They were employed chiefly as runners, one of the most dangerous duties in the war. The 1/4th Battalion pipers numbered eight when they landed on Gallipoli : when the battalion left the peninsula there remained but two—six having fallen in action, of whom five were lads from Kelso. Of the two survivors, Pipe-Major Forbes was to fall in France, while Piper Lockhart, promoted to commissioned rank, survived.

The pipers of the 1/5th Battalion were more fortunate. On the evacuation of the peninsula the pipes and drums were sent home, the pipers and drummers being armed with rifle and bayonet or put on duty as runners. In that capacity two of the pipers gained distinction : Piper M'Minn being several times mentioned in despatches and receiving the M.M. for bravery in the battle of Gaza ; Pipers A. Erskine and J. Diamond mentioned in despatches. Diamond was also promoted sergeant and was awarded the Serbian Gold Medal of Kara George. He fell in action in the second battle of Gaza, April 1917, when there was also killed a promising young piper named Donald M'Kellar, holder of the Scottish Juvenile Pipers' Championship.

The death in action of another young piper of the 7/8th Battalion was long deeply deplored by his comrades, who regarded his few compositions as meritorious and held him in deep affection. As he lay dying his one request was that his beloved bagpipe might be sent to his father.

PIPERS OF THE CAMERONIANS
(SCOTTISH RIFLES)

UNIQUE among the regiments that constitute the British Army are the Cameronians who, as the Angus Regiment or " 26th Foot," long represented the adherents of the Covenanter, Richard Cameron, one of the leaders who preached and fought for freedom to worship, against the Forces of Charles II., at Rullion Green, Drumclog, and Bothwell Bridge.

Like the 25th, or King's Own Scottish Borderers, the Angus Regiment owes its origin to the Government of 1689, but unlike the former unit, it was called forth, not for defence of the City of Edinburgh, but for the " resistance of popery and prelacy and arbitrary power, and to recover and establish the work of the Reformation in Scotland, in opposition to popery, prelacy, and arbitrary power in all their branches."

Had it not been for the religious persecution which these Covenanters had endured at the hands of the ministers of Charles II. and of James VII. and II., and the promise of relief from the Dutch successor of the throne, the regiment could not have come into existence. The nucleus of the Angus Regiment to the number of 500 had marched to Edinburgh in March 1689, along with a delegation to the Convention, for a settlement of Church and State in consonance with their ideas. The

Convention, then sitting in the Parliament House, made use of the 500 stalwarts as a defensive force, and on the termination of these services, for which they refused payment, they were invited to become part of the New Army. They were to be formed into two battalions, one under the command of the Earl of Angus, the other under that of Lieut.-Colonel William Cleland.

After some hesitation the men agreed, and "without beat of drum or expense of levy money" they were enlisted as regular soldiers of the Crown. Many of the customs of their covenanting days they preserved and preserve to this day. They carried their muskets along with their Bibles to church, when in camp or in billets, and all the strict habits of Sabbath-keeping were maintained. Alone of Infantry regiments they still bear as the regimental device the mullet of their first colonel, the Earl of Angus, though every other regiment had to surrender those private emblems in deference to an Army Order of 1751.

It is hardly likely that they had pipers when, in 1689, they marched to Dunkeld, their first engagement, where the 500 Cameronians under the brilliant leadership of young Cleland, poet and scholar, as well as soldier, repulsed a force of 5000 Highlanders, and nullified the success of the Jacobites at Killiecrankie. It was the victory of Dunkeld which enabled the Government to dispense with the large army then in Scotland; and in time to allow of the Cameronians being sent from the Highlands, where they were stationed, to Leith where they embarked in February 1691 for Flanders. In all the stiff fighting there and in Holland, they upheld the high reputation which they had won at Dunkeld.

Again, one asks, did they have pipers there? Were they, like so many of the stern Calvinists, opposed to secular music of any sort? Did they share Wittenbold's aversion to "Torphichen's Rant" as recorded by Niel Blane in *Old Mortality*?

It is just possible that they allowed themselves the solace of pipe music in the intervals of fighting, if they did not avail themselves of the battle music in the actual fighting to which they were called.

May we not infer from the fact that the regimental Pipe Quick Step—the Cameronian rant or reel—is a seventeenth-century composition, that it had been played by the pipers of the regiment since the year 1689? All doubts might have been set at rest if one could rely on the accuracy of a coloured print in Carter's *History of the* 26*th*, where a piper with a bagpipe having two drones is said to be of the period 1713. In spite of the correctness of the two drones there is good reason for suspecting that the illustration is not that of a piper of the Cameronians of 1713. And yet the old Muster Rolls—which make mention of forty drummers on the strength— suggest that some of these were actually pipers in disguise, as in other regiments.

Nor does Sterne in *Tristram Shandy* refer to any pipe music or piper in the regiment with which he is so well acquainted. Their name then was like the name of every regiment of the Line known by the name of the Colonel—Angus. In

1754 it became the 26th Foot, and in 1782, when territorial titles were introduced to most corps, the ancient name of Cameronians was reintroduced.

It is not until 1830 that reference is made in the regimental records to pipers. Even then we should not have had that had it not been for correspondence that passed between the Officer Commanding and General Headquarters. A tight little piper—Cosmo Cameron—had been refused admission to the regiment on account of his inches. His piping must have been good to judge by the letters that passed. In the end Cosmo was allowed to enter as a piper, provided his health and physique otherwise were satisfactory. This incident proves that pipers were not at that date a new institution, otherwise Cosmo would have had no chance.

Curiously the difficulty of 1830 was not recalled in 1862 when Headquarters requested to know on what authority the Cameronians had pipers. On that occasion the Colonel brought forward the oldest soldier—the Bandmaster with thirty-five years' service—as one who recollected seeing and hearing pipers in the battalion from the day when he joined. This evidence evidently satisfied G.H.Q., for the pipers were continued as a regimental institution.

Though they do not figure prominently in the history of the regiment it is not the pipers' fault. They have participated in all the campaigns in which the Cameronians have fought, fighting in the field and playing their companies out and in.

How many excellent pipers the regiment has

had none can say, only the record of one such being available, namely, Donald Campbell.

The pipers of the 2nd Battalion have a widely different career, that is prior to 1882, when as the 90th Perthshire Volunteers (Light Infantry) they achieved fame as fighters without any association with the stern Cameronians. Formed in 1793 by Thomas Graham of Balgowan, who, because of brilliant leadership in the Peninsular War was created Viscount Lynedoch, the men were recruited from rollicking, light-hearted "blades" who sought adventure in battle. It seems singular that until 1882 there is no mention of pipers in a regiment raised in Perthshire—bugles alone, the indispensable instruments of music in Light Infantry regiments, being apparently sufficient to meet their needs when on the march. All this was changed when, by the reorganisation of the Army in 1881, the 90th were linked with the 26th as the 2nd Battalion, and both, on the reputation gained by the 90th as having among them the best shots of the Army, were constituted "The Scottish Rifles." The battalion was then allowed to have pipers—to be paid for by the officers—but no drums were permitted to destroy one of the characteristics of all Rifle and Light Infantry corps. The large bugle bands of the " Rifles " and " Highland Light Infantry " needed no assistance from drums ; but pipers, having more to do than buglers, and being numerically weaker, have a much greater strain on their lungs than have the buglers, when playing on the march. To make their task easier by a supply of drummers was the plea put forward by successive pipe-majors; but not until 1888 was a drum issue granted to the Scottish Rifles. But again their short step—as Rifles—does not conduce to good pipe music, which is perhaps the reason why the tune known as "The Black Bear" is so popular in the battalion, and because it is an Atholl regiment why the famous marching tune of "The Atholl Highlanders" serves as its marching-past tune.

In the Great War the pipers of several battalions of the Rifles played their companies into action, while in other battalions, pipers were in the ranks. The practice of playing into action was stopped after the severe casualties sustained by the pipers. Of the ten pipers who led the 2nd Battalion into France, four were killed in February or March 1915, while a fifth was wounded, and a sixth fell in action in 1916. The popular and intrepid pipe-major, Alexander Cameron, fell while leading a platoon on 5th February 1915. That duty he had volunteered to do, to the dismay of his fellow pipers who had anticipated the consequence. But Cameron was a born soldier, as well as a good piper, and performed his combatant duty with his accustomed *élan* and resourcefulness, and when he was interred beside the colonel and the adjutant the battalion felt that they had lost one of their greatest mainstays. No more cheering words, no more invigorating pipe melodies before and after battle, from that "pukka" soldier. And in missing the commission which would have been his had he survived, King and Country lost at once a piper of merit and an officer who would have made his mark.

Of the two pipers—Horne and Robertson—
who played their respective companies over the
parapet at Loos, to the lightsome "Atholl
Highlanders" some notice may be taken. Horne
was a "crack shot"—was indeed the best shot of
the battalion in 1913. He fell in action on 31st
July 1916. Robertson was luckier. Employed
now on wiring parties, now in fighting, he did
everything with the greatest coolness and gallantry.
"It was owing," wrote his O.C., "to Robertson's
ability as a leader that we were able to maintain a position which we had captured from the
enemy." The Military Medal awarded him was
a slight recognition of his services, as was
also his promotion to the rank of company
sergeant-major.

The edict against pipers playing their companies
into action fretted many a piper throughout the
service and was disregarded whenever an opportunity offered. Pipers Whitelaw and M'Gurk,
for example, of the 9th Battalion, defied the order
during a bombing raid at Arras in April 1917,
by playing their companies over the parapet
and into "No Man's Land"—a spectacle that
thrilled all beholders of other battalions in the
vicinity.

Of quite a different category was the experience
of Piper J. Thomson of the 11th Battalion, when
stationed in Salonica. The glowing reports of the
Scots pipe music had reached the ears of the king of
Rumania, who, curious to hear for himself, begged
that a piper might be sent to him for an afternoon
and evening. Thomson, who in civil life is a
miner in Lanarkshire, was selected, and so

delighted the Rumanian king with his pipe tunes, that he was entertained to dinner with the king, queen, and royal family—an honour that is unique in the annals of the Scottish Rifles.

PIPERS OF THE BLACK WATCH
(ROYAL HIGHLANDERS)

OLDEST of Highland regiments, the 42nd Royal Highlanders, The Black Watch, owes its origin to no outbreak of war, civil or foreign, but to a combination of several "independent" companies which did duty in the Highlands in the second half of the seventeenth century against "thieves and broken men." The freebooting habits of certain lawless clansmen had become so serious a social menace that in 1667 Charles II. granted a commission under the Great Seal to the second Earl of Atholl to raise a company for the express purpose of putting an end to their predatory practices. Other companies were formed in different parts of the Highlands by various chiefs, and in 1739 they were all consolidated into the regiment known in subsequent years as the 42nd Royal Highlanders, The Black Watch. Thus the honour of forming the first of the companies which grew into the famous regiment belongs to the House of Atholl, the men of that company being Atholl Highlanders and the pipers men of the same clan.

It is curious that on the Roll of the Atholl Company the names of the pipers are not given, while in several other companies they appear along with the names of the officers. Among the pipers named are a Patrick M'Grigor and a

Donald M'Crimmon, whose daily pay of ten shillings Scots was exactly half the pay of an ensign and more than thrice the three shillings paid to a private or sentinel. The number of pipers in a company was usually in the ratio of one to every fifty men.

Besides the freebooters, Jacobites and other disaffected subjects came under the surveillance of the new-formed companies which, it is not surprising to learn, proved inadequate for the tasks imposed, and had to be reinforced by companies of the Foot (now Scots) Guards whose bright red coats, white breeches, and white belts were a striking foil to the black-belted, tartan-garbed Highland Watch. From that contrast sprang the name first given by the Highland public—the name which the regiment prizes above all others—"Am Freiceadan Dubh," "The Black Watch," in contradistinction to the "Saighdearan Dearg" or "Red Soldiers."

After several vicissitudes the companies had been disbanded in 1717, but, reformed in 1725, were incorporated in 1739 into the regiment commanded by the Earl of Crawford and Lindsay; and one year later, were assembled in the field between Taybridge and Aberfeldy, now marked by a monument commemorative of the event. In the companies of that regiment were many Campbells, Grants, Macphersons, and Frasers, whose pipers sounded the "Assembly" tunes of their respective clans. The regiment was, after inspection, dismissed to their former duties, and in 1743 were again mustered at Perth and informed that they were to proceed to London for review by George II., who, it was reported, had been much impressed by what he had been told of the social standing and magnificent physical appearance of the rank and file. It was a momentous occasion in the light of later events; Lord Sempill, who had succeeded the Earl of Crawford as colonel, knew that the "Watch" was a home defence regiment or police, and that the order to proceed to London was not for the purpose of being admired by His Majesty, but for official inspection prior to embarkation for foreign service; the men, probably aware that the king had specially sent for three privates to show how broadsword exercise was done, were flattered by the royal interest taken in their regiment. These feelings were soon changed after arrival in London where, instead of His Majesty, they found they were reviewed by General Wade, and, from various unofficial sources, learned that they were bound for the American plantations, where they would serve, not as a regiment, but scattered in various English units.

The Highlanders had reason to resent their shabby treatment. Though they considered themselves a Home regiment, immune from foreign service, they would not have demurred to active service against a European foe, provided they were together, as one unit. But to be scattered among English regiments in obscure islands of the West Indies was repugnant. Smarting under this strong sense of injustice and suspicious of their officers who had not paid them, 107 of the regiment decided to march back to Scotland. The leaders of that movement were Cpls. Samuel and Malcolm

Macpherson, Private Farquhar Shaw, and Piper Donald MacDonald. It was a stealthy march which the 107 undertook, through country which they did not know and where the pipes dared not be heard, and not until they had entered Northamptonshire were they intercepted by a body of cavalry which had been ordered to capture them.

Imprisoned in the Tower of London the ring-leaders were kept apart from the rest until the close of the Court-Martial: their fate was a foregone conclusion—they were condemned to be shot; while the others were flogged and sent out in detachments to several regiments in the West Indies. Only one of the ring-leaders had his sentence commuted—and he was the piper. At the earnest intercession of Captain Robert Munro his life was spared, but he had to join the draft of thirty-seven of his comrades who were embarked for the Leeward Islands as part of Lieut.-General Dalziel's regiment.

The tragedy of 1743 might have been avoided had the men been properly treated at the outset; as it was, the consequences of the Mutiny were not confined to the actual sufferers but to many Highlanders at home who took their stand for Prince Charles mainly because of this regrettable "incident."

Piper Donald MacDonald, who disappears from the subsequent history of the Black Watch, has his niche in the temple of fame, and survives in the drawing of a contemporary artist, and in the print published in H. D. MacWilliam's *Official Records of the Mutiny of the Black Watch*. The

PIPER DONALD MACDONALD, 42ND HIGHLANDERS, 1743.
By kind permission of H. D. MacWilliam, Esq.

authorities did one notable service in transferring
Lord Sempill, the colonel of 1743, to another
regiment, and getting in his place one of the best
officers that the regiment ever had, Lord John
Murray, a son of the Duke of Atholl, who was
to lead it in many of its glorious actions for forty-
two years. Their first battle was Fontenoy, where
the dash and gallantry of all ranks was the talk
of the officers of other regiments there and
the "theme and admiration of all Britain." The
pipers were in action but no mention is made of
them, not even by " Edie Ochiltree " and " Francie
M'Graw," those veterans of the 42nd at Fontenoy.

The regiment returned to England and was
kept in Kent while other regiments were hurried
north to take part in the actions at Prestonpans
and Culloden. Some desultory fighting in the
Netherlands, succeeded by a period spent in garrison
in Ireland, filled up the time of the 42nd till it
was sent to North America where, in the war
against France, it was to experience its greatest
hardships. There in the battle at Fort Ticonderoga, where the bagpipes were heard above the
din of firing, the 42nd Highlanders made repeated
but unavailing attempts to beat down the fort,
their desperate onslaughts costing the regiment
no fewer than 647 casualties—314 killed and 333
wounded ! It was fortunate that the regiment
had been shortly before then 1300 strong. The
" laments " and the old pibroch of Clan days,
" The Desperate Battle," which the pipers played
after the battle were heard by many of the
Canadian contingent. Parkman, the historian of
Canada, has described the " romantic beauty of

the scenery, the sheen and sparkle of the waters, the countless islets with pine, fir, and birch, and the bordering mountains where the notes of bugle, trumpet, bagpipe, and drum were answered and prolonged by a hundred woodland echoes"! One of the pipers present was John M'Donald of the 42nd, who retired on pension sometime later and obtained the post of piper to Glengarry, where he assumed the dignity proper to a Chief's piper. The considerable leisure which was his he kept as a sacred rest. "Why don't you do something in your spare time, John?" once inquired Lady Glengarry. "Ma'am," answered the piper, "it's a poor estate that cannot keep the laird and the piper without working."

That piper doubtless recalled the terrible time at Ticonderoga (for their gallantry at which the 42nd received the honour of the prefix "Royal" to their name of Highlanders) and two years later —1760—of their share in the capture of Montreal; it was the Fraser Highlanders' pipers who were the turning point in the successful issue of the battle on the Heights of Abraham.

The transfer of the 42nd Royal Highland Regiment to the West Indies and thence to Cuba, where Spain was the enemy, appears to have been uneventful so far as the pipers were concerned. The regiment was then shifted to New York and from 1763 to 1767 was engaged in the trying warfare against Indian tribes, after which they were sent to Cork, where they remained until 1775, obtaining recruits by means of recruiting parties sent to Scotland. The regiment was next sent to its old battleground in North America, where their enemies were the colonists whom they had formerly assisted. The rank and file had then received a complete change of arms. Instead of the time-honoured claymore and pistol they were given musket and bayonet, except the pipers who continued to carry the claymore. The War of Independence cost the regiment two pipers who were killed, one of them while playing on the summit of a high hill overlooking New York being struck by a bullet which caused him to fall from crag to crag in his long descent to death. In 1779 a draft of recruits for the 42nd and the 71st, which had been sent from Stirling to Leith for embarkation, mutinied on learning that they were to be drafted to the 82nd Regiment. In the shooting which ensued a piper was shot in both legs, rendering him useless for the army. Descendants of that unfortunate piper are Pipe-Major George S. M'Lennan, late of the Gordon Highlanders, and his younger brother, Pipe-Major Donald M'Lennan, 1st Seaforth Highlanders.

In the recapture of the two British guns from French cavalry at Guildermalsen by some of the 42nd, the pipers cannot claim a direct share though all gloried in the honour meted out in the wearing of the "red hackle" for the bonnet that still marks the episode of 1795.

In times of peace the pipers were generally keen to try their skill with civilian and other regimental pipers. In 1800 Piper William Forbes succeeded in winning second prize for piping at the Highland Society's competition in Edinburgh. In 1801, while he and the other pipers were animating the 42nd in the battle of Alexandria, the honour of the old regiment was being upheld in the competition of the Highland Society by worthy John M'Donald, the veteran of Ticonderoga, who was then almost 80 years old. He is said to have "attracted particular attention and received from the judges a suitable premium; he had been piper to the Glengarry family for some generations." It seems a pity that the venerable pipe-major was unable to revisit the city in the following year when his old regiment was in garrison in the Castle. The pipe-major of that day was John Buchanan, an excellent piper who, from among thirty competitors, won first prize at the annual competition of the Highland Society. That was the last opportunity for many years which the pipers of the 42nd had of displaying their skill in competitions, for, in 1803, they were ordered to the south of England in anticipation of a threatened French invasion; thence to Gibraltar where they remained until 1808, when they were sent to Portugal, arriving shortly after the battle of Vimiera. Attached to the army of Sir John Moore, the 42nd and the other regiments were insufficiently supported against the vastly larger army of France and had to retire along roads covered with snow, over mountains and through defiles for 250 miles, the pipers playing their best for the encouragement of the troops, harassed and weary. Then at the close of that trying march with its rearguard actions, was fought the battle of Elvina, where the 42nd and the 4th and 50th Foot bore the brunt of the day, and where was killed Sir John Moore. Corunna followed, the pipers

playing alongside their companies.   Shipped for
England and thence to the Walcheren expedition,
the regiment was represented in the Peninsula by
its 2nd Battalion which took part in the battles
of Busaco, Fuentes d'Onor, and the sieges of
Ciudad Rodrigo and Badajoz, until 1812, when
the 42nd proper arrived.   Just before the battle
of Salamanca the regiment had the surprise of
their lives in the capture of a French *piper*!
What the 42nd pipers thought of the *musette*
cannot have been exactly complimentary and they
seem not to have deprived the foreign piper of his
instrument.

The honours which the regiment won for the
actions in the Peninsula—Pyrenees, Nivelle, Nive,
Orthes and Toulouse—were also the honours of the
pipers.   Still greater distinction was to be theirs
in 1815 when they accompanied the 42nd to
Quatre Bras and Waterloo in the brigade commanded by Sir Denis Pack.   The gallantry of the
pipers there had not failed to meet the eye of
the brigadier, who showed his appreciation by
presenting to the regiment a set of pipes, which
successive pipe-majors of the 42nd played for the
following thirty years at least.

Alexander [1] M'Tavish, who had been pipe-major
at Quatre Bras and Waterloo, may have been
as good a player as his predecessor, Buchanan,
but he was less fortunate in the competition of
1817 held by the Highland Society.   The regiment was then back in Scotland and M'Tavish,
who had lost no time in entering, was placed
third.   In 1819 he did better, getting second

[1] In Angus M'Kay's *Collection* he is styled Duncan M'Tavish.

place, and two years later was voted the "extra prize, an elegant mounted dirk."

The foreign service which occupied the time of the 42nd from 1825 to 1836 was spent in Gibraltar, Malta, and the Ionian Islands. A few years in garrison in Dublin and the 42nd were again in the Ionian Islands; in Malta and the Bermudas, whence they were sent to Nova Scotia, which they left in 1852 for home. In their next great campaign, the Crimean War, the 42nd were brigaded with the 79th and 93rd. The most notable episode there was the advance, in echelon formation, up the slopes of Alma, the massed pipers of the three regiments marching in silence like the rest. That impressive picture of the tall, feather-bonneted Highlanders and the Guards in their high bearskins, emerging and halting at the summit, appearing to the opposing Russian troops like an army of giants, struck the imagination of one piper—Pipe-Major William Ross of the 42nd—who interpreted the emotions of Highland soldiers in a march which he named the "Heights of Alma." Ross had the good fortune to be appointed in 1854 piper to Her Majesty Queen Victoria, a post he retained till his death in 1891.

In 1858 the 42nd were in the Indian Mutiny where, in the charge on the first position in the Siege of Lucknow, the pipers rushed on with their companies, the rout of the enemy being announced by the pipers' playing: "The Campbells are Comin'."

The pipers could not complain of inactivity any more than the rest of the regiment, for in

December 1873 they were sent to Ashanti, where
King Koffee Kalcali and his stalwarts had been
attacking British settlements.

Landing on the Gold Coast the 42nd had to
traverse large tracts of country, where dense trees
and bushes made excellent cover for the spear
throwing enemy and impeded the progress of
our men.

That expedition—with the battles of Amoaful,
Becqueh, Ordasu and Coomassie—seems relatively
unimportant in the light of the Great War, yet
it made a deep and wide impression on the
public of that time. The chief newspaper of the
United States had sent H. M. Stanley as one
of its war correspondents to report its progress,
and the troops whom Stanley chose particularly
to observe were the Black Watch—the name
which the regiment had retaken in 1861. The
long, tortuous passage through the jungle where
men fell from time to time, the loss of others
in the bush — including Piper Honyman, who,
however, found his way back—was all described
by the American reporter. Stanley admired the
Black Watch, was thrilled as he stood and watched
them "as they marched past the ambuscades, the
bagpipes playing, the cheers rising from the throats
of the lusty Scots, until the forest rang again
with the discordant medley of musketry, bagpipe
music, and vocal sounds." That long, trying
march through the jungle was the most memorable part of the campaign and the only part
that found expression in a pipe melody. In the
" March to Coomassie" the pipe - major, John
M'Donald, depicted the sentiments of the pipers

on the eerie journey. The fighting which followed
must have seemed of less moment for there is no
pipe tune to commemorate any of the actions.
Yet they were prominent in all these actions,
playing the charging tunes, by order of General
Sir Archibald Alison, an order which Piper James
Wetherspoon disobeyed to some purpose. For,
a corporal who was standing beside Wetherspoon
falling wounded, the piper dropped his pipes,
seized his comrade's rifle and made so excellent
a use of it that his valour was later the subject
of much praise. He, too, fell wounded but
not seriously; and on recovery was considerably surprised to find that he was awarded the
Distinguished Conduct Medal.

In 1881, under the New Army scheme the
73rd (Perthshire) were made the 2nd Battalion,
an ideal partnership, for the 73rd had been raised
in 1780 as 2nd Battn. of the 42nd, severing its
connection in 1786 when the 2nd Battalion was
constituted the 73rd. It had made its reputation
as early as 1784 by its defence of Mangalore—
one of the "noblest examples in history"—in
the nine months' siege of which one piper had
been killed and one wounded. The most notable
piper of the 73rd in the early days of the nineteenth century was Hugh M'Kay, a notable
composer as well as an intrepid soldier-piper.
One of the sergeants of the 73rd who published
his *Recollections of the Campaigns of* 1813-15
told how, "during our forced marches through
Germany the most serviceable man we had was
our old piper Hugh M'Kay, who, when the men
were tired and straggling, would fall back to the

rear, and, striking up some lively air, would soon have them about him like a cluster of bees."

That testimony of an English sergeant—and most of the 73rd were English in the early years of the nineteenth century—is interesting so far as it goes, but there was no chronicler to succeed Sergeant Morris in any of the subsequent campaigns — in the Kaffir Wars, the Indian Mutiny, in China, and again in India. As 2nd Battn. The Black Watch the pipers were not so likely to be overlooked as they had been, when the majority of the officers and men were English or Irish.   In India, the 73rd was the best qualified of regiments to be partner of the 42nd, who were shortly afterwards sent to the Egyptian War of 1882-5.   There the pipers, still under Pipe-Major John M'Donald of Coomassie fame, played the charging tunes at Tel-el-Kebir, El Teb, and Tamai. The wearers of the medal with the blue-and-white barred ribbon and its companion bronze star with blue ribbon, given by the Khedive, are comparatively few nowadays, and there were not many of the rank and file who wore them in the succeeding campaign, namely, the South African War, 1899-1902, where the 2nd Black Watch shared with the other units of the Highland Brigade some of the hardest fighting in the war. In addition to the notices of pipers playing at Elandslaagte, Magersfontein, and other engagements, there is one picturesque incident, not so well known, which has a piper of the Black Watch as its leading character.   The Modder River, then in spate and pronounced unfordable, had to be crossed in order that our men might

get to close quarters with the enemy, who were
sniping under cover. Without hesitation Piper
Donald Cameron jumped in, found that the water
reached only to his waist, upon which discovery
the officer in charge gave the order for the men
to cross the river in tens, each man holding his
neighbour's hand. Thus the smaller soldiers were
enabled to keep their feet and all got across
safely, Piper Cameron being first.

This episode has its romantic parallel in the
French wars of almost two centuries ago, when
the company of exiled Jacobite officers—all Scots
—served as privates in the army of France.
They were on their way to storm a stronghold
of the Germans on an island of the Rhine.

> The ford is deep, the banks are steep,
>   The island shore lies wide;
> Nor man nor horse could stem its force,
>   Or reach its further side.
> See there! amidst the willow boughs
>   The serried bayonets gleam.
>
> .   .   .   .   .
>
> No stay—no pause.   With one accord
>   They grasped each other's hand
> And plunged into the angry flood,
>   That bold and dauntless band.

Piper Donald Cameron, who probably had never
heard of "The Island of the Scots," had his valour
appreciated by the officers, who, in addition to
mentioning him and Piper George Burns in dis-
patches, were the means of obtaining for Cameron
the D.C.M.

It may not be out of place to record that the
gallant piper, who retired from the army on the

conclusion of hostilities and settled in South Africa,
rejoined on the outbreak of the Great War as
pipe-major of the South-African Scottish, but,
finding that the pipers were not in the forefront,
resigned his post for a place in the ranks and rose
to be company sergeant-major.

In the Great War the 1st Battn. of the Black
Watch were in the Retreat from Mons and in the
engagements that followed. Of the six pipers
who played the battalion in those actions three
were wounded, a fourth was transferred to another
battalion ; while to make good this depletion four
pipers were sent to the battalion, of whom, however, only one escaped casualty.

The fierce fighting at Aubers Ridge, 9th May
1915, found the pipers coolly playing amidst all
the rain of shot and shell, a waste of energy—since
the strains of " Hielan' Laddie " were inaudible—
but memorable as witness to the intrepidity of the
pipers of the Black Watch in battle.

The pipers of the 2nd Battalion who played
their companies during the War in France and
Flanders—October 1914 to November 1915 and
during the Mespot. and Palestine campaigns—were
remarkable for the large number of marksmen
they contributed to the battalion's credit, and of
these no fewer than five were " best shot " of their
respective companies. The " Admirable Crichton "
of the battalion was Piper Peter M'Nee, a very
handsome man who, besides being a splendid
" shot," was an excellent bomber. When placed
on trench mortar work he was equally distinguished. " Let me have M'Nee and the 'goods,'"
remarked a certain stalwart Irish officer, " and

I'll keep back a whole Army Corps!" Alas! the brave M'Nee, after valiantly assisting to repel one of these attacks, was killed at his post.

Piper Wilson was a daring and successful scout, gaining the D.C.M., an award that was also bestowed on Pipe-Major Keith "for conspicuous gallantry under most trying circumstances."

Four pipers won fame by playing their pipes in action at Loos. Alec M'Donald and David Simpson were determined to keep by their platoons, playing their music until the final trench was captured. They had reached and passed the first line trenches and the second line, and were about the parapet of the third, when Simpson fell mortally wounded and M'Donald was severely wounded. Their gallantry had deeply impressed the battalion, all of whom rejoiced to learn that Alec M'Donald, whose leg had to be amputated, had been awarded the D.C.M. Poor M'Donald, however, did not survive the war.

Armitt, another piper of the battalion, was also playing his platoon into action, but on reaching bombing range Armitt put down his pipes and took a hand in bombing the Germans back.

The most surprising piper was probably the boy piper, Wishart, who, like his friends, played his platoon into action, entirely rapt in his martial music, heedless of the deafening roar of artillery, machine-gun, and rifle fire, and regardless of wounds, until some shrapnel silenced his pipes for ever. Boy Wishart was much surprised when, lying in hospital, he learned that he was being publicly praised as a hero, and still more surprised when he received a command to appear before

His Majesty. That is always a great honour for a soldier, a landmark in one's military experience, and one surely unique among boy soldiers! Boy Wishart must have felt highly pleased with himself and with the world when he heard His Majesty tell him that he was "the bravest boy he had heard of."

Of such excellent material are all good Army pipers made!

The pipers of the New Army and Territorial battalions of the regiment were no whit behind their friends the pipers of Regular service; like them they were relieved of the duty of playing in action after Loos. Some served as stretcher-bearers, a duty in which the pipers of the 1/4th Battalion particularly distinguished themselves, earning the publicly expressed thanks of Generals Sir J. French, Willcox, and Anderson. Piper—later Pipe-Major—Dan M'Leod was awarded the Military Medal for bravery in the field, and Pipe-Major Alec Low had his disregard of danger and his devotion to duty officially recognised in the award of a D.C.M.

Daring and ingenious were the pipers of the 7th Battalion, who, as runners, seemed to bear a charmed life in that exceedingly dangerous duty, their worst spell being probably that at Beaumont Hamel, where several fell while bearing orders from Headquarters to the battalion, and in consequence of which much muddle was caused. Several pipers were recommended for commissions, one transferred to the Tank Corps, another who as a marksman, was accepted by the Lovat Scouts as a sniper, and three—Pipe-Major Thomas

Macdonald, George Galloway, and David Swan—
were awarded each the Military Medal.

Captain Edouard Ross, a Scoto - French
interpreter who was present in the advance in
August 1918, on the Albert - Arras Road,
described in *The Scotsman* how the Germans
who occupied the heights endeavoured to check
the oncoming British Force. The Black Watch
were determined to clear them out and one
company had advanced to within 120 yards of
the Germans when a murderous fire was opened.
Though every one of that company was wounded
they managed to win a trench, but they were far
from the rest of their battalion and the smoke of
the guns prevented the other companies from
locating their position. The piper who was in
that trench, however, knew how to direct them.
Standing up he played one of the regimental
tunes with the desired effect : the companies
charged in the face of the terrific gunfire and
captured the position, while the retreating Germans
were cut off by the Gordons on their right.

The pipers of the Black Watch on the Eastern
Front were looked upon by their officers in much
the same light as the old-time clan piper was
looked upon by his chief; he occupied a high
place in the hierarchy of heroes. The official
historians of the regiment make the point quite
clear by frequent reference. "To men of the
Highland Battalion "—an allusion to a temporary
union of Black Watch and Seaforths — these
officers write, "there was no sound like the
sound of the pipes. Men of both battalions
might well recall how they had charged forward

in France and in Mesopotamia, the pipers leading
the way—and no body of men had shown greater
gallantry or inspired others with their spirit more
than the regimental pipers. Yet, even in war,
the days of battle are few and the days of trial
many; and often at Reveillé and Retreat, on the
march and in camp, did the sound of the massed
pipers stir the memories and strengthen the spirit
that inspired the men of the Highland Battalion
to face all and every danger that lay before it"
(Wauchope, *The Black Watch*, vol. i., p. 232).
Elsewhere the authors remark: "On the many
long marches the music of the pipes gave fresh
life to weary columns . . ." and, "in many battles
men have followed where the pipers led, and
great were the services, though heavy the toll on
the pipers playing the way along the smoke-hidden
trenches in France and putting fresh life into the
men during the hard-fought battles near Kut and
Baghdad. . . ."

They pay tribute to Pipe-Major J. Keith who
was awarded the D.C.M., and to Piper, later Pipe-
Major MacLeod, but the officers were particularly
proud of their pipe-corporal, D. MacMaster, one
of the oldest soldiers in the 2nd Battalion.
MacMaster was out with a patrol party on the
Palestine Front in 1917 when they were attacked
and the captain was wounded. The old pipe-
corporal then took charge of the party, and though
they were again attacked he managed to bring it
back to battalion lines. The officer-in-command
was delighted and extolled the "coolness and
determination of the pipe-corporal which was ably
seconded by the remainder of the company."

When decorations were later conferred the old pipe-corporal was awarded the Panama Medal.

For many years the soldiers of India have looked upon the members of Highland regiments as allies, friends, "big brothers," fraternising with them and excluding all other kinds of regiments. The Gurkhas and Pathans and Sikhs esteemed in particular the bagpipe, so much so that they too obtained their own bagpipes, and, having learned from the pipe-majors of the different Highland units stationed among them the commoner tunes, "took on" all the mannerisms of their kind instructors.

It was thus a pleasing order of the authorities which placed the 1/8th Battalion of the Gurkha Regiment beside the Black Watch in Mesopotamia. The old-time interchange of courtesies knew no change in their close co-operation during the Great War; and when the day arrived for the Black Watch men and the Gurkhas to bid each other farewell they took leave like the Greek heroes of old by an exchange of gifts. To the Black Watch the Gurkhas presented a pair of kukris, while the Scots in return gave—what the Gurkha takes delight in—a set of bagpipes, mementoes of the War and of two distinguished regiments.

(For the above report of the Gurkhas and the Black Watch I am indebted to the splendid narrative of the *Official History of the Black Watch*, edited by A. G. Wauchope.)

PIPERS OF THE HIGHLAND LIGHT INFANTRY

Possessors of more battle honours than any other Scots regiment, the Highland Light Infantry owe much to their pipers. Long years before 1881, when the 74th Highlanders were added as their 2nd Battalion, the pipers had materially assisted to make the high reputation of the regiment. The 71st, or 1st Battalion, had been raised in 1777 by John (Mackenzie) Lord MacLeod, eldest son of the Third Earl of Cromartie, who had been "out in the Forty-five."

Mustering at Elgin the regiment, comprising 681 Highlanders and 260 Lowlanders, were sent to India to repel the French and natives who were then attacking the British settlements. After a weary voyage which lasted twelve months they were disembarked at Madras and very quickly had the misfortune to be too near an ammunition wagon which had exploded, just as they were going into action. Several officers and men were wounded and made prisoners by the large army of Hyder Ali, one of the 71st's officers being Captain Baird who was later to attain to much fame as Lieut.-General Sir David Baird and of whose capture Sir Walter Scott used to relate the following story. Baird's mother, on being informed that her son had been chained to another officer like all those who had been captured, ejaculated: "Lord peety the chiel wha's chained to oor Davie!"

That indignity was, however, spared Captain Baird, who was badly wounded and whose services were in consequence lost to his regiment for some weeks.

It was the battle of Porto Novo, 1st July 1781, which introduced the pipers of the 71st to the admiring notice of soldiers far and wide. The 71st, the only white battalion engaged, held the post of honour on the extreme right of the first line. The whole force under Sir Eyre Coote numbered but 8000; while the enemy had 25 battalions of Infantry, 400 Europeans, and about 45,000 Cavalrymen; and more than 100,000 matchlock men and 47 cannon.

The position looked hopeless for the small body under Sir Eyre Coote. All the brunt was on the Scots, everything depended on them, and that seemed to be realised not only by the commander-in-chief but by one of the pipers who accompanied the 71st. For eight hours the fight went on and all the time that piper kept playing all that he knew of battle tunes. The 71st put up their hardest and best and, surprising as it must appear, actually won the day.

What the men and their officers actually thought about the piper one cannot tell, but they must all have felt considerably astonished and delighted when, at the close, Sir Eyre Coote rode up to the piper, shook him heartily by the hand, "Well done, gallant fellow, you shall have

a silver set of pipes for this!" The promise was
kept and the pipes are to this day an heirloom
at Headquarters of the 1st Battalion of the
regiment.

One engagement after another found the 71st
and their pipers achieving brilliant victories until
the whole series terminated in favour of British
arms at Seringapatam in 1799. Then the 71st
was sent off to fight the Dutch in South Africa,
thence to South America where the fighting
was still against the Napoleonic regime.

There, too, the pipers proved of value to their
friends. One soldier whose term of service had
expired, confided to a comrade his intention to
remain in that sunny land; the comrade said
nothing—merely hummed a pipe tune, "Lochaber
No More." It was enough; "Ach, no, I could
not . . . no, I must go back."

After the street fighting in Buenos Ayres
in 1806 the pipe-major discovered that he had
lost his pipe banner. How it had gone, whether
by capture or by his own carelessness, none could
say. The loss was soon forgotten in the press
of other affairs. Judge, then, the surprise of
the successors of these officers and pipers when,
eighty years later, they were informed that the
old pipe banner had been all that time a treasured
relic in an old family in Chile and that it was
to be restored to the regiment. The circumstances were these: In 1882 Sir John Drummond
Hay, H.M. Chargé d'Affaires at Valparaiso,
wrote to Her Majesty Queen Victoria stating
that Santiago D. Lorca, Admiral of the Chilian
Navy, had a British banner which had been in

H

the possession of his family since the days of his grandfather, who had enjoined his sons to treasure it until circumstances should permit of its safe return to the British nation ; and that he now proposed to hand it over to the Chargé d'Affaires. This was the long missing pipe banner of the 71st. Her Majesty, regarding it as valuable as a regimental colour, gave order for a warship to be sent for the delivery of the precious relic. That was done, and the Queen having inspected it, handed it to the representatives of the 71st, who placed it in their Headquarters, where it still reposes, showing a thistle and rose, the emblems of the regiment, embroidered on a field of crimson silk fringed with gold.[1]

If the 71st won fame by its piper in India it was destined to achieve more fame in the Peninsular War by the valour of another piper. At the battle of Vimiera, 21st August 1808, Piper George Clark set the example so often followed in later actions, of continuing to play, in spite of severe wounds, the regimental charging tune, "Up and waur them a', Willie." Clark played when he fell wounded and played for some time, the while his comrades, animated by his play, fought on. Officers and men fêted the wounded piper and would have urged the Authorities to bestow a decoration on him had such things been customary then. They did their best, however, for they told of the heroism of Clark, and that was lauded by civilians at home to so great an extent, that on the return

[1] Another pipe banner of the 71st still hangs in Santo Domingo Church, Buenos Ayres.

of the regiment to Scotland, the Highland Society
held a reception in honour of Piper Clark and
awarded him a gold medal and a set of pipes.
Moreover, when their piping competition was
about to be held they dissuaded him from com-
peting, probably because they did not wish to
see him second to any ; and having awarded him
a special gold medal, appointed him piper to the
Society.

In 1813 the pipers of the 71st were at Vittoria,
where they played " Johnny Cope " in the brilliant
uphill charge against the French—a fact alluded
to by a Forfarshire poet, William Glen, one of
whose stanzas runs as follows :—

> If e'er they meet their worthy king,
>   Let them dance roun' him in a ring,
> And some Scots piper play the spring
>   He blew them at Vittoria.

The renown of the regiment which had relied
so much on the prowess of its pipers had more
than a transitory effect on its fortunes. Because
of its brilliant conduct in the various actions in
the Peninsula, the 71st was, in 1809, promoted
to be a Light Infantry regiment which, among
other details, meant an alteration in dress and
accoutrements. Light Infantry corps were not
as other regiments, but wore a distinctive uniform
which permitted of greater freedom in their quick
movements and skirmishing duties ; and they had
a bugle band to cheer them on their way. These
were very fine for ordinary regiments of Foot,
but hardly good enough for a Highland regiment
that prided itself on its picturesque dress and its

own form of musical instrument. Accordingly Colonel—later General—Sir Denis Pack appealed to Headquarters that the 71st might be allowed to retain the title of "Highland" before the new designation "Light Infantry," and that it might continue to wear "such parts of the national dress as might not be inconsistent with their duties as a light infantry corps, including the 'bonnet cocked'"; finally, he urged, "that they keep their pipers in all their customary dress. It cannot be forgotten how these pipers were obtained and how constantly the regiment upheld its title to them. These are the honourable characteristics alluded to, which must preserve to future generations the precious remains of the old corps, and of which I feel confident His Majesty never will have reason to deprive the 71st Regiment."

This eloquent appeal had the desired result. The letter of 12th April 1810, from Whitehall, contained an assent to all Colonel Pack's requests, and as the "71st Highland Light Infantry" it shared, with the 90th Perthshire Regiment—now 2nd Battn. Scottish Rifles—the distinction of a Light Infantry regiment, and of being the only light infantry corps in possession of pipers—all the other light infantry corps being English. This right to pipers was confirmed in 1854 when Headquarters permitted each Highland unit to have a pipe-major and five pipers. Yet, here again, there continued for many years a difference between the pipe band of the H.L.I. and that of every other regiment; there were no drums in light infantry units and the H.L.I. carried on without these great assets until 1905, when there was appointed a pipe-major who, coming from the Seaforth Highlanders, deplored the lack of the sheepskins. The officers acceded to the earnest representation of Pipe-Major James Taylor by getting the necessary number of drums.

The pipers had then a long list of battle honours : Waterloo, Sebastopol, the Indian Mutiny, Tel-el-kebir, Crete and South Africa, 1899-1902, being the successors of the eighteenth century engagements. It was in the last-named war that two pipers of the H.L.I., Pipe-Major Ross and Piper J. M'Lellan, were both awarded the D.C.M. for conspicuous gallantry in the battle of Magersfontein where, in the most exposed part of the field, they played the regimental "Assembly" with such excellent effect that the scattered soldiers were brought together. M'Lellan was poet and composer of several melodious tunes, one of which received—while the battalion were stationed in Egypt—the name of "The Burning Sands of Egypt," and, after doing duty in South Africa as "The March to Heilbron," it was adapted to the words of a song which is yet popular : "The Road to the Isles." Such at least is the proud claim of the H.L.I.

The 2nd Battn. the 74th Highlanders has an equally notable record of distinguished pipers, the earliest noted of whom is George Maclachlan, who was among the first to scale the twenty-foot-high wall at the siege of Badajos. Several were killed in the attempt and many more were wounded but Maclachlan escaped ; only his bagpipe was hit just as he had reached the top and had started

"The Campbells are Comin'." Maclachlan coolly sat on the ramparts, heedless of the bullets that went whizzing past, repaired his bagpipe, tried it, and resumed his advance and the stirring tune. It was he who averted disaster from his regiment at Vittoria, where the 74th had gone to the rescue of the 88th Regiment. The adjutant had tried in vain to recall his men; they heard him not. Without direction of any kind Piper Maclachlan promptly played the "Assembly" while he stood by his officer's side, and the men, hearing the old, familiar notes, came towards him at the "double."

That successful exhibition of native wit and initiative became the talk of the officers and was reported to Headquarters; the grateful adjutant promised the piper a reward of value, but alas! that promise could not be redeemed, for Piper Maclachlan shortly afterwards was killed in the thick of battle.

In the Great War the Highland Light Infantry had all its nine "New Army" battalions, six territorial and two regular battalions engaged in one or other of the theatres of war; and in every unit the pipers were conspicuous either as pipers, runners, ration and ammunition carriers, stretcher-bearers, or with rifle and bombs.

The 2nd Battalion was the earliest in action. As part of the Second Division it fought in all the actions from Mons to Festubert, December 1914. It was then that the 1st Battalion arrived from India. The pipers of the 1st Battalion numbered twenty-eight, twenty-two of them being "acting" pipers; the 2nd Battalion had a pipe

PIPER OF THE 74TH HIGHLANDERS OF 1850
(now 2nd Bn. Highland Light Infantry).

band of fifteen, of whom nine were "acting" and accordingly these reverted to the ranks in accordance with Army regulations. The six "full" pipers of the 2nd Battalion—who became stretcher-bearers, and at times ammunition carriers—were all casualties by the close of the year 1914, their places being taken by pipers sent from the depôt. Festubert accounted for some severe losses to the pipers of the 1st Battalion—two were badly wounded, two were captured, and the pipe-major and four of the acting pipers killed in action. One piper—Morrison—was long remembered for the gallant fight which he made against hopeless odds and for his refusal to surrender to a number of Germans who surrounded him He fell at last with seventeen bayonet wounds.

The shell-swept field of Richebourg also forms one of the vivid memories of the H.L.I. pipers, one of whom, Pipe-Sergeant Godsman, carried bombs throughout the battle, to the surprise of his comrades who entertained few hopes of his survival. The pipe-sergeant, however, did escape, though wounded, and had the satisfaction later of learning that his devotion to duty and disregard of danger had been recognised in the award of the Cross of the Russian Order of St George, a distinction shared by another piper.

The Territorial battalions began their war experience in Gallipoli, where the casualties among the pipers were heavy in consequence of their position at the head of their respective battalions. So great were these casualties, that on the eve of evacuation of the peninsula, pipers could not be obtained except after an exhaustive search among

men in the trenches who had not enlisted as
pipers. The pipers who had played their
companies forward were in many cases found
lying dead on the battlefield with their pipes by
their side.

Piper Kenneth M'Lennan of the 7th Battn.
H.L.I. was more fortunate, though he had his
pipes blown out of his hands by a shell in the
action of 12th July 1915 when he was at the head
of his company; piping being over he became
stretcher-bearer, tended the wounded under heavy
fire, and had his gallant services recognised by the
award of a D.C.M.

The pipers who had been found among the
rank and file were formed into one pipe band for
the Division and were utilised for the marches
through Egypt and Palestine, their music being
appreciated not only by the Division but by all
who were near enough to hear them. Men
writing home mention how the sound of the pipes
reaching their ears over wide expanses, seemed
like a whiff from the homeland where they had
thought little of pipe music. These improvised
pipers carried on until they were brought to
France where they became stretcher-bearers or
runners, or ammunition and ration carriers.

In the "Kitchener" battalions of the H.L.I.
the pipers were at times playing their companies
into action, at other times they fought in the
ranks, and very often they were stretcher-bearers
and runners. Young Gilbert, the pipe-major of
the 17th Battalion, was one of those who took
each of these duties in turn, and for a considerable
time he was actually Regimental Sergeant-Major.

It was, however, for his work as a runner from Headquarters to battalion lines that he received the Military Medal.

In the Somme offensive of July 1916 the pipers were with the battalion of the H.L.I. which penetrated farthest into the enemy lines. There Piper Hugh MacArthur had been as a rifleman and at the close of the day returned to Headquarters for rest. He was not long there when the Headquarters Company was almost surrounded by German troops who were strenuously bombing. Neighbouring battalions were being pressed back and everything looked "black" for our troops. Piper MacArthur pondered the situation and promptly decided that only a stirring air on the pipes could have any chance of averting disaster. Accordingly he got his pipes, stood on the top of a trench and played as loudly as he knew how, with the anticipated result—the repulse of the enemy !

On the glad occasions of Divisional Games the pipers of the different battalions proved their skill by winning prizes for pipe-playing. The pipers of the 2nd Battalion won the first prize in 1917 for marches, strathspeys, and reels, and the 7th (Territorial) Battalion were first in 1919 in competitions open to Brigade, Division, and Army Corps.

A unique departure from the old Army pipers' ways was made in consequence of the American army's entry into the War. Their authorities had requested the services of some officers and non-commissioned officers as instructors, and no one was surprised ; but when they also asked for

the "loan" of pipers the request seemed odd.
Pipers were sent and those selected were from
the 14th Battn. H.L.I.   Very soon these pipers
learned to their considerable surprise that the
gentlemen with the nasal twang were not all so
ignorant of pipe tunes and pipers' ways as they
had imagined.   After all it was not so surprising,
for the Yankee hat and the nasal twang often
disguised the ubiquitous Scot.

PIPERS OF THE SEAFORTH HIGHLANDERS

THE 72nd, Duke of Albany's Own Highlanders, and the 78th, Ross-shire Buffs, both hailing from the county of Ross and both raised by a Mackenzie of Seaforth, had nothing in common until they were united, in 1881, as the 1st and 2nd Battns. The Seaforth Highlanders. Their records being equally distinguished, none expressed dissatisfaction with their official co-partnership. " Honours were easy."

Yet—in the very year in which they were formed, namely, 1778—the 72nd were within an ace of wrecking their corporate existence as a regiment, and by nothing less than open mutiny ! The men, among whom Clan MacRae was well represented, under the firm belief that they were about to be betrayed by both Government and their own officers, and smarting from the more immediate effects due to neglect of pay and of bounty, flatly refused to embark for India, and, forming themselves on the quay of Leith into column of fours, with pipers in front, marched off to the King's Park, ascended the heights of Arthur's Seat, and made preparations for surprise attack by entrenchments and the posting of sentries. There they stayed for several days, supported morally and materially by the citizens of Edinburgh, whose visits, with hampers of food, they naturally much appreciated.

How long they might have withstood the long arm of authority is matter for surmise, but the authorities, conscious probably of their own shortcomings, despatched two generals, who, along with the Earl of Seaforth, their chief and colonel, interviewed the mutineers and promised to redress their grievances. Their confidence thus restored, the Highlanders forthwith marched down the hill, the colonel and the pipers leading. The battalion was then embarked for service in the Channel Islands, some in Jersey, and the rest in Guernsey, after which the whole body was transferred to Portsmouth and sent to India, 1100 strong. Transport ships then were vile, owing largely to lack of accommodation, and that, added to the length of time taken to accomplish the voyage, and the want of vegetables, made the death-roll of the unfortunate Seaforths very heavy. When the regiment disembarked at Madras after eleven months at sea, 247 men had died of scurvy and many more were too ill to bear arms, leaving but 369 fit to march, and these, although depressed by the death of their chief and colonel, the Earl of Seaforth, were immediately sent up country and attached to the 71st. The 72nd did not take the field as a regiment until April 1783.

In their early battles in India, summed up in the name Hindoostan—an honoured name on the regimental Colour, the battle tunes of the Clan Mackenzie — "Blar Strom," and "Cabar Feidh" — must have rung out clear and often, but the mere fact of these tunes being part of the regiment's programme in action makes all allusion to the pipers unnecessary. It is only when an unusual incident occurs, such as that at the siege of Pondicherry, that the annalist makes note. There the French troops were having the best of it—for a time. With the strong sun behind them and right in the eyes of the 72nd, there seemed no chance for our troops, whose fire was weak and desultory. The volleys of the French were rattling merrily and the officers of the 72nd were powerless to stem them or to infuse energy into their men. Then the O.C. had an inspiration. He would have a pibroch played. A pibroch at such a time! Everyone was amazed at the order, and none more so than the French soldiers who, when they heard the first few notes of that unnamed composition, slackened their fire, then actually ceased firing, and from over their stockades their puzzled eyes looked at the equally puzzled Highlanders. The ruse had succeeded, and the hostile gunfire died down for the rest of that day. The slow notes of the pibroch played by the piper of the Grenadier Company had undone the enemy!

In 1806 the regiment was sent to South Africa where the pipers proved an immense asset, sometimes exchanging the bagpipe for the claymore. Their prowess was praised and sung wherever Scots were gathered. The Highland Societies of London and Edinburgh vied with each other in giving publicity to their deeds. It was mainly due to the stirring tunes which they played in all the actions in South Africa, especially in the capture of the Cape of Good Hope, that these were so successful — at least such was the opinion of the officers and men of the regiment.

There was one incident remarked by the English soldiers of the 59th Regiment, who were associated in several actions with the Seaforths. Both units had made an exceptionally long march, and at the close the Englishmen were glad to lie at rest; everyone, they thought, would be equally glad. But to their amazement they heard the pipers of the Seaforths playing their pipes, and looking up they saw the stalwart Grenadiers of the Highlanders dancing to the pipers' playing!

The departure from the regiment of their chronicler, Lieut. Campbell, was a loss to the 72nd—and especially to the pipers, in whom he was keenly interested. The facts relating to them are not noted with the same frequency by his successors, until the present century, when ample amends are made by the historian of the pipers of the Seaforths, Major Mackay-Scobie, whose *Pipers of a Highland Regiment*, full of interesting material, is narrated in delightful fashion. From that work the following episode in the Kaffir War of 1834-35 is taken. A Kaffir chief who had been captured by the 72nd, manifested a surprising interest in the bagpipe, asked all manner of questions regarding it, and was told, among other facts, that it could sound all kinds of signals except that of " Retreat." The chief, thinking this was a defect in the instrument, generously offered to his captors his wooden whistle which, when blown at one end indicated "Advance," and when blown at the other end, "Retreat."

For many years the regiment had forty-seven pipers and drummers. They were in the Crimea and in the Indian Mutiny, where two pipers played alternately for thirteen hours on a forty-two mile march; and the pipers led the charge on Kotah, which was captured. They were in the Afghan War, where the storming of the Peiwar Kotal was immortalised by Piper Stark in his well-known "72nd's Advance on the Peiwar Kotal." The famous march from Kabul to Kandahar was disastrous for the pipers, only two surviving when Kandahar was reached—the rest having literally "played themselves to death." In 1882 the 72nd were in action in Egypt where, in the battle of Tel-el-Kebir, each piper played his company into action and after the battle entertained the regiment on its thirty-three miles long march to Zag-a-Zig.

Deprived of the Highland garb in 1809, like other Highland corps they tried again and again to have that order rescinded. In 1823 they were allowed to resume all the characteristics of their nationality, except the kilt. In their trews of Royal Stewart tartan the 72nd were conspicuous in all engagements. In recognition of their valour they were privileged to style themselves, "The Duke of Albany's Own Highlanders," which, with the cipher and coronet of that Prince, still finds an honoured place in all their appointments.

Their 2nd Battalion (from 1881), the old 78th Highlanders or Ross-shire Buffs, had been raised in 1793 by a cousin of the founder of the 72nd, who, in course of time became Lord Seaforth. Like the 72nd, the Ross-shire Buffs won their fame in India; so much so that they were, after the Mutiny there, termed the "Saviours of India," and their pipers, even more than the pipers of the 72nd, had a due share in the honours accorded the regiment by the public. In one of their earlier actions the pipers, or rather one of them, had a mortifying experience, a two-fold affront. Just before the battle of Assaye, an order was issued for all musicians to go to the rear to be in readiness for casualties which they would carry to the surgeon. Accordingly all the bandsmen retired and with them a Company piper, who rightly deemed himself a "musician." When the battle was over that unfortunate piper was subjected to the taunts of his comrades and his officers. "Whoever heard of a piper going to the rear! Disgraceful!" "But I was ordered to go; the order said all musicians were to go," pleaded the injured piper. "That's all very well for the flutes and hautbois and the like," was the answer, "but for a piper who should always be in the forefront of battle to go to the rear with the *whistlers* is a thing unheard of." The insult to his art had to be swallowed, but only let him get an opportunity and he would show them whether he was not a piper worthy of his gallant predecessors. Order or no order, he decided he would keep in the forefront in future. His opportunity arrived in a very short time when the battle of Argaum was fought. There the piper was seen and heard in the thick of the fight, deaf to all but his fierce notes. So insistent was he that the officers had difficulty in restraining the men from charging. The piper's honour was vindicated completely.

Twelve years later the 78th were in the Netherlands where, in an action in the village of Merxem, Piper Munro was badly wounded; he could sit however, and, despite the pain, urged on his fellows by playing "Hey, Johnny Cope," and "Hielan' Laddie," as several pipers have done in more recent days—with more tangible recognition. In a still later engagement in Holland the 78th ascribed their victory over a French force which numbered three thousand, to the gallantry of the pipers.

The 78th were denied a place in the Peninsular War and at Waterloo; their romance and renown centre in the Indian Mutiny, one episode of which, finding its way into the public press, was spoken about for many years throughout the English-speaking world. "Jessie's Dream" commemorates in a well-known song the experience of Mrs Jessie Brown, one of the imprisoned residents of Lucknow, to relieve whom the 78th were marching forward, their pipers, as usual, playing at their head. The song represents Mrs Brown[1] announcing to her despondent companion the approach of the British with the pipers playing.

It is at once curious and ridiculous that in later years much controversy should arise over this evidently perfectly reasonable basis of fact for the song. One newspaper correspondent had

[1] Said to have been a Scot, the wife of a soldier in the 32nd Regiment.

even the temerity to state that the 78th had no
pipers with them and that the story had originated
in France!

Fortunately there are preserved two books
relating to the pipers at Lucknow, which completely refute the allegation of falsehood.   One of
these, *The Personal Narrative of the Siege of
Lucknow*, by L. E. L. Rees, a survivor of the
siege, contains the following passage : " The
shrill tones of the Highlanders' bagpipes now
pierced our ears ; not the most beautiful music
was ever more welcome or more joy-bringing.
As Havelock's force came nearer the enemy
found some of us dancing to the sound of the
Highlanders' pipes.   The remembrance of that
happy evening will never be effaced from my
memory."   That is surely strong enough evidence
on the point.   The other work is *Reminiscences
of the Mutiny*, by Forbes Mitchell, who devotes
much space to the story of Jessie Brown, whose
companion in the same compartment in the
Residency was a Mrs Gaffney, the wife of a
brother sergeant of Mitchell.   Mrs Gaffney described to Mitchell how Jessie Brown had heard
the bagpipes long before anyone could believe
that a force was coming to their relief.   The
pipe-major of the 78th, the well-known Norman
M'Leod, a Raasay man, who, among other
compositions, has to his credit " The 78th's
March to Lucknow," took Mitchell aside to
listen to the pipers play " On wi' the Tartan,"
which they did out of compliment to the Scottish
residents.

If the story of Jessie Brown's vision of the

approaching Highlanders and their pipers is the
most romantic in the estimation of women, the
extraordinary stratagem of Piper Gibson of the
78th is, for soldiers, by far the best feat achieved
by any of the pipers at Lucknow. Six sowars
(troopers of native cavalry) had spurred their
horses, prepared to charge three isolated Seaforths
and Piper Gibson. The Scots had no ammunition,
but with fixed bayonets were ready to receive
the enemy's charge. The sowars galloped to
within twenty paces of the party; the piper,
who had no arms, presented the drones of his
pipes, blowing at the same time one long note.
The enemy stopped immediately, turned and
"flew like the wind, mistaking the bagpipe for
some infernal machine."

One occasionally hears from the lips of older
people narratives of the Indian Mutiny, and from
them gathers some notion of the deep impression
which the Seaforth Highlanders made on the
people of Scotland on their return in 1860.
When they marched into Edinburgh as the
garrison battalion, they were fêted as heroes and
called the " Saviours of India." Until 1859 their
pipers had worn the buff doublet, a colour which
was then changed for green, and that, along with
the red sash and a dirk at the waistbelt, made
the pipe-major look "unco smart inteet" as the
pipe-major of the time expressed it—a dress that
"weel becomes one with the rank of pipe-major"
(Mackay-Scobie, *Pipers of a Highland Regiment*).
The speaker was Pipe-Major M'Donald, one of
the 72nd's best heavy athletes in tossing the caber,
throwing the hammer, etc., of whom the officers

were very proud, and whom they honoured on his retirement to pension by having his portrait painted for their mess and presenting him with a set of pipes.

Very fortunate in their pipers and pipe-majors, the officers expected all their guests to appreciate the music which the pipe band rendered for their benefit. The pipe music being excellent, the officers in 1875 obtained a complete set of new pipe banners, with all the honours, mottoes, and regimental devices beautifully embroidered in letters of gold.

The bandmaster was inclined to resent the attention lavished on the pipers. One bandmaster used to tell how he had on one occasion pre-pared a most attractive musical programme for a distinguished visitor. Although the band played very well no word of appreciation fell from the officers. The artist's thirst for praise impelled the bandmaster to ask the colonel whether the performance had given satisfaction. Judge of the musician's feelings when he was told that he had done well enough, but that the band did not matter so long as the pipers were all right.

The pipers continued to maintain their high standard of pipe-melodies, and in 1878 their pipe-major, Alexander M'Kellar, who had held the rank since 1860, improved a pipe melody which has become one of the greatest favourites everywhere. "The Barren Rocks of Aden" owes its origin to Piper James Mauchline of the 78th who was with the regiment in Aden in 1844. Mauchline recognised that his composition had been improved by M'Kellar. Ronald Mackenzie, who succeeded M'Kellar, accomplished much, but none of his works have the wide appeal of the classic "Barren Rocks."

It is remarkable how strong is the enthusiasm for bagpipe music among soldiers in Highland regiments. In both the regular battalions of the Seaforths many had qualified as "acting pipers," thus making the band assume enormous proportions. When the Great War opened these acting pipers reverted to the ranks in terms of the Service regulations, while the "full pipers" played their companies into action until the havoc wrought at Loos. There the pipers of most of the battalions of Seaforth might have been seen—and heard—playing the regimental charging tune "Cabar Feidh" at the head of their respective companies, but the results were disastrous. Of the two "New Army" battalions of the regiment, the 7th had lost four killed, and three wounded; and the 8th had also four killed and five wounded, two being captured. The 2nd Battalion, which lost six pipers, killed, and five wounded, before the close of 1915, used to recall the "leadership" of Piper M'Lean. It was he who, in the advance on the hill held by the Germans at Loos, shouted during one of their brief halts: "At them, lads," then putting chanter to his mouth, he dashed along with the men, playing the regimental charging tune, "Cabar Feidh," until the objective was taken.

All this indifference to danger, and the high mortality which it entailed, led the officers of the Seaforth and other units to ban the piper from playing in action, an order which was not always observed. The 1st Battalion pipers, who were more fortunate in the earlier stages, counted several who, in prowess, skill, and versatility, maintained the pipers' reputation. There was Neil M'Kechnie, for example, who was one of the acting pipers whose services in the opening stages of the war took the form of a bomber. M'Kechnie's exploits in that capacity had earned for him the Russian Order of St George — and a wound. On recovery he took part in Loos and emerged unscathed, and then turned to his pipes, playing his battalion into Mesopotamia. There he was noticed playing his company into the attack on a Turkish position at Sheikh Saad, where he was again wounded. After recovery he returned to his battalion, and on this occasion was put into the trenches. The officers deemed the trenches safer than the places usually taken by the pipers who played their companies into action. The majority of pipers were placed on stretcher-bearing, or on ammunition carrying, or kept as runners. Some were in the transport lines. The runner and the stretcher-bearer were generally looked upon as doing the most hazardous work of all ; the sight of small parties of stretcher-bearers tending the wounded under heavy fire and bearing them off to the rear was too often a thrilling experience for those who not seldom saw the gallant stretcher-bearers struck down with their helpless burdens. It was after several trying experiences in seeking the wounded at the battle of Port Arthur that the tireless energy, whole-

hearted devotion, and utter disregard of danger
of Pipe-Major D. B. Mathieson were recognised
by his officers, who recommended him for the
Distinguished Conduct Medal, and that was in
due course awarded him. Every piper who was
engaged in this heroic work might with justice
be said to have earned a like distinction. But
of course there was a limit to awards. Of the
pipers of the Territorial battalions of the Seaforths,
the 1/4th, a Ross-shire unit had six killed, and
ten who had to be discharged because of wounds.
The pipers of the 1/5th Battalion who hailed
principally from Caithness and Sutherland, went
to France twelve strong, and at the close of the
War numbered but four—their losses being, like
those of the 1/4th, due to their services in carrying
messages under fire and bearing wounded off the
field. The officers of the 1/6th Battalion (Elgin),
realising how stretcher work accounted for many
of the casualties to their pipers, released them
from that work and placed them and the drummers
on ration and ammunition carrying. Some of their
pipers, however, elected to go into the trenches
and others to volunteer as runners. Two young
pipers of the 1/4th Battalion were sent off to a
cadet school and duly obtained commissions. One
piper of the 1/5th was likewise promoted, and
another in the 1/7th; while the 1/6th had two of
their pipers promoted to commissioned rank. The
D.C.M. and the M.M. were not uncommon on
the breast of the pipers of the Seaforth battalions,
but probably the most popular award was that
meted out to Pipe-Major William Taylor of the
7th Battalion, a well-known ex-pipe-major of the

1st Battalion, whose first-class piping is now at the service of the boys of the Queen Victoria School at Dunblane. Taylor got both the Meritorious Service Medal and the Croix de Guerre.

PIPERS OF THE GORDON HIGHLANDERS

THE Gordon Highlanders owe much to their pipers. When the regiment was raised in 1794 the beautiful Duchess of Gordon did not rely entirely on her magic kiss for the recruits required; she went forth on her recruiting expeditions preceded by six pipers. So, at the risk of being considered ungallant, one may deem that in many instances it was the pipers, and not the dainty kiss, which lured the simple countryman from his peaceful paths to a soldier's stirring life.

Throughout the early campaigns of the regiment—in Egypt, where the Gordons and the 90th (now 2nd Scottish Rifles) distinguished themselves, winning the battle honour of Mandora for their Colours—the pipers were a recognised institution, except by Army Headquarters. In the regimental Orders of June 1805, drummers are directed not to beat when the regiment marches past in open column, but "pipers may play." It was also a recognised custom for the pipers to play the tune "Salute to the Prince" ("Failte am Prionsa") as they marched on the flanks of their respective companies past the saluting base. Marching past was then performed in slow time, while the brass band played "The Garb of Old Gaul"—all which ceremonial was abolished after the Crimean War.

Drummers were long the highly privileged members of all regiments with their penny a day more than the pay of a private. They were officially established; the pipers were not; hence the stratagem to which most Highland regiments resorted, of styling their pipers "drummers." In the regimental Orders of 1805 there is the candid statement: "Alexander Cameron, the piper, is to be taken on the strength of the Grenadiers as "drummer." Cameron was a notable piper, whose name and exploits were long the talk of the regiment. Colonel Greenhill-Gardyne had the privilege of interviewing a very old ex-Gordon who had been a comrade of Cameron throughout the Peninsular War and at Waterloo. The old soldier mentioned to Colonel Gardyne that his heroes were :—the Duke of Wellington; Colonel Cameron, or "Fassifern," as he was styled, from the name of his estate; Norman Stewart, a private with the reputation of an unmatched marksman; and Cameron, the pipe-major, who had a lofty contempt for all generals and colonels who imagined that the music of the pipes was of secondary importance. Only when the pipes were absent was there risk of losing battle, was Cameron's theory. In the engagement of Fuentes d'Onoro in 1811 he received the greatest insult he thought a piper could have; his pipebag was pierced by a musket shot from the enemy. Cameron was enraged and, tying his instrument around his neck, he seized the musket of a wounded comrade, loaded it and fired. Firing was too slow a business, however. Throwing the weapon away the fiery pipe-major drew his

trusty claymore and dashed into the thick of
the enemy "amid the cheers of the battalion"
(Gardyne, p. 253).

Cameron occupied a prominent position in
the history of the regiment at that period. An
account of each action seems incomplete without
reference to the special activities of the sturdy
pipe-major who seems to have played when and
where he liked. It was his firm belief that if
he did not play the troops would suffer; nothing
would shake that belief.

In the battle of Maya in 1813 the enemy
were too strong numerically for the Gordons,
being 3000 to the Gordons' 200. Forced to
remain quiescent on the slopes of a hill until
supports arrived, the Highlanders had no peace
from the impatient pipe-major, who argued that,
with his music going strong, the enemy would
be quickly overcome. Starting up the " Pibroch
Donuil Dubh " he had the satisfaction of witnessing the Gordons rise to their feet, ready for
action. But the general had not come to that
stage. Ordering Cameron to stop and the men
to lie down, General Stewart went back to his
post; but Cameron, pointing to the enemy who
were mustering at the base, assured his friends
that it was a waste of time to stay there idle.
Again he began a stirring air and again the
men got a-foot, which once more brought the
irate general to the recalcitrant piper. " If you
play again without orders, I'll have you shot,"
thundered the general, and as he went off, the
undisturbed musician told his friends, as though
it were a personal grievance: " He'll no' let

me play, and noo every man in France will be here."

Just then the long-waited-for supports, in the shape of the 6th Foot and some Brunswickers, arrived. The men rose to cheer them and the pipe-major, regardless of the terrible threat of the general, set the men off with his best rendering of "The Haughs of Cromdale," their own charging tune. On they rushed, men and pipe-major, before the word of command had been given, and drove the enemy before them. The victory was overwhelming, and all, curiously, gave the glory to the insubordinate pipe-major who had defied the orders of a general!

In December 1813 the pipers of the 92nd at St Pierre made themselves famous by their constant play throughout the attack by an overwhelming force of the enemy on the British troops. Backward and forward surged our troops until the order was given to retire. Still the notes of "Cogadh no Sith" sounded, but they were the notes of one piper alone, for the others had been killed whilst playing that pibroch. The 92nd had suffered severely, but the fate of the pipers and the doggedness of the surviving piper had apparently impressed the colonel (Cameron) more than all else. Reports of the pipers' conduct reached the Highland Society, the news distributing agency then of all things Highland and military, and the pipers of St Pierre, who could have had no idea that their courage would be lauded far and wide, live in the painting that has been reproduced so often from the original in the British Museum. That shows the battlefield of St Pierre and the central figures are the three pipers, one of whom stands playing while his disabled comrades lie beside him. The standing piper probably represents Pipe-Major Cameron. In 1815 the pipers of the 92nd added to the gaiety of the scene at the famous ball given by the Duchess of Richmond at Brussels, where the pipe music and dances were the principal features of that historic evening. On the following day the pipe music was of a sterner kind. Led for the last time by " Fassifern " the pipers played the regiment to Quatre Bras to the tune of " The Camerons' Gathering." " Fassifern " was hit and fell, mortally wounded. As he lay he requested his friends to fetch the piper for one more melody before he died. What that melody was none knows, though James Grant, in his graphic *Romance of War*, gives it as "Oran an Oaig," the Death Song of Skye. That, however, is not accepted by skilled pipers as at all likely, since it is not within the ambit of the bagpipe.

The death of the gallant colonel made a deep impression on all the battalion, particularly on the pipers, who looked upon " Fassifern " as the great patron of them and of their music. One piper at Waterloo swore he had a vision of the old colonel in the " Scotland for Ever " charge—where Highlanders and the Greys and the Inniskillings rushed on together—waving his bonnet in front as of yore. That fancy inspired D. H. Buchan to write :—

> Of vision keen and versed in spells,
> Strange tales the Colonel's piper tells.
> How he with more of joy than fear
> Again beheld his chieftain dear

High riding in a misty cloud
While war's artillery thundered loud,
    And broke o'er Waterloo.
That though he heard not there his voice,
He saw him wave his bonnet thrice.

Just as the pipers had introduced the Duchess of Gordon and her novel recruiting idea to the notice of all Scotland; as they had led the van in all the campaigns of their regiment since; so, at the termination of the momentous period 1793-1816, it was appropriate that the last "word" should be the piper's—that is to say, so far as the 92nd Highlanders were concerned. For the farewell tune played by the pipe-major to the land of France was that same "Cogadh no Sith" which Lord Cathcart requested should be played for the benefit of the Emperor of Russia, an account of which is given in the chapter on the Cameron Highlanders.

Pipe-Major Cameron, who died on 18th October 1817, while with the regiment in Belfast, had the honour of receiving from his officers a handsome silver medal on which was engraved, "Presented to Pipe-Major Alexander Cameron." The historian of the Gordons, writing so recently as 1894, thus describes the accomplishments of Cameron:— "Well versed in Highland lore and legend, the notes of his bagpipe suggested these more vividly than words. In the pibroch "Tarbh breac dearag" ("The Red-spotted Bull") he told of Keppoch's feud with Lochiel. "Mnathen na Glinne so," or "Women of the Glen," recalled the massacre of the MacDonalds at Glencoe. When he turned to the more joyful measure known as "Ochd fir

Mhuidart," or "Eighth Man of Moidart," he was recalling the historic landing of Prince Charles and the joy of seven peat-cutters who celebrated the occasion by dancing a reel, with a spade stuck in the ground as eighth man."

Duncan Smith was another Waterloo piper whose skill in pipe-playing was overshadowed by his eccentricities, one of which was his hatred of trousers. In "fatigues," when everyone else was suitably clad in trews, Duncan was always found in the kilt. It was alleged that on one occasion, having received the present of a pair of trousers, he put them on wrong side foremost and became so indignant that he pitched them away and would never tolerate mention of them afterwards. He had also a theory that pipe music ought never to be dispensed to the " Sassunnach." There was a time when part of the regiment was stationed at barracks along with parts of other units—all being under the command of an English colonel. When the composite battalion paraded Piper Duncan Smith was with his company which, on the march, was at the rear of the column, quite glad of the piper's music. The colonel one day sent word for the piper to come forward and play at the head of the column. Duncan obeyed so far as to come forward and march ; but his pipes were under his arm. "Play up, piper," called out the colonel. To which the piper replied, " No more wind, sir." " All right; fall-in with your company." And Duncan went back and tuned up merrily, and the colonel, understanding, left him alone.

"How did you feel at Waterloo, Duncan ? "

inquired a fresh young ensign. "Och! I shust plaw awa' an' no gie a tawm whether I be shot or no'!" That very question was again asked of the piper many years later in a law court, where he was a witness, except that it took the form of, "I believe you fought at Waterloo?" Duncan, with much contempt for all lawyers, rudely replied, "How could I pe fighting when I wass plawing the pipes aal the time?" adding still more rudely, "It wass more wind than work wi' me—like a lawyer."

Yet, in spite of all his vagaries, Duncan quitted the regiment with the rank of pipe-major and with pension, gratuity, Good Conduct, Long Service Medal, and with a set of bagpipes which was presented by the officers.

In those days all the ancient regimental pipe customs begun by Colonel Cameron were maintained inviolate. They had tunes which one always associates with the Cameron Highlanders, pipe tunes of Clan Cameron, the reason for their popularity in the 92nd being explained by the presence of many of that clan among the *personnel* of the 92nd. It used to be a rule that one pibroch had to be played at officers' mess, and, on guest nights, nothing but pibroch. On parade the pipers played without drum accompaniment, and, while the battalion was being inspected, the men marched past the saluting base at slow time, each piper on the flank of his company, playing a salute to the general, most of which usages went into disuse after the Crimean War.

Two years before that war the 92nd were inspected by Major-General J. E. Napier, who dropped a "bomb" on all ranks by his disapproval of pipers as being contrary to regulations. His subsequent report to the commander-in-chief, the Duke of Wellington, in which he mentioned that "these were not authorised by Headquarters," brought forth a stinging observation from the "Iron Duke" which benefited not only the 92nd but every other Highland regiment. "I am surprised," wrote the Duke to Napier, "that an officer who has seen, as you must have seen, the many gallant deeds of Highland regiments, in which their pipers have played so important a part, should make such a report."

The Duke of Wellington died in that year, but it was in all probability owing to his letter and action that, two years later, an Army Order was issued authorising an establishment of one pipe-major and five pipers for every Highland regiment, the daily pay of a pipe-major to be 2s. and that of each piper 1s. 2d.

The Crimean War saw officers and men in action—not as a battalion, but scattered in several other units, an arrangement which naturally was disappointing to the 92nd. In the Indian Mutiny they were also present and there the pipers under Pipe-Major M'Phail were reported to be of great assistance in maintaining the *moral* of all ranks.

It was not, however, until the Afghan War of 1878-80 that the 92nd had an opportunity of exhibiting that marvellous combination of "dash" and steadiness which characterised them in action in the early days of the nineteenth century. The Afghan War of 1878-80 provided occasions in many engagements where,

K

under two distinguished officers, Sir Frederick
Roberts, later the famous Lord Roberts, and
Sir Donald Stewart, the Gordons with their
major, George S. White, who was destined to
attain the pinnacle of his profession, won the
admiration of all.   As in the Peninsular War
Sir John Moore had selected a Gordon Highlander as one of the supporters for his coat-of-
arms, so in the Afghan War Sir F. Roberts
paid a like compliment to the regiment.   There
is no room here to epitomise the stirring events
of the period, but space must be made for one
episode or two in which the pipers were prominent.
In the turmoil and rapine occasioned by Ayub Khan
and his rebellious subjects it became necessary
to relieve Kandahar, and to effect this, troops had
to be sent from Kabul, some 320 miles distant,
through a dense forest country and sand-swept
areas.   The heat was torrid and only the strongest
of the army were considered fit for service.   Four
brigades were formed, and of the infantry battalions
composing these only three were white—the 60th
(King's Royal Rifles), the 72nd (Seaforths), and
the 92nd (Gordons)—all the others being made
up by Gurkhas, Sikhs, and Punjabis; while the
9th Lancers was the only English cavalry corps.

These 10,000 men were expected to overawe
all the rebels in the intermediate villages between
Kabul and Kandahar, as well as put down the
insurgents in Kandahar.   Accompanying the
force were twenty pipers and drummers, whose
music was never more appreciated than during
the trying stages of this journey, which, remarkable as it was for many episodes, was long

remembered for one dramatic incident, and that
one due to the magic spell of the bagpipes. It
was in March 1880 that the 92nd marched
through the streets of Ghazni in Afghanistan,
and as they passed through the lines of natives,
with pipes and drums ringing, the unexpected
happened. A tall young man, apparently an
Afghan, darted out from the crowd, gazed wist-
fully on the pipers, as he marched alongside,
and danced at intervals to the lively airs of
the pipes. He kept looking at the Gordons as
though he had found his long-lost brothers.
The soldiers were strangely moved, rightly suspecting in the peculiar behaviour of the man
some mystery relating to his nationality. They
made inquiries and learned that he was a Scot,
named Dawson, who had, when a child of four,
been kidnapped from his home in Peshawar by
Afghans. Dawson had apparently lost all the
habits of his race, all the ways of the ordinary
Briton, but the sound of the bagpipes and the
drums had awoke some chords in his memory.
He clung to the regiment ; the officers gave him
a post in their mess, and there he remained until
the eve of action. Then he disappeared, none knew
whither; though it was suspected that he could
not endure the thought of deserting his adopted
friends the Afghans, still less to be with those
who were to fight them. Thus the Scot who
was reclaimed by the medium of the bagpipes,
was again lost for ever.

In all the battles that were so soon to follow,
the pipers were generally in the forefront ; on the
one occasion when, at Pir Paimal village, they were

in the rear, the battalion was doing badly against an overwhelming force of Afghans. "Fetch up the pipers," called General Macpherson to the officer-in-command. The pipers were soon at the front and the familiar notes of "The Haughs of Cromdale" floated around each Gordon. It was there that one canny piper had a bullet shot through his bag, a fact unnoticed at the time when his music was cut short, the piper inquiring of a neighbour, "Fat's wrang wi' the auld wife the day?"

Among the casualties was one young piper from Strathspey, Grant, whose right hand had two fingers shot off. "Cheer up, my lad," said the surgeon, "the pain will soon be gone." To which the lad sadly answered, "It's no' the pain I mind, sir, but that I'll nevermore play the pipes."

In 1881 the battalion took a distinguished part in the disastrous action at Majuba Hill, South Africa, where, among those who died of their wounds, was Piper David Hutcheon, a Kincardine man. It was also in that year that the 92nd received as their first battalion the 75th (Stirlingshire) Regiment, which, though not a Highland unit, had performed much excellent service since it was raised in 1787 by General Robert Abercromby. In the wars in India at the close of the eighteenth and the opening decades of the nineteenth century, the 75th had won much merit, which they later increased by their valour in South Africa and again in the Indian Mutiny. Though the 75th had thus many claims to be considered a highly suitable partner for the 92nd, bringing with them, as they did, the battle honours: "Seringapatam,

Guzerat, South Africa, 1835," and the badges of the Tiger and Sphinx, there was the customary grumble among many of both regiments.

It is unlikely that the 75th had then pipers. Until 1809 it was dressed in the Highland garb, but that had been taken from the corps—as from other units similarly termed "Highland." The 75th, however, had no grounds for complaint as their members were either Lowland or Irish; in 1863 the round Kilmarnock bonnet with diced border had been issued to show its nationality, but these were apparently all the Scots characteristics of which they could boast. When in 1881 it became the 1st Battn. Gordon Highlanders, almost the first step taken was the appointment of Pipe-Corporal M'Lean of the 2nd Battalion as Pipe-Major of the ex-75th. M'Lean doubtless took with him some of the spare pipers of the 92nd.

It was the 1st Battalion which was sent to the Egyptian War of 1882-84, where, in the battle of Tel-el-Kebir, its pipers played during the advance through a hail of bullets from the enemy who lined the ramparts. Over the ditch in front of the parapet and up and over that parapet the Gordons with their pipers went; after close hand-to-hand fighting the enemy were routed within twenty minutes.

For their gallant conduct there the 1st Battn. Gordon Highlanders were authorised to bear among their battle honours "Egypt, 1882" and "Tel-el-Kebir."

Two years later (1884) the 1st Battalion was again employed in war—on this occasion against the

Mahdi and Osman Digna. This was a protracted affair consisting of several severe engagements. During one of those intervals of fighting, when opportunities offered of rendering aid to wounded friend and foe, one of the Gordon pipers, Macdonald, while handing cold water to a prostrate Soudanese, was well-nigh scalped. The enemy did not know the golden rule.

Of all the campaigns in which the Gordons have borne a distinguished part, none outshines the Dargai war of 1897. The eyes of the world were drawn to it; the successful ascent by the 1st Battalion of the steep hill, dominated by the tribesmen who had till then been masters of the situation, provided one of the dramatic thrills. The Gurkhas and the Dorsets had attempted to storm the enemy's entrenchments but had to give up; and their commanding officer reported it impossible, owing to the great numbers of the enemy lining the edge of the plateau. It was then that the general officer commanding the 2nd Division ordered the brigadier-general to move up the Gordon Highlanders and the 3rd Sikhs. The task was great and the odds seemed all against the successful achievement. The general, however, had deputed it to the Gordon Highlanders and the pride of the regiment was touched. The words of Colonel Matthias to his battalion, "The General says this hill must be taken at all costs—the Gordon Highlanders will take it," sounded like a clarion and rang in the ears of all who heard them. In his despatch, General Sir W. Lockhart wrote: "The dash of the Gordons—headed by their pipers, and led by Lieut.-Col.

Matthias, C.B., with Major Macbean on his right and Lieut. A. F. Gordon on his left—through a murderous fire, had, in forty minutes, won the heights" (quoted by Gardyne, vol. ii., p. 350). Up the precipitous path leading to the crest they went, "the men cheering like mad"; it was then, during this dash, that Piper Findlater won his world-wide fame. Wounded and unable to move, he continued, amidst all the heavy firing, to play the regimental march. So, too, did Piper Milne, in spite of a bullet wound in the chest. The hill was won; the enemy did not wait for the last of our reinforcements, but fled.

It was rightly deemed a brilliant affair in which several officers and men had been preeminent in valour. Pipers Findlater and Milne were singled out for particular praise, but a discrimination was exercised between the respective claims of each for a suitable decoration, Findlater being awarded the V.C., while Milne got the D.C.M. Never before had there been so much enthusiasm expressed upon a feat for which the bronze cross "For Valour" had been given. In the words of Colonel Gardyne, "The incident of the wounded piper continuing to play, being telegraphed home, took the British public by storm, and when Findlater arrived in England he found himself famous. Reporters rushed to interview him; managers offered him fabulous sums to play at their theatres; the streets of London and all the country towns were placarded with his portrait; when, after his discharge, he was brought to play at the military tournament, royal personages and distinguished generals shook him by the hand; his photograph was sold by thousands; the Scotsmen in London would have let him swim in champagne, and the daily cheers of the multitude were enough to turn an older head than that of this young soldier."

Piper Milne, too, had a most enthusiastic reception on rejoining his battalion, and the honour of a telegram addressed to the O.C. from Her Majesty Queen Victoria in which she inquired for the health of Milne.

Findlater had to "weather" many trying storms of adverse criticism. To play his pipes on the stage was deemed derogatory to the distinction of a V.C. holder, but, then, man cannot live on a mere bronze cross and a title alone. And so it arose out of all the discussions in the newspaper Press and in Parliament, that the authorities decided to grant, along with the Cross, an annual payment of a sum that might range, according to the needs of the recipient, from £10 to £50. The piper's V.C. was thus a landmark in the history of the most coveted distinction in the British army.

The South African War of 1899-1902 saw the 2nd Battalion with its pipers actively engaged. Honours there were few and hard to gain, yet two pipers of the battalion succeeded in having their gallantry fittingly rewarded. At Elandslaagte Pipe-Major Charles Dunbar and Piper Kenneth M'Leod, a burly man from Stornoway, emulated the pipers of Dargai by playing during the advance and the fighting after being wounded. Both were awarded the D.C.M. M'Leod had, while serving in India, come under the notice of

the Crown Prince of Germany, and that future
enemy of our country had, rightly regarding the
doughty piper in the handsome dress of his rank
as a most important personage in the regiment,
conferred on him the Order of the Red Eagle.
That distinction, unique among pipers, M'Leod
proudly wore, in the form of the Cross of the
Order, until the outbreak of the Great War, when
he grew much ashamed of it, vowing, on his way
to rejoin his old regiment, that he would throw
it away.

All the old pipers of the Gordons were also
on their way to renew their acquaintance with
the rigours of war. Many were absorbed by the
new army battalions and not a few who had gone
abroad were found later in one or other of the
pipe bands of a Canadian or an Australian unit.

Their successors in the two regular battalions
and the pipers of the territorial battalions were
no whit behind the old school of pipers in all
the actions of the Great War. Those of the
1st Battalion who had escaped the fate of their
comrades who had been trapped in the thick
mist of early morn while holding the left flank
of the troops at the Condé Mons Canal on
23rd August 1914, suffered four days later in
the action at Bertry, where two pipers were
killed and five were captured. In the first
battle of Ypres the 2nd Battalion pipers were
with their companies during the three weeks
that they held the line against a force six times
their numbers. It was not, however, until the
engagement of Neuve Chapelle in March 1915
that the pipers were particularly mentioned for

conspicuous bravery. There Pipe - Sergeant Robert Stewart proved the hero in the eyes of his battalion, playing all the favourite battle tunes of the Gordons, utterly regardless of the hail of musketry fire and artillery. At Loos he was equally daring in playing before his company in the advance. It was madness, the men told him and his brother pipers, but in vain. The pipers strode on with "The Haughs of Cromdale" announcing that the Gordons were astir. One piper after another fell in that advance and Stewart was one of these; he had been, it is said, marked out for a D.C.M. but that distinction did not materialise; posthumous distinctions were not then given.

"Wee Stumpy," as his friends in the battalion called him, was another piper who marched with his company, playing as though the issue of the battle depended on him. The men with the rifle and bayonet however had other views. "Come oot frae there, Stumpy, till we get at thae d—— ruddy Jerries. . . . Come oot, ye'll be killed, I tell ye. . . ." Stumpy heeded them not, playing valiantly until he was hit and went down. When the battle was over and the survivors, gathered in groups, made lamentation over friends who had fallen, they deplored the passing of the pipers, Stewart and "Stumpy," whose music they "would hear no more." Then they learned that the little piper was not killed, but wounded, and that not severely, whereupon the Gordons rejoiced.

Not only at Loos, but at Festubert and Neuve Chapelle, the pipers of the 1/6th Territorial

Battalion were conspicuous as pipers, and like the pipers in other battalions they sustained many casualties. The pipe-major, Isaac Howarth, did not use his pipes in any of these actions, but instead applied all his energies to succouring his comrades who lay wounded on the battlefield. Right fearlessly and tirelessly did he perform these duties, binding wounds, then bearing the stretcher from field to base and back for more. More than once his exceptional gallantry was remarked upon by officers and men alike, and in recognition of his outstanding bravery and devotion, Howarth, a veteran with a piper son in the battalion, was awarded first the D.C.M. and later had a bar added to that medal.

Medals did not often come the way of the pipers, who risked their lives many times each day in their duties as ammunition carriers and as runners, but they (the pipers) were much appreciated by all those whom they served. Sometimes a piper found himself relegated to some minor work behind the lines, as was the case in one battalion, whose entire band was so placed—a slight that was resented by the pipers who promptly applied for transfer to other units where they were allowed to share in the dangers and glories of the combatants.

The pipers of the 1st Battalion had entered the War with pipes playing amidst the heavy fire of battle, and they ended their term of campaigning in like manner. In the very last action in 1918, they went over the top alongside their respective companies to the tune of " The Haughs of Cromdale." At that time the 2nd

Battalion were on the Italian front, whither they had been sent in 1917. Their pipers and drummers had there rendered many important services, one of the most curious being given while they stood waist deep in a swift-flowing channel. There they stood for hours on end waiting for the wounded whom they had to bear across, each stretcher having four pipers or drummers, with other four to steady them. "Yet they never hesitated," wrote the colonel; "they formed a living line to help those who were slightly wounded. . . . But for the work of the pipers and drummers it would have been impossible to evacuate the wounded that night."

Much pleasanter was their duty some months later when pipers and drummers were ordered to proceed to the quarters of the King of Italy, who had asked as a special favour for a concert of pipe music. His Majesty had then the delight of listening to the marches, strathspeys, and reels of the Highlands of Scotland and the regiment's own marching tune, "Hielan' Laddie." Probably both King and pipers were quite unaware that about 2000 years earlier the pipers of the army of Imperial Rome were engaged somewhere in England or Scotland in playing to their respective Legions the classic marches of ancient Italy.

PIPERS OF THE QUEEN'S OWN CAMERON HIGHLANDERS

THE Cameron Highlanders are enthusiastic about piping and their pipers; the officers used to strive to maintain the traditions of the regiment even to the extent of having a couple of bearded pipers for the flank men of the front rank, but not even an extra penny on the day's pay will tempt the fashion-loving, shaven piper of to-day to forgo the use of the razor.

There are many customs of the regiment not noted in the Orders, and many creditable deeds of pipers and others which find no place in the regimental records; the old-time chroniclers did not see the necessity of recording more than was absolutely imperative and refrained from any display of undue pride in their personal performances. There are many things that might have been told. To this regiment is ascribed the introduction of the green doublet which is worn by the pipers of all regiments, but no credit is claimed for the idea. They do not permit the pipers or the band to play on Sundays, though there is no written order against Sunday music. Nor is it stated why, on the first march of the original regiment in 1794, from Fort William to Stirling, for official inspection, the "79th" pipers played, not "Pibroch Donuil Dubh," their marching tune, but "Gabaidh sinn an Rathad Mhor," which

means, "We'll keep the High Road." It was
certainly a more appropriate melody for the
occasion, besides being one with historical associa-
tions, for it was the MacIntyres' clan tune before
the Stewarts adopted it in the sixteenth century.
As there were many Stewarts in the regiment and
among the pipers in 1794 and for many years
afterwards, the choice of the marching tune is
easily accounted for.

"Gabaidh sinn an Rathad Mhor" had, moreover, sounded loud and clear on the field of
Sheriffmuir in 1715, and was in consequence long
remembered as "The Sheriffmuir March," and it
was that very tune that rang through the Canon-
gate of Edinburgh when the hundred pipers of
the Jacobite army announced to the panic-stricken
Hanoverians the entrance of Prince Charles to
the capital of Scotland.

We have no record of what the pipers of the
Camerons did in the campaign in the Low
Countries and in the Peninsular War, but it
can be safely assumed that, opportunities for
heroic deeds failing, they brightened the tedium
of the long marches and stirred the blood of the
soldier in battle.

Not until the eve of Quatre Bras do we hear
again of the pipers as a force in the regimental life,
and the report comes from the outside, how in the
early hours of a June morning in 1815, the citizens
of Brussels were awakened by the pipes of the
Camerons, and looking from their windows they
saw rank upon rank of warriors in waving tartans
led by their pipers, marching towards Quatre Bras.
Meaningless to the Belgians, the tune "Bonnie

Loudon's Woods and Braes" reminded the troops of Scotland. The foremost poet of the age has described the scene in the famous lines :—

> And wild and high the "Camerons' Gathering" rose,
>   The war note of Lochiel, which Albyn's hills
> Have heard, and heard too have her Saxon foes :
>   How in the noon of night that Pibroch thrills,
> Savage and shrill. . . .

Now the reticent chronicler was forced to take note of one of the pipers, for everyone who had been present at the battle of Waterloo told of the heroism of Piper Kenneth Mackay of the Camerons. When the regiment had been formed into hollow squares, ready with fixed bayonets to receive a charge of the French cavalry, the pipers being inside the squares, Mackay coolly stepped outside the square of his Grenadier Company, and marched round and round the bristling bayonets of his comrades, playing "Cogadh no Sith" ("Peace or War"). The incident thrilled all who saw it and all who heard of it, even to the old King George III. himself, who testified his admiration of the gallant deed by sending a handsome set of silver-mounted pipes to the piper. Piper Kenneth Mackay's action was the subject of a spirited painting, which was exhibited in the Royal Academy in 1893 by the late Bogle Lockhart, A.R.A. The picture was afterwards purchased by the officers of the regiment for their mess. When the Czar of Russia was in Paris in 1815, he asked to see some Highland soldiers at close quarters. General Lord Cathcart, the British Ambassador, a soldier

and a Scot, ordered Piper Mackay to play
" Cogadh no Sith " for the benefit of the Czar, but
his Imperial Majesty did not ask for an encore.

On the return of the regiment to Scotland the
pipers of the Camerons entered for the Highland
Society's competitions, and acquitted themselves
with credit.   In 1818 the pipe-major, Alexander
Sutherland, won fifth place.   Six years later Piper
Donald Stewart was placed second, and he won
the first prize in 1825.   The name Stewart is long
found on the roll of pipers of the Camerons, and
each bearer of the historic name appears to have
been an expert player, John Stewart, in 1837,
maintaining the reputation of his clan by winning
the " handsome Highland sword " of the Highland
Society.

In the following decade greater honour was
brought to the regiment, and pipe music was
enriched by Pipe-Major John Macdonald, whose
" 79th's Farewell to Gibraltar," composed on the
departure of the regiment from the " Rock " in
1848, is still a favourite melody with regimental
and civilian pipers.

No record of the pipers in the Crimean War
has been preserved, beyond the fact that they
took part in the display provided for the benefit
of the Turkish commander-in-chief, Omar Pasha,
who was accompanied by Lord Raglan and
Marshal St Arnaud.   The last item in the pro-
ceedings was a charge of six battalions of infantry,
in which the Camerons rushed forward cheering
wildly, with drums beating and pipers playing.
This incident delighted the Turk who dropped
his reins and clapped vigorously.

The hardships of the campaign told heavily on all, and two pipers, Charles Donald and Andrew M'Rae, died between November and the end of 1854. Although the 79th shared with the 42nd, the 93rd, and the Guards the glory of carrying the heights of the Alma, their pipers could only share in the silence of the victorious advance, and it was a 42nd piper who celebrated the event in a classic melody.

Nothing is known of the doings of the pipers of the 79th in the Indian Mutiny. Of the five who were with the regiment one did not survive the campaign.

In the Coomassie campaign 135 volunteers from the Camerons served with the Black Watch, but it is not among the Battle Honours of the regiment. In the same year (1873), however, Queen Victoria granted the title, " Queen's Own Cameron Highlanders," a distinction which entailed a change in the facings and the " Colour " from the previous green to dark royal blue, and the substitution of eagle feathers for black cock in the glengarries of the pipers, but did not alter their dark green doublets.

From its formation in 1793 the regiment seems to have been a specially favoured corps. When certain Highland units had in the first decade of the nineteenth century been compelled to give up the kilt for trews, the Camerons were excepted ; and when in 1881 the whole army was reorganised, regimental numbers being dropped for a territorial or other distinctive title, and all line regiments were linked in pairs as first and second battalions, the Camerons were allowed to continue as one

L

battalion, not sharing the glory of the name with a less distinguished battalion. Some misgiving was caused in 1893 by a proposal of the Secretary for War to convert the regiment into a third battalion of the Scots Guards. The scheme was dropped when, after strong protests from the various Highland societies, the Queen expressed her disapproval to the Duke of Connaught who promptly informed the War Secretary.

The formation of the second battalion of the regiment in 1897, as the result of direct recruitment, gave great satisfaction to the Camerons, for it was an evidence of the popularity of the corps.

At that time there were still some serving who had been in the Egyptian War of 1881-84, and these veterans told of the long, silent, tiring march over the loose sand of the desert, guided through the darkness by a naval officer. Coming unexpectedly upon the enemy's forts at Tel-el-Kebir at early dawn, they made a wild rush upon the entrenchments, Private Donald Cameron ahead of all. According to the reports of newspaper correspondents the pipers struck up "The Cameron Men," but pipers who were there said they were quite unprepared to play anything and simply rushed forward with the rest of the battalion, and that Pipe-Major Macgregor Grant did not play till they had cleared the first barrier. Interviewed by the chaplain, the Rev. Patrick Mackay, the pipe-major said that he played "The Standard on the Braes o' Mar," and after that "onything that cam' into my heid." That is definite enough, and the colonel expressed his

admiration of the piper's action, speaking often
of Grant and his pluck. Grant died of cholera
a year later.

The pipers who heard these tales in 1897
were to have experience of battle in the following year. They were placed in the rear of the
battalion in the advance on the dervish zariba
at Atbara, where they played "The Earl of
Mansfield." In the action Piper James Stewart,
emulating Mackay at Waterloo, stood close to
the most formidable of the enemy's stockades
playing "The Cameron Men" for the encouragement of his comrades. He presented an easy
mark for the dervishes and fell, hit not once but
seven times. That, and the saving of General
Gatacre's life by Private Cross who killed a
dervish about to spear the general, were the outstanding actions of the rank and file of the
Camerons in that engagement. Cross, who was
killed later, was recommended for the V.C., but
there were soldiers who maintained that Piper
Chalmers, one of the best shots in the regiment,
and also one of the most notorious defaulters, had
a share in Cross's act, but was debarred by his
" conduct sheet" from receiving any reward.
Many stories are told of that excellent but
misguided piper.

The regiment sailed from Egypt for South
Africa in January 1900. At Lagos, where their
transport anchored for a day, the men were disembarked and paraded through the town, where
the main interest of the natives centred in the
pipers. The conditions were not favourable to
pipers in the South African War, for silence

throughout the operations was as a rule imperative.   Only during the entry into a town—as
at the capture of Pretoria—did the pipes and
drums call out the inhabitants to see the rooi-
neks pass to the strains of "The March of the
Cameron Men."

On the outbreak of the Great War the 1st
Battn. of the Cameron Highlanders marched
down the Castle Hill of Edinburgh, with pipes
playing amid all the emotion aroused by the
spectacle of a regiment leaving for the front.
On entering France the pipers had to lay aside
their pipes and act as runners.   On this service
two of them were killed before the close of 1914,
and three were wounded.   One of the two left
unhurt, Piper Henderson, hearing that one of
his officers was lying badly wounded and unable
to move out in "No Man's Land," ran out to
his aid and succeeded in bringing him into safety,
for which act of disinterested gallantry he was
awarded the D.C.M.

Only two pipers with the Cameron Highlanders!   More were sent out from the reserve,
but not to play, for these fresh pipers were
put into the trenches for some considerable
time.

All the pipers of the 2nd Battalion had to
put away their pipes on entering France, for
every one of them was a marksman, and was
therefore required for sniping.   At St Eloi,
Hill 60, Ypres and Armentières they were actively
engaged, but escaped lightly, only two pipers
being wounded.   On their removal in November
1915 to the Balkan front, the pipers were again

snipers under the leadership of Pipe - Major
Mathieson, "best shot" of his company in pre-
war days. Sergeant-Piper James Johnston, also
"best shot" of his company, shone as a guide,
sniper, and scout, and thoroughly deserved the
D.C.M. and M.M. which were awarded him.
Only in rest billets could the pipers practise their
art, and there one of them, Piper Gillon, composed two pipe tunes—"The Battle of Arras,"
and "The Balkan Hills." No further contribution
was made by the four pipers of the 2nd Battalion
on the expedition to South Russia to assist the
Loyalists against the Bolsheviks. Russia does
not seem to have inspired any piper of the Royal
Scots or Camerons to compose a pibroch, a salute,
or a march.

The 4th (Inverness) Territorial Battn. of the
Camerons marched out of Bedford for France
in 1915, their six pipers playing "Lochiel's Awa
to France." A young officer of the Seaforths,
Lieut. E. A. Mackintosh, M.C. (killed in action
in 1916), has expressed in the opening verse of a
spirited poem his feelings on the occasion—

> The pipes in the street were playing bravely,
>   The marching lads went by,
> With merry hearts and voices singing,
>   My friends marched out to die;
> But I was hearing a lonely pibroch
>   Out of an older war,
> "Farewell, farewell, farewell, MacCrimmon,
>   MacCrimmon comes no more!"

Many of these young "MacCrimmons" "came
no more!"

Not allowed to play their companies, the

pipers were either in the ranks or bearing stretchers, though they sometimes resumed their pipes when their companies were going into action. Donald Patterson fell at Festubert in 1915. Two very young pipers—W. F. Macdonald, a son of ex-Pipe-Major Macdonald, Seaforth Highlanders, and Robert Tolmie—were promoted to commissioned rank in the Seaforths, and two years later, in 1918, both fell in action.

The 5th (Lochiel's) Battalion pipers were duty men when they landed in France, Pipe-Major Beattie becoming R.Q.M.S., while the pipers went into the trenches. In the battle of Loos, which caused the loss of so many pipers, three pipers of the 5th were killed, three were wounded and one was gassed—the whole pipe band gone! The officers tried to repair these losses by drafts from the 1/4th and 8th Battalions, but death and wounds continued to play havoc among the pipers, only six of the twenty-five so added being with the battalion at the close of the war.

The pipers of the 6th and 7th Battalions were mainly occupied in ammunition and ration carrying, after the action of Loos where three pipers of the 7th were killed and several wounded. In consequence of these losses the remaining pipers were transferred to the carrying of rations and ammunition and to stretcher work. The change did not altogether please the pipers who sighed for the return of the times when they played their comrades into action. Their opportunity arrived at the battle of the Somme in 1916. Battalion after battalion had tried in vain to capture a German trench. The pipers thought they knew why all the previous attempts had failed, and when it came to the turn of the 7th Battn. Cameron Highlanders to make the attempt, the pipers were ready, with the drones of their pipes decorated with the Scottish colours. On the order to advance the pipers stepped out to the tune of "The March of the Cameron Men"; the 7th Camerons took the trench, and the four pipers who returned unscathed stoutly maintain that the success was due to the music of their pipes.

The inhabitants of a certain village not many miles from Mons entertain very pleasant memories of the 1st Battalion, and in these memories the pipers have a large share. For it was there that, during the Retreat in 1914, the Camerons found themselves for a time. During their sojourn the natives made friends with the regiment and loved to listen to the piper who taught them to distinguish "The Cameron Men" from all others. The Camerons marched away to fight at the Marne, the Aisne, and all the other earlier battles of the Great War, and their numbers were still further reduced in the subsequent actions. In 1917, by a curious coincidence the same battalion was again in the village, but only one or two of the original battalion were with it. There were the natives who had been under the yoke of the Germans till then, and their joy at finding themselves relieved by the Highlanders was heightened when they heard the old familiar tune of "The Cameron Men." Till then they did not recognise the newcomers as their old friends—or at least, as the representatives of their old friends—but the tune settled it.   It is one more "honour" to the long list already ascribed to the pipers of the Queen's Own Cameron Highlanders.

PIPERS OF THE ARGYLL AND SUTHERLAND
HIGHLANDERS

THE two regiments the 91st and the 93rd
Highlanders, which ran their separate courses
until they were linked together in 1882 as "The
Princess Louise's Argyll and Sutherland Highlanders," have each an interesting story to tell,
one which owes not a little to their pipers.
Almost the first item in the opening chapter of
the 91st, which was raised in 1794 by the 5th
Duke of Argyll, is one that concerns pipers.
That reference occurs in a letter which his kins-
man, Duncan Campbell of Lochow, a captain in
the Scots Guards, who was to become the first
commandant of the 91st, wrote to a friend,
requesting: "If you can meet with one or two
good pipers, handsome fellows and steady, you
might go as far as thirty guineas for each."

In due season the pipers, "handsome and
steady" no doubt, obligingly came and piped
the majority of the rank and file from the various
clachans of the county, to the territorial tune of
"The Campbells are Comin'." The regiment was
soon clothed in complete Highland dress with a
tartan of dark green, blue and black set.

It continued for some years as a Highland
regiment, but its distinctive title and Highland
characteristics alike were to be lost, with the
exception of the pipers, for about fifty-four years.

The pipers were actively engaged as pipers during
the regiment's campaign in South Africa in 1795
and throughout the Peninsular War. In the
second year of that protracted campaign the
military authorities ordered the kilt to be with-
drawn from the 91st and some other Highland
units, and tartan trews to be issued instead. A
year later (1810) tartan trews also were with-
drawn in favour of the grey trousers worn by all
English and Lowland regiments. Their name,
too, was changed from the "91st Argyllshire
Regiment" to "91st Regiment of Foot." By
the year 1821 the old customs and characteristics
had all disappeared, losses that were deplored by
some ex-officers of the 91st who visited their old
regiment that year as it lay at Maryhill. These
officers said that they particularly missed the
piper at mess, and everything about the barracks
suggested an English regiment rather than a
Scottish one. That, indeed, was then its trend,
for some of the rank and file volunteered for
service with other Highland regiments and their
places were taken by Irish and Englishmen. The
officers sought to stem the change and appealed
to Headquarters for permission to resume their
old title and dress of the Highland soldier, but
to all their appeals the authorities were adamant.
" If you can guarantee that all the regiment is
composed of Scots, your appeal will be sustained
—not unless." That was how the matter was
disposed, and as no such guarantee could be given
the 91st continued to be badly handicapped. Yet,
strangely, the pipers continued and were with the
regiment throughout its service on the island of

St Helena, 1836-40, where its duties consisted in the guarding of Napoleon's tomb and in preparing for the removal of his body to France.

The lack of the Highland characteristics told heavily on the regiment; those who would otherwise have joined, gave a wide berth to the 91st, and Major M'Neill, a typical Highland officer, finding in 1842 that he could not get the Highland dress for the corps exchanged with Major Lindsay of the 78th Highlanders, an exchange that was for the benefit of the 78th and the disadvantage of the Argylls. The annalists of the period make no secret of the unpopularity in which Colonel Lindsay was held by officers, non-commissioned officers and men alike. He had closed the officers' mess, in violation of the Queen's Regulations, and "allowed the corps of pipers to die out."

The lack of pipers was a most grievous complaint, one which irritated all members of the 91st for several reasons, one of which was the nickname which it earned in the forties of the nineteenth century.

The 74th had been sent to the same station as the 91st, and as fresh arrivals, expected to be escorted to the neighbouring camp from the station by a party of pipers from the resident Argylls. No pipers, however, were seen or heard, but instead there fell on their ears the sound of clattering camp kettles, as the cooks and orderlies of the Argylls ran to make ready the meal for the strangers.

"That must be the band of the Argylls," remarked a wag in the 74th, and from that time the pleasantry was bandied about, to the intense disgust of the injured Argylls. Efforts to make good the deficiency in bagpipes, in spite of the ban by the colonel, resulted in some ex-piper getting a set, borrowed probably from one of the 74th, and with these the Amatola hills were made to resound with the melodies of the Highlands.

That was, however, only a makeshift, but better times were in sight; the unpopular Colonel Lindsay was censured by the commander-in-chief for some failing in administration, and shortly after retired in the same year, 1847.

What a relief! Major Glencairn Campbell, an officer of the best type, was promoted and intro-duced his reform of the old 91st by searching out the bagpipes, chanters, and pipe banners that had been hidden in some chests in the quartermaster's stores for many years.

These were found none the worse, the pipers were regarbed, equipped, and posted to their duties as pipers, and soon the old familiar pipe tunes were heard from Reveillé to Tattoo and "Lights Out."

One can realise the relish with which the regimental chronicler of 1847 entered in his book, "Once more the regiment was able to march out with its pipers dressed in green tunics and Campbell tartan trews and plaids and with diced bonnets—all that they had to remind the men of their Scottish nationality."

The regiment's recovered sense of gaiety was however short-lived, for another "ogre" in the form of an inspecting officer, catching sight of the pipers on parade, sternly ordered their removal from the strength of the corps. That was in

1850; the regiment, officers and men, were indignant, the chronicler fell into despondency as he wrote, "The regiment had clung to the pipes as the last relic that remained of the origin, the history, and the nationality of the corps. They had been handed down from the period of its formation without objection. (The ban by Colonel Lindsay was not noticed by the chronicler.)

Better times were ahead, but not for some years was there an opportunity afforded of disobeying the edict against the pipes. The 91st went to Ireland in 1851 and remained there till 1854, when they were sent to one of the most interesting series of stations, namely the different islands in the Mediterranean, visiting among other historic places Mars Hill, listening to lectures on that and other scenes of St Paul's missionary work. Once in India, which the 91st reached in 1858, Colonel Bertie Gordon lost no time in sending to Scotland for sets of bagpipes for which he paid £86. The old pipers had all left the regiment, except one, William W. Cameron, a private. To him the colonel entrusted the training of those willing to learn the rudiments of the piob mhor. In a few more years' time the regiment heard with delight that "Her Majesty was graciously pleased to approve of the 91st (Argyllshire) Regiment of Foot resuming the appellation of the 91st Argyllshire Highlanders and being clothed and equipped as a non-kilted Highland corps, the tunic as worn in all Highland corps, the trews of Campbell tartan." Thus the year 1864 was a landmark in the annals of the regiment. It was remembered by many others not connected with the regiment because of the newspaper correspondence that ensued in regard to the "Campbell tartan." No one seemed to know exactly which was the set used by the original members of the 91st, although, as it turned out, the only one who was right was the Duke of Argyll. The consensus of opinion by those deemed most expert was in favour of the set showing the red stripe, which, though resembling too closely the tartan of the Atholls, the old enemy of the Campbells, was the tartan adopted and used by the 91st until their union with the 93rd. The pipers and the regiment altogether were on the upward way toward official favour. The marriage of H.R.H. the Princess Louise to the Marquess of Lorne in 1871 meant very much to the personnel of the 91st, which, as the regiment of Argyll, had its representatives present at the marriage, at Windsor. There the pipers played alternately with the band of the Grenadiers, and of the small party of officers who had the honour of being received by Her Majesty Queen Victoria and Princess Louise the pipe-major, M'Dugall, was one. Her Majesty was an admirer of pipe music and took the opportunity of requesting that the regiment should march past on all occasions to the tunes of the pipers, and that when marching past the pipers would fall in in front of the military band. When asked what favour he would like to be bestowed on his regiment, Colonel Sprot replied that he should like it to bear the title of "Princess Louise's," and if possible that it should have once more the kilt as part of its uniform. That long-cherished hope of the regiment would also have been realised then, had it not been for the objection taken by the commander-in-chief that the kilt "would cause difficulty in recruiting and add to the expense."

The pipers were wage-earners for the regiment, or rather for the public at large. When the 91st moved into Edinburgh Castle in 1873 the band and pipers were in great request as entertainers. Once each week in the winter of 1873-74 they played in the Assembly Rooms, and the profits gained from the prices of admission, amounting to £42, were put towards the cost of the handsome drinking well at the south-west corner of the Esplanade. When the regiment was sent in 1879 to take part in the Zulu War the bandsmen were put on hospital orderly duties, while the nine pipers along with some drummers and fifers accompanied the battalion into action.

At last the regiment attained its long-cherished desire—its rehabilitation as a kilted unit. The union of the 91st and the 93rd in 1882 made that a matter of course, and the question of tartan which had caused so much anxiety in 1864 was quickly settled by the adoption of the latter corps's tartan, which was identical with the tartan worn by the original 91st. The combination of the two battalions was a necessary one, though the officers and men of each unit were not disposed at first to think so. For some time it was the habit of the officer responsible for sending drafts from one battalion at home to the other abroad, to send the smallest and the least desirable, a practice which was later amended, as in other corps.

The 91st, or 1st Battalion, had been winning renown for some time, and during its sojourn in South Africa in 1883 it attracted the notice of a much wider public merely because the piper of " D " Company, which had been converted into a mounted infantry company, was also mounted. A piper on horseback announcing on his pipes "The Campbells are Comin'" was an event which aroused the greatest degree of curiosity on the part of the general public as well as the battalion, the members of which turned out to witness the debut of Piper Loudon as an equestrian piper. Thanks to the great age and mild character of the steed the piper managed to retain his seat in the saddle while he rather anxiously essayed a pipe melody. The battalion was satisfied, if not proud of their mounted piper, and took the opportunity of sending him some time later to meet the commandant and play him from the station to the mess-tent. Pressmen and artists made the most of the picture, which they sent to various newspapers, one illustration finding its way into the pages of the *Illustrated Times*, another getting an honoured place in the officers' mess. The pipers were of excellent quality, a fact borne out by their successes in 1885 in the Caledonian Sports of Durban, where they were awarded first place for pipe-playing and for dancing. A much greater tribute to the value of pipers was rendered at the conclusion of the army manœuvres at Aldershot in 1893, when it was reported that among all the battalions that had taken part, the 91st alone had had no casualties; that during the whole period none had fallen out. This admirable record military critics puzzled to account for, several holding that it was due to the stamina infused by the music of their pipers.

There is no doubt that the men themselves placed great store by the pipers: no test of physical endurance which they entered upon ever took place without the accompaniment of the pipes. In 1895, for example, a party of N.C.O.'s and men of the battalion marched from Aldershot to Hyde Park Corner, London, in full marching order, with the object of making a record. They were accompanied by two of their pipers, M'Kay and Robb, who played alternately most of the way. That distance of thirty-five miles they accomplished in twelve hours thirty-five minutes, or in terms of actual marching, nine hours.

Four years later the battalion was in the thick of the South African War, the pipers with it, ready for any emergency. That emergency did arise in the terrible battle of Magersfontein, where the heavy fire on the Highland Brigade in close formation proved devastating. Sergeant M'Innes, whose description has been used by Mr Dunn-Pattison in his *History* relates that the men of the different battalions " were converted into a dismayed mob, running to seek cover anywhere, and yelling, shot by the score as they did so. . . . I witnessed one of the bravest deeds I ever saw, for suddenly there broke forth the strains of 'The Campbells are

M

Comin',' and there was Jimmy M'Kay, the
corporal piper of the 91st, standing up fearlessly
playing the regimental tune, facing the storm
of bullets in a valiant attempt to stop the
retirement from becoming a rout. The pipers
of the various regiments broke out playing
almost immediately after, and there can be no
doubt that this altered the aspect of the fight
considerably." A noble tribute to the pipers!

The town of Johannesburg after the war
came to know the band and pipers of the 91st
pretty well. In August 1902, both band and
pipers marched through the town playing "The
Barren Rocks of Aden" to the joy of the
residents, and they led the battalion as it formed
part of the units which paraded before Lord
Milner; and in December 1902, the small detachment from the 91st which was present at the
unveiling of the monument to the Highland
Brigade at Magersfontein, included James M'Kay,
the piper of Magersfontein then pipe-major.
Three ex-pipers of the regiment were observed
in the pipe band of Kimberley Town Band.

When the band and pipers left Johannesburg
the town authorities raised a subscription for the
bandsmen and pipers and drummers in recognition
of their entertainments in the town gardens each
week.

The 91st was making up for all the slights
and scurvy treatment which it had received in
the earlier part of the nineteenth century, when
it was the "Cinderella" of Scottish regiments.
In 1908 it was especially honoured in being
selected to furnish the guards for the King's

residence at Buckingham Palace and at St James's Palace, while the Foot Guards were on manœuvres. For a battalion that had never courted the lime-light, it was a novelty to find themselves gazed upon by crowds of Londoners who had never till then looked on kilted sentries at Buckingham and St James's. The dismounting of each guard provided further entertainment for the Londoners, as it was done to the accompaniment of a piper who played off the guard in slow time with "M'Kay's Farewell to the 71st," and then changed into a quickstep.

The 91st had really proved a partner altogether worthy of its 2nd Battalion, the old 93rd, one of the most distinguished battalions of the army. In its early days it had been Presbyterian to a man, and was, with the probable exception of the Cameronians, the only battalion with its own elders and its own communion cups.

The 93rd had not the opportunity of sharing in the thrilling episodes of the Peninsular War and of Waterloo, as it served at the Cape and then in fatal New Orleans. It was the Crimean War, and particularly the engagement of Balaclava, that marked it out as a great battalion. In the "Thin Red Line" and at Inkerman six pipers were present, Pipe-Major John M'Leod, Angus M'Kay, Roderick M'Kay, Hugh Connachar, George M'Donald and James Sinclair. Of John M'Leod, the regiment—officers and men—were immensely proud. A first-class piper, soldier, and comrade, he was never known to grumble though everyone else indulged in that luxury when cold, hunger, and other hardships oppressed all. M'Leod, like the true philosopher that he was, spoke little but shared all his goods with his more immediate comrades. Everyone knew that when the hamper of food and drink which his relatives sent him at regular periods arrived, he would divide the whole equally among his tent comrades. One defect however he had, in the eyes of the junior officers—there was no animation in face or body as he played. Long would they sit listening to his splendid rendering of pibroch, march, reel, and strathspey, but when they looked on his face they would have liked to protest. When he walked his admirers could have prodded him, for he walked as no piper and no soldier walked. When about 1855 the piper's doublets were changed to green, the officers took the opportunity of putting the walk right. "Look here, John," said one, "when you get that doublet you must really put on some swagger; every other pipe-major has it." To which M'Leod made answer: "Na, na, I'm no guid-luiking eneuch for that." And without the swagger the pipe-major proved his valour in the Indian Mutiny more than once. There, in the assault on the Secundrabagh, General Sir Colin Campbell, turning to the colonel of the 93rd, shouted "Bring on the Tartan, let my own lads at them," an order which Pipe-Major M'Leod and seven pipers quickly translated by playing "On wi' the Tartan" ("Haughs o' Cromdale"). Like one man the seven companies leapt over the wall, quickly silencing the enemy. When the fight was over Sir Colin Campbell made his way to the pipe-major to compliment him on his spirited playing. "Thank ye, sir," replied honest John, "I thought the lads would fight better wi' the national airs to cheer them." A similar compliment was paid M'Leod by Sir E. Lugard, commanding the division, after the hot two hours' fighting in the Begum's palace. During all that time the pipe-major played, to the astonishment of all, "as calmly as if he had been in the officers' mess tent" (Forbes Mitchell's *Reminiscences;* Munro's *Reminiscences*). M'Leod was certainly a remarkable man.

To an officer about to rebuke a reckless young soldier who cursed and raved before the attack the pipe-major said, "Don't mind the puir lad, sir, he's not drunk, he is fey! He will never see the sun set!" a prophecy that came true.

At the siege of Lucknow M'Leod was first into the breach, and no sooner in than he played and continued doing so throughout the fighting in places perfectly exposed, doubtless to the astonishment of the sepoys (*Burgoyne,* p. 256).

Dr Munro tells an amusing episode regarding a Maharajah of Patiala and the pipers of the 93rd:—

The regiment had been on the march (one of 616 miles when accomplished) and halted for one day near the residence of the Maharajah. "His Highness, on being made aware of our presence, sent his vakeel to invite us to an afternoon entertainment, and to request that we would bring the band with us. Accordingly several of us went, and the band attended as requested. The Maharajah, a very young man, received us with the politeness which Oriental princes understand so well, and conversed with us in English. He paid little, if any, attention to the music of the band, but when the twelve pipers struck up a reel and strathspey his countenance brightened up and his eyes sparkled. He listened with evident pleasure, and, when they ceased to play, exclaimed: 'Beautiful! That is the music for me. Can I get such a band? Can I buy it?' He was informed that it might be possible to purchase the discharge of one of the pipers and engage him to instruct his own men. This suggestion the Maharajah gladly accepted, and John Mackay,[1] one of the 93rd pipers, being pleased with the liberal terms offered by the Indian prince, was at length transferred to his new charge. Some time afterwards, on the occasion of a Durbar held at Umballa, a number of Indian princes with their military retainers were present. The Maharajah and a very large body of his troops attended along with their pipe band. Dr Munro, whose house was near, was surprised to have a visit from a gorgeously dressed soldier in scarlet tunic covered with gold lace, blue cloth trousers with general officers' gold lace down the sides, a splendid blue and gold turban or paghri on his head, and a broad heavy sash to correspond round his waist. This was ex-Piper John Mackay, head musician of His Highness of Patiala. John treated the doctor to some tunes on the pipes by the fourteen Indian pipers whom he had taught on pipes supplied by Glen of Edinburgh. The doctor was

---

[1] *Fionn* says the name of the piper was Henry Sinclair M'Kay. Mackay in "Sutherland and Reay" gives it as John Mackay.

surprised at their proficiency. The men were dressed in green cloth tunics and 93rd tartan trews. . . . 'The Maharajah had at first intended to dress the pipers in full Highland costume, but,' said Mackay, 'I couldn't stand seeing a native dressed up in a kilt and insisted on trews instead.' Mackay was delighted with his post and with his master, who paid him much more than the sum mentioned in the agreement. 'I have also a good house, several cows, a horse and buggy, and whenever my services are required to play either to amuse or soothe His Royal Highness to sleep I always get a handsome present in money.' Mackay remained five years in the Maharajah's service and then owing to illness returned to Scotland where he set up a fine business" (Munro's *Reminiscences*, pp. 318-19).

Meanwhile his old regiment had been on the march through India on their way to the Easofzai Campaign (1863). In their progress the stalwart natives, who regard themselves as descendants of Joseph the son of Israel, took scarcely any notice of the men until the pipers began to play. Then "every man, woman, and child within hearing flocked to listen" (*Burgoyne*, p. 301).

The 2nd Battalion was engaged in the war in the North-West Frontier of India in 1897-98 while it was the 1st Battalion that marched from Dublin in 1899 on their way to the South African War. No opportunities for gaining distinction came the way of the pipers whose duties lay in stretcher-bearing.

It was not until the Great War that the

pipers were given the chance of showing their
great versatility, ingenuity, and courage in tight
corners.   Counting all the Territorial and New
Army battalions of the regiment, twelve of the
fourteen were in the field.   The pipers of the
1st and 2nd Battalions did not have their pipes
on entering France; every piper and every
drummer was then a rifleman, taking his place
in the trenches alongside the rest of the battalions.
The 1st Battalion which had come from India had
arrived in France in November 1914, and fought
there till December 1916, when it was sent to
the Balkans along with other units from Indian
stations, to form the 27th Division.   During the
fighting in France only one piper had fallen but
soon after the campaign in the Balkans had opened
they sustained several casualties.   That led to an
order by the O.C. requiring all pipers to leave the
trenches and repair to Headquarters, where they
were to stay until the battalion went to the front
lines when they were to play them as far as was
deemed safe.

    The pipers of the 2nd Battalion had been
fighting for ten months in France when it was
learned that eleven of the twenty-one pipers who
were on the Peace Establishment were casualties,
one of the killed being a sixteen-year-old boy.
The officers thereupon withdrew the remainder
of the band from the trenches and placed them
on ammunition carrying, with intervals when they
played the battalion into action and from the front
line trenches.   One piper who did not conform
to the rule was Peter Dean, considered one of
the best all-round soldiers in the battalion.   Dean

was not only a piper but a machine gunner whose
skill and daring made him conspicuous among
officers and men alike. It came as no surprise
to his comrades to learn that he was awarded a
D.C.M. They looked for more and they were
not disappointed. For soon afterwards he was
awarded a bar to that medal, then he was
promoted to a commission, was transferred to the
Machine Gun Corps, where he secured an M.C.,
and finally he was further promoted major in his
own battalion, the only instance in the Great War
of a piper becoming a major in his mother
battalion. His old comrades among the pipers
were naturally proud of Dean, none more so than
Leonard A. Planner, one of the most popular of
the band. "Jim," as he was named, had gone
to the regiment as a boy from the Duke of York's
School, which was rather astonishing in respect
that he had no ties with Scotland. He had
escaped all manner of casualties until the 9th
November 1918, when, to the dismay of his
friends in the battalion, he was killed—the last
piper to fall in action.

The pipers of the New Army and Territorial
battalions were no whit less distinguished in action.
One of the romantic episodes of Beaumont Hamel
was the complete rout of a force of Germans
by a piper! A subaltern with a sergeant and
a piper found that they had lost touch with
their fellows and were in the immediate rear of
the Germans, who were resisting an attack by
our men who were at the far end of the village.
It was a decidedly awkward situation for the three
"Argylls," but the piper saved it. Striking up

the regimental tune "The Campbells are Comin'," he and his officer and N.C.O. had the satisfaction of seeing the enemy retire in disorder, under the impression that the piper heralded another party of attackers in the rear.

Of the Territorial battalions the 1/5th Battalion pipers had many adventures as runners, ammunition carriers, and stretcher-bearers in Gallipoli, Egypt, Palestine, and France, and suffered many casualties in consequence. Piper William Carlyle, 1/6th Battalion, who had been mentioned in despatches, met a hero's death in trying to rescue a wounded comrade. Piper George Flockhart of the 1/7th (Falkirk) Battalion seemed to bear a charmed life, for, surviving the second battle of Ypres, where five of his piper comrades were killed and the pipe-major was wounded while acting as platoon sergeant, he distinguished himself by his gallant leadership, for which he was awarded a D.C.M. After passing through all the vicissitudes of war Flockhart resumed his pre-war occupation as a miner in Carnock Mine and was killed while at work just a month after the Armistice.

The 1/8th (Dunoon) Company had two pipers who were distinguished in different spheres. William Laurie, the pipe-major, has been reckoned one of the most accomplished pipers, and his work, the "Battle of the Somme," holds first place among the Great War compositions. The hardships of the campaign proved too much for Laurie's constitution; he was invalided home, where he died on 28th November 1916. John M'Lellan, a piper in the same band, had won the

D.C.M. as a piper in the H.L.I. in the South
African War. M'Lellan was a poet who found
inspiration at the cannon's mouth so to say,
several of his poetical effusions which found
places in the newspaper columns having been
actually composed and written in the front line
trenches. He has also to his credit several
popular pipe melodies, one of which, "The
Taking of Beaumont Hamel," expresses the
piper's feelings in that memorable action.

Probably the most unfortunate of all the
Territorial battalions of the regiment was the
1/9th (Dumbarton) Battalion, whose pipers were
almost entirely made casualties soon after their
arrival in France. Two were killed in the first
battle of Ypres and three so severely wounded
that they had to be discharged ; three others fell
sick and had to be invalided out. The few who
remained were then transferred to other units.

In the New Army battalions the pipers were
put to one or other of those indispensable
duties — ammunition carrying, stretcher work,
running messages, and occasionally serving as
duty men. In the 10th Battalion the pipe-
major, Thomas Aitken, a veteran of the pre-war
Argylls, tended the wounded under heavy fire
and had his devotion and gallantry rewarded by
a D.C.M., while Piper Duncan M'Sporran, who
later was promoted pipe-major, forgot that he
was regarded as a very good pibroch player but
remembered that the old-time piper went into
battle at the head of his men, and so kept that
place in many an engagement, including that of
Longueval. M'Sporran may not have won any

decoration but he did earn the warm approval of
the men who marched to his stirring strains. In
the storming of the Hindenburg line the runners
and ammunition carriers had arduous and trying
times and one of those who excelled on that
occasion was Lance - Corporal Piper Gammack
who, in consequence, was awarded the Military
Medal.

Far different conditions governed the pipers
of the 11th Battalion, whose colonel, the late
Malcolm M'Neill, a distinguished officer of the
regular Argyll and Sutherland Highlanders, with
a passion for pipe music and some ability as
a player, tried to shelter his pipers from all
unnecessary risks. A good piper of the Camerons
is said to have called forth the admiration of
Colonel M'Neill, who promptly offered the
officer commanding the Camerons three privates
in exchange for that piper, an offer which was
not accepted. Once M'Neill had to leave his
battalion, and on his return learned that the
pipers had been put on ammunition carrying in
consequence of which eight pipers had become
casualties. The colonel was inclined to be angry
and the officer responsible had to listen to a
lecture on the value of pipe music in war and
the consequent necessity for conserving as far
as possible the providers of that music.

For the Republic, Raymond Desvarreux, one
of the foremost painters of France, made an
excellent portrait of a fine-looking, magnificently
proportioned piper, of the A. and S. H., James
M'Niven, a native of Tiree.

PIPERS OF THE LOVAT SCOUTS

THE kilted pipers of the Lovat Scouts, in hunting Fraser tartan of their chief and colonel, Lord Lovat, are a feature of every peace time parade of the regiment. In time of war they are not so easily discerned for they have donned the khaki breeches and equipment of the troopers and are in the ranks with pipes strapped to their kits; for the Scouts rightly deem pipe-playing in action or in scouting quite out of place.

Raised in 1900 by the Lord Lovat for service in the South African War the Scouts, under their founder and colonel, Lord Lovat, D.S.O., an ex-officer of the Life Guards, made a great name alike as fighters, cragsmen, and keen-eyed scouts, qualities which they owed in large measure to the presence in the ranks of many deer-stalkers, shepherds, and gamekeepers of the Highlands. They were particularly commended for their successes at Diamond Hill and Naaupoort Nek, which they helped to win.

Like the Scottish Horse, with which regiment they have much in common, the Scouts were after the war placed on the army establishment as a regiment of Yeomanry—a tribute to their excellent work in the South African campaign.

The outbreak of the Great War found the Lovat Scouts mobilised, their well-filled ranks quickly swelled to overflow, fresh recruits and

past members arriving in such large numbers as
to necessitate the formation of additional regiments.   The   1st   and   2nd   Regiments   were
despatched to the Dardanelles, the 2/1st kept
as "feeder" or reserve and the 2/2nd sent to
Lowestoft,   where,   instead   of   the   threatened
German invasion, that English east coast town
had to endure several severe bombardments.   That
2/2nd Regiment of Lovat Scouts was a very much
different body of men from those in the other
units for they were neither so exclusively Scottish
nor had they a pipe band.   It was therefore with
much delight that the Scots in the regiment
welcomed the arrival one day of a piper of note
who had come to fill the post of pipe-major—
unaware that there was no pipe-band.   The pipe-
major searched for his pipers and, failing to find
them, inquired of the adjutant, who had to make
the sad admission that there was no piper in
the regiment but the new pipe-major.   A pipe-
major and no band!   The thought was unendur-
able to Pipe-Major Donald A. Campbell, who
shook the dust of the piperless Scouts from his
thick brogues and departed, and with him vanished
the last hope of the Scots in the 2/2nd Lovat
Scouts for the old pipe melodies of Scotland.

The members of the 1st and 2nd Regiments
were more fortunate, for in all intervals of
rest during the fighting in the East the combatant pipers were accustomed to untie their
pipes and entertain their comrades behind the
lines in billets and in dug-outs.   How much
these concerts were appreciated may be imagined.
Sometimes   a   pipe   enthusiast   belonging   to   a

neighbouring unit, hearing a pibroch or a march floating out towards his camp, would wend his way to the source to ascertain who was the "good piper," and then learn that it was Pipe-Major Donald Macmillan of the 1st Regiment or Pipe-Major John Campbell of the 2nd. The crowded audiences of the dug-out concerts were always mindful of the lonely Scout at the Observation Post, and him they would invite by telephone to listen; and the O.P. man, with his ear to the 'phone, would then dream he was back to the hills and glens of his native land, in the strains of the piper's music.

Thus the Lovat Scouts progressed through the fighting of Gallipoli, Egypt, and Macedonia, where, in September 1916, they were converted into the 10th Battn. Queen's Own Cameron Highlanders, retaining the title through their next field of fighting, namely France and Flanders.

They are once more the Lovat Scouts, and, along with the Scottish Horse, have the signal honour of being placed as the only two regiments of Scouts in the British army; and the pipers, under Pipe-Major William Ross, late of the Scots Guards, do duty as pipers in tartan kilt and belted plaid.

PIPERS OF THE SCOTTISH HORSE

Like the Lovat Scouts, the Scottish Horse owes its origin to the South African War of 1899-1902. It was in the autumn of 1900 that Lord Kitchener accepted the offer made by the Caledonian Society of South Africa to raise a corps of Scots from the various provinces, provided that the name should be "The Scottish Horse." Practical shape was given to the proposals by the message sent forth by Lord Kitchener to the Marquess of Tullibardine, D.S.O.—now the eighth Duke of Atholl —who was then a captain in the Royal Horse Guards, offering him the command of the new regiment, and requesting that the "Fiery Cross" should be sent around for recruits.

The recruits, to the number of four squadrons, were got together by February 1901, a feat which so pleased the Marquess that he applied for and obtained leave to raise a second regiment of Scottish Horse to be recruited from Scots in Scotland and in Australia. The pipers arrived early in 1901 with John Macaskil as pipe-major.

The excellence of their soldiering and scouting in some of the "hottest" battles of that war was recognised by all the generals under whom the Scottish Horse had served, and was such that when the war was over and the regiments were disbanded, it was thought advisable to perpetuate the name, in a new formation to be recruited from the shires of Perth, Argyll, Moray, Banff, and Aberdeen. In the recruiting campaigns throughout these areas the pipers were of considerable value. On the long marches across the veldt of South Africa the pipers, mounted on trained Russian ponies, played cheerful airs for the men. They have of more recent years remained on foot, forsworn the breeches, and kept to the Atholl Murray tartan kilt and plaid. The pipers are mostly Atholl men, pipers also of that unique corps known as the Atholl Highlanders, the private regiment of the Duke of Atholl. The Scottish Horse have a marching-past tune called "The Scottish Horse," composed in South Africa in 1901 by the Duchess of Atholl, who about the same time wrote another pipe melody entitled "Brothers Three," in honour of her husband and his two brothers, all on active service.

The outbreak of the Great War found the regiment mobilised; soon its ranks were overflowing with fresh men and with men who had left its ranks in earlier years. The two regiments expanded into nine—three brigades—and each regiment with its own band of twelve pipers.

As battalions of infantry the 1st, 2nd, and 3rd Regiments went to Gallipoli, where they took part in all the fighting until the evacuation of the Peninsula; thence to Egypt and successively to Palestine, Salonika, and France. During their service in the East the Scottish Horse had, in addition to marching and fighting, made roads, and, from being dismounted Horsemen, were, about the close of September 1916, converted into members of that famous regiment The Black

N

Watch, though even then they were allowed
to retain their identity in dress and in the official
designation "13th Battalion The Black Watch
(Scottish Horse)."

In all the adventures of the regiment the
pipers were handy men, now assisting the quartermaster, now in transport, and, when the regiment
were on the march, refreshing them by tunes on
the pipes, which they resumed for these occasions
and for times in rest billets.

In Gallipoli, in 1915, the pipers took a leading
part on a notable occasion. Lord Tullibardine
wished to prove to the Higher Command that the
Turkish trenches, in front of his line—which he
had been ordered to take—were fully occupied,
though "Intelligence" had reported them empty.
News of the victory at Loos gave an excellent
opportunity. The men were ordered to fix
bayonets, show them over the top of their
trenches and cheer. The pipers were sent into
the trenches with orders to play and then lie
low. Just as they were about to begin, an
officer asked a piper what he was going to play.
"The De'il's in the Kitchen, sir," answered
J. A. Gordon. "Capital . . . most appropriate,"
was the laughing comment of the officer. And
"The De'il's in the Kitchen" and other tunes
rang through to the Turkish trenches, the tenants
of which, though they probably did not understand the message, were considerably startled.
"It so much startled them," wrote an officer of
the Scottish Horse, "that for forty-five minutes
they put down a rifle fire barrage on our trenches of
terrific density—while we laughed." Incidentally

it may be added that the affair thus started, developed into a fine pyrotechnic display, as the field and larger guns on both sides hearing the "battle," joined in without in the least knowing what it was about.

One point was made clear: the order for the Scottish Horse to occupy the Turkish trenches was cancelled.

Except for that most extraordinary episode the pipers were kept at Quartermaster's Stores or on transport, and while so employed on the Eastern Front suffered severely in health, nine pipers having to be invalided out of the service. Pipe-Major Peter Stewart, aged 61, head stalker in the Atholl forest, was an indefatigable sniper, and had the good fortune to be awarded the Serbian Cross of Kara George, a much coveted distinction among troops in the Near East.

With the transference of the Scottish Horse to the Western Front the pipers had to endure the hardship common to pipers of all units, of seeing some of their number posted to one or other of the fourteen battalions of their temporary regiment—The Black Watch.

PIPERS OF THE LONDON SCOTTISH

WITH a history ranging from 1859 the London Scottish, or 14th London Regiment, is one of the best-known units of the Territorial Force in the Kingdom. The battalion, dressed in the Highland garb, with glengarry, doublet, and kilt of Elcho grey, blue-grey hose, and white spats, is a familiar sight throughout London. The pipers are as well known as are the rank and file and are invariably part of every expedition which the battalion or a part of the battalion is accustomed to make. The war service of the "Scottish" dates from the South African War, 1899-1902, when many volunteers attached themselves to the Gordon Highlanders, and among these were several pipers.

On the outbreak of the Great War the battalion was mobilised, and in very short time had countless applications from ex-Territorial members and freshmen for admission to the ranks. In this way the Scottish grew to three battalions, the first being ready for active service soon after the opening of hostilities. Indeed, the 1st Battalion, which left on 14th September 1914, was one of the earliest, if not the first, Territorial Infantry unit to reach France. Marching through the streets of Havre, the pipers saluted France by playing on their pipes "The Marseillaise." On the 31st October the men had

entered battle at Messines, where they drew
considerable praise for their steadiness. The
first anniversary of the War the pipers celebrated
by playing "God Save the King," a performance
which immediately brought "Die Wacht am
Rhein" from the band in the German trenches.
The pipers who had played the battalion overseas were not content to remain as pipers. Their
quick promotion to commissioned rank may strike
those who are not acquainted with the personnel
of the "Scottish" as phenomenal; but the pipers,
like the rank and file, are capable soldiers,
and the majority of them are equipped with
the necessary certificate for commissioned rank
from O.T.C. units. The scattering of these
embryo officers to different regiments is in itself
interesting. Pipers Edgar and Mackinnon were
posted 2nd lieutenants in their own corps;
Campbell went to the Scottish Rifles; Piper
Pennington, after remaining with the Scottish
until he had been twice wounded, became a
lieutenant in the Royal Navy; Mackay, who was
commissioned to the Black Watch, fell in action
with that regiment. Pipers L. D. Henderson[1]
and Sutherland Graeme went to the Seaforth
Highlanders, 4th Battalion. The twin brothers
Porteous put down their pipes and parted
company on receiving commissions—one going
to the R.A.S.C., the other to the R.G.A.;
Piper Zambra was made a lieutenant in the
Royal Flying Corps, and B. R. Nicol in the
Labour Corps; while five others, Greig, Hare,
Grant-Crawford, Gordon Forbes, and Joss, who

---

[1] Now (1927) Major, London Scottish.

on one occasion rendered great service to the
battalion by guiding it to its front line trenches,
graced the company of officers in that highly useful corps—the Royal Army Ordnance Corps.

Of those who elected to remain as pipers
eleven were killed in action, one of them being
a sixteen - year - old Edinburgh Academy boy,
named Angus. Indeed, that list of killed included many who had made or were making
their mark in various fields. Harry Latham, a
lance-corporal piper, was one of the most distinguished rifle shots in the Territorial Force;
his name will be found near the top of the
King's Hundred for several years until 1914.
Latham's gallantry was remarked in battle and
he was mentioned in despatches. Piper James
Carey, who hailed from Dundee, lost his life
while trying to save the life of his company
officer. Pipers Andrew B. Paton, a Glasgow
man, and Sam Campbell, from the far Hebrides,
were carrying a wounded man from the battlefield, when both were struck by a shell and killed.
Piper Connolly died from illness contracted at the
front, whilst Piper Pratt had a distressing wound
which caused blindness. Piper Pratt is now an
inmate of St Dunstan's and maintains his old
cheery ways and his fondness for pipe music with
which he entertains his friends. His correspondence he conducts himself by typewriter.

The 2nd Battalion had a more varied experience
of war than their comrades of the 1st. Landing
in France in June 1916 they left for Salonica at
the close of November, where owing to their
bagpipes having gone bad in the excessive heat,

they were forced to fall back on dried goatskins soaked in whale oil, which made admirable bags for the pipes. In their next field of action—Egypt—the troubles of the pipers were caused by the sand which got into the reeds and prevented them from doing justice to themselves or giving satisfaction to their comrades on the long marches through the desert. The bags, moreover, became dry and no honey or treacle being available as emollients, the only means of keeping the bags moist for play was the scanty drinking-water with which each man was provided.

Matters were better when the battalion moved into their most interesting theatre of campaign, namely Palestine.

There pipers and battalion generally experienced a curious thrill in marching to the tunes of the pipes through the old Biblical lands—the Jordan, the land of Gilead, and Jerusalem. The pipers had played the battalion into the Holy City on 9th December 1917, and later, when the drums went bad, they managed to replace them with Turkish instruments captured at Nebi Musa (Moses' Tomb) the drum-sticks being fashioned from Turkish tent pegs found in the Turkish tents.

Back once more in France in May 1918, the pipers were fortunate in escaping wounds and sickness, and also in the fact that the battalion had appreciated the music of their pipes played throughout the Eastern part of their campaign.

PIPERS OF THE LIVERPOOL SCOTTISH

(10th BATTALION THE KING'S LIVERPOOL REGIMENT)

THE Liverpool Scottish is probably the only unit in the British Regular or Territorial Army that owes its inception to a piper.

During the progress of the South African War, 1899-1902, the Scottish readers of the Liverpool newspapers were roused to action by a letter which had been written by Mr Forbes Milne, a Scots resident in the city, in which he urged the formation of a Volunteer battalion from the Scotsmen settled in Liverpool. As a result of that spirited appeal to his fellow-countrymen the young Scots quickly responded. A committee was then formed, and very soon the necessary authority of the War Office was given for raising a battalion of Liverpool Scottish. In January 1901 the battalion was an accomplished fact—an integral part of the Territorial, or rather, Volunteer Army, and with kilted uniform and pipe band complete.

Mr Forbes Milne, the promoter of the scheme, was a piper, and was appointed pipe-major of the battalion, but did not live long to enjoy the privilege, for he died that very year. He was succeeded by one who was much better known in the piping world, namely Pipe-Major John Mackay, composer of "The Badge of Scotland" and other compositions.

The Liverpool Scots have another proud distinction: they were one of the first, if not the very first, Territorial unit to enter the battle zone in November 1914. The eleven pipers who led them overseas had to put by their pipes and take up the duties of stretcher-bearers and first-aid men, though some elected to revert to the ranks. No matter to what duty they had gone, hardly a piper remained to the battalion a year later. The pipe-corporal had been killed in action in December 1914; two pipers were badly wounded and three others had been invalided out. Two had been promoted, viz. Pipe-Major Stoddart, who became R.Q.M.S., and Piper N. Hampson, who went to the South Lancashire Regiment as a 2nd lieutenant.

Thus many months passed without a note of pipe music on the march or in rest billets. Then, in 1916, appeared five pipers who were welcomed by the battalion. In 1917 there was embodied a 2nd Battn. Liverpool Scottish who joined the 1st Battalion. But the pipers, who were set to ration carrying, found some of their number selecting other jobs in preference. Pipers Johnston and Gilfillan, for example, became Lewis gunners; Piper Service went into the trenches; and Rae was kept busy as a despatch rider. Yet they one and all kept a look-out for any occasion which might justify the use of the pipes; they desired to play their companies into action, but to all their entreaties for this "privilege" the officers turned a deaf ear. None was more chagrined by these refusals than a gentleman from New York, Piper Worthington, who had to be content with more useful but less picturesque duties. One piper did manage to evade the edict against playing into action, by attaching him self to a raiding party which proceeded over "No Man's Land" to the tune selected by that enterprising piper of the Liverpool Scottish.

PIPERS OF THE TYNESIDE SCOTTISH

In the north-east province of England, the Territorial area of the Northumberland Fusiliers and the Durham Light Infantry, are many Scots. Unlike their brethren in London and Liverpool, they had never banded themselves together for military purposes until the outbreak of the Great War. Then it was that the old clan spirit manifested itself. The Scots there, who would otherwise have joined one or other of the local regiments, were so early as August 1914 made aware that an effort was being made to form a battalion of Tyneside Scots. The modern " Fiery Cross " was sent through the various towns and villages, through Newcastle, Sunderland, North and South Shields, the two Hartlepools and elsewhere, wherever there were Scots, or sons of Scots, calling upon them to join a new formation which would indicate the Scots origin of its members : " The Tyneside Scottish." The Scots responded so well that in time there were formed three battalions of the Northumberland Fusiliers made up of the "Tyneside Scottish."

One of the early steps in the formation of the 1st Battalion was to secure pipers and drummers. In answer to the invitation to all pipers and drummers of experience the necessary numbers quickly enlisted and were then equipped with bagpipes, drums, and Highland dress—the gifts of influential Scots and others of the district, among whom were Lord Armstrong, Colonel Joseph Cowen, Sir Thomas Oliver, Colonel John Reed, Mr Angus Watson, and Professor J. Wight Duff.

The question of a tartan was much debated, and finally one with set like the Campbells of dark green and white stripes, was adopted.

To the reader north of the Tweed there is something significant in the choice of the first camping ground of the Tyneside Scottish. At Alnwick, 821 years earlier, there fell in action against the English that warlike King of Scots, Malcolm Caenmhor. Alnwick in 1914 was a training ground for Scots and English, united against a common foe, but even it did not suffice for the extensive operations which were part of every battalion's exercises. They were sent to Salisbury Plain in August 1915, and in both camps the pipers were of the greatest moment. Indeed they were held in the highest esteem by both battalions of the Tyneside Scottish, the men of each battalion claiming to have a better pipe band than the other, and each pipe band doing its best to justify the claim.

After what seemed to the battalions concerned an unconscionably long time, they were at last sent to France in the beginning of January 1916, as part of the 34th Division. The pipers, who had hitherto led their battalions, were ordered to stow away their instruments, and, with rifle and full kit, take their places in the ranks and in the trenches. Thus they fought until the eve of the battle of the Somme, 30th June 1916, when an important alteration in the status of the pipers was made. They were permitted to resume their instruments, take their place at the head of the battalion or companies, and play them into action.

The Tyneside Scots pipers were proud of the honour and right gallantly did they maintain the old traditions of the heroism of the Highland pipers in battle. They played with all their wonted verve into "No Man's Land," till five fell mortally wounded and two more were severely wounded, leaving but four pipers of the 1st Battalion untouched.

The pipers of the 2nd Battalion were more fortunate, for out of their complement of thirteen pipers there were lost but two killed and four wounded. Of the pipers in that historic battle Brigadier-General Trevor Ternan wrote: "The majority of the pipers fell at La Boiselle on the 1st July 1916, and the pipes in which they took such pride, and played with their last breaths, were lost, or only now exist as torn and bloody fragments preserved as treasured relics of that band of heroes, the 'Tyneside Scottish pipers.'"

The surviving pipers were appointed stretcher-bearers and they performed their new duties with all the bravery and solicitude for the wounded which the regiment expected of them. No matter how heavy might be the shelling that went on, the pipers were there devoting all their mind and energies to the care of those who lay wounded. It was in circumstances like these that the tireless zeal of three was observed and led to the award of the M.M. to Pipe-Major Wilson, Lance-Corporal Taylor, and Piper Phillips. Piper T. Shaw won his M.M. as a bomber.

But the lack of pipe music was at length badly felt and was much deplored by officers and men. No music on the march and none when the battalion was in rest billets! The rousing tunes about which they used to talk, were like to become but dimly remembered. Fortunately in the early part of 1917 the colonel informed the Tyneside Scottish Committee at home of the need for more bagpipes, and, in response, there were sent out sufficient sets wherewith to complete a fresh pipe band for each of the battalions of the "Scottish." But though the pipes were there the pipers were not, except the pipe-major and one or two others. Volunteers were then asked for, and many willing to learn the ways of the bagpipe were quickly taught enough to satisfy the uncritical audiences of the Scots over the Border; though many averred that the preliminary stages of that limited musical education were more painful to the ear than the noise of the largest shell.

The new-found music of the pipes cannot have lasted many months when the battalions and the pipers were sundered, the battalions being disbanded and the pipers finding themselves privates in the King's Own Yorkshire Light Infantry, two ex-pipers falling in action a month later.

A very interesting set of pipers were the Tyneside Scottish, if only for the pipe-majors. Munro Strachan, pipe-major of the 2nd Battalion, was over fifty years of age when he proceeded to France, his son, an ex-Regular piper of the K.O.S.B., also of the 2nd Battalion, being a

pipe tutor not only for his own recruits but also
for the large number of tyros of the Tyneside
Irish. The pipe-majors of the other battalions
were the Wilsons—a father and his two sons.
John Wilson, senior, town councillor as well
as pipe-major, had also the honour of being
selected first pipe-major of the Tyneside Irish,
in 1915.

IRISH PIPERS AND PIPERS OF IRISH REGIMENTS

As pipers in battle, Irish pipers have a very long history. They are said to have been with the Irish troops that crossed over into Gascony in 1286 in the cause of Edward I.; they were at Crécy in 1346 and played in support of their 6000 comrades in arms in that memorable fight, and doubtless commemorated the victory of Edward in some pipe salute. Irish pipers may also take pride in the knowledge that one of their predecessors was chosen by Albrecht Dürer as a subject for his art, the woodcut of that warrior piper of 1514 being considered one of the finest executed by the great artist.

Like the Scots bagpipe of 1745, the Irish war pipe was long frowned upon by all hostile authorities as provocative of war, and, consequently, one of the steps taken by Edward III. for securing the pacification of Ireland and the establishment of good order, was the enactment forbidding the practice of pipe music—an edict which can have had little effect.

Cromwell took the same view in regard to the potency of the bagpipe, and threatened any who dared to transgress the law against playing the bagpipe with banishment to the Barbados. What a punishment for pipe-playing! There is, how-

ever, no record of any piper having been
"found out."

In every feud, every battle fought on Irish
soil, the pipers were present to urge on their
respective sides to victory as well as to serve the
purposes of a bugler. In the siege of Kinsale,
for example, in 1600, when Earl Tir Owen
found himself, in the darkness of night, surprised
by a superior force, his signal for retreat was
made by the piper on his bagpipe; and in 1647,
when the garrison of Ardlonan Castle had to
surrender, there was among the number one
bagpiper.

In that same year there was in Ireland a
company of Scots under Sir Alexander M'Allister
or M'Allisdrum, *alias* M'Donell, who had gone
to the assistance of an Irish chief who had some
accounts to settle with another chief. The
Scots were annihilated, and all that remained
to mark their service in that land was the
pipe melody which their pipers were wont to
play. The Irish, who had memorised the tune,
made use of it under the name of "M'Allisdrum's
March."

One of the most remarkable regiments of
Ireland came into being about the year 1661,
when His Majesty's Regiment of Guards, or Irish
Guards, was raised for Charles II.; and that
regiment had, in addition to its complement of
officers, 1200 soldiers, and 24 drummers—one
piper for the King's Company. From their headquarters in Dublin the Irish Guards, with their
piper, marched to Derry and fought at the battle
of the Boyne, where the medley of tunes played

by the pipers of the opposing armies must have
been formidable.

The Irish Guards were then on the eve of
their extraordinary career; after the victory for
the troops of William of Orange the Irish Guards
were given their choice of a sovereign, and, with
the exception of seven, they elected to follow the
fortunes of the deposed king, James II., in exile.
In the army of France they won a great name for
valour in various battles. They assisted the
French troops in 1702 to drive out the Austrians
from Cremona, the city famed for violins, a feat
which the pipers commemorated in a pipe melody
which has yet a high place in the pipe music of
Ireland—"The Day we beat the Germans at
Cremona."

Better known then by their successive colonels'
names—Ruth's, Dillon's, Roscommon's, Walsh's,
and Berwick's, and as the "Irish Brigade," the
Irish Guards fought at Fontenoy with distinction,
their pipers playing "The White Cockade" to the
disturbance, no doubt, of the Royal Scots, the
21st, 25th, and 42nd Regiments, on the other side.
Their success stimulated the French authorities to
despatch detachments of the Guards to the aid
of the Jacobites in Scotland, where, in the battle
of Culloden, they were all either killed in action
or taken prisoners.

It was the French Revolution that put an end
to the service of the Irish Guards, or Irish
Brigade, in the cause of France. The colonel
declined to serve the Republic, and his men
accepted the invitation of the British military
authorities in 1794 to become a distinct regiment

in the British Army, with leave to retain their old uniforms with the light blue facings and badge of St Patrick.

The Irish Guards, however, had fallen on evil times. Their reserve of recruits from the homeland they could not obtain, for rebellion was ripening in Ireland—to culminate in 1798—and the Guards, unable to fill up the gaps in their ranks, were forced, after a period of active service in North America and the West Indies, to endure the necessary hardship of being transferred to other regiments.

The Irish Guards had ceased to be—but not altogether. A century later the extraordinary valour of Irish soldiers throughout the course of the nineteenth century was officially recognised by the formation in 1902 of His Majesty's Regiment of Irish Guards, which was placed on the same footing as the Grenadier, Coldstream, and Scots Guards; but, unlike the Scots Guards, they had no pipers until 1916. The prominence in active service of pipers in Scottish units had reminded the Irish Guards that they, too, used to have pipers, and once the memory of their old-time pipers had been awakened, steps were taken to form a pipe band. The first to present a set of Irish war pipes — that is the ordinary bagpipe with two drones—was the patriot John Redmond, M.P. Pipers were enlisted, were taught by the pipe-major of the London Irish, and were clothed in the time-honoured saffron-coloured stuff, dress of Ireland's ancient warriors, with dark green stockings, saffron tops, saffron garters and knots, dark green jacket, and service bonnet with the white metal bearing the star, and on their "dress bonnet" the badge, of the Order of St Patrick on the right side of the bonnet, and with the St Patrick's blue hackle above the badge.

The pipers of a Scots regiment would probably take exception to the dress of the Irish Guards' pipers on several grounds: there are no spats, no sporran, no black shoulder-belt or belted plaid, and no dirk. The black braid across the front of the jacket of the pipers, though alien to the idea of the Scot, might pass, but not the silver braid, silver pipings, and silver chevrons of the sergeant-piper or pipe-major. Nevertheless, the pipers are debonair and smart, and, like the pipers in Scots regiments, have their allotted duties throughout the day. At Reveillé they play "Dawning of the Day." Breakfast requires no warning, nor tea; but at dinner-time they remind all good soldiers of the "Little House under the Hill," and the notice for "Lights Out" on the pipes is the tender "Oft in the Stilly Night."

The famous old Irish pipe melody called "Garryowen" summons the Irish Guards to parade, and the regimental march past is to the tune of the equally old and renowned "St Patrick's Day."

Their smartness in dress and piping abilities were not so marked, naturally, in 1917, when they were sent to France to join the two battalions, though they were even then, after their year's training, shaping well. On their first appearance at the regiment's Headquarters, the officers thought that something was wrong in

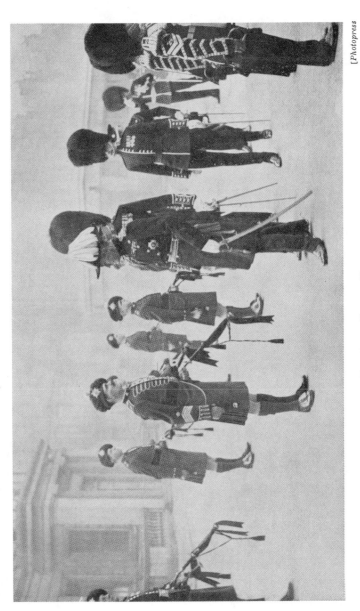

THE IRISH GUARDS PIPERS.

the "hang" of the kilt, and, jealous for the
honour of the Guards, sent for the pipe-major of
a battalion of the Gordons to examine and report
what should be done to improve that defect.

Their sartorial appearance having been put
right, the officers, according to Mr Rudyard
Kipling, "solemnly invited Captain Hugh Ross
of the Scots Guards to tea, in his capacity as a
pipe expert, to pronounce on their merits. And
Civil War did not follow." Mr Kipling was
amazed to find the Irish pipers play without
displaying any of the animation that characterises
the Scots pipers, and, on his inquiring of the
pipe-major the reason for the "immobility," was
informed that it "was one of the secrets of the
regiment."

The pipers of the Irish Guards were a success
and played before the King of the Belgians and
"an unlimited amount of British generals."

The officers who had financed the pipe band
out of their own pockets were, in 1918, relieved
of the expense, the pipers being placed on the
establishment like their colleagues of the Scots
Guards and other Scots units.

Other regiments—the Royal Irish Fusiliers,
Royal Dublin Fusiliers, Inniskilling Fusiliers,
Leinster Regiment, and the Royal Irish, now
Royal Ulster Rifles—had pipers, but not all full
pipe bands. Certain "Service" Battalions of
these aiming at having pipes and drums, had to
seek their recruits among the youth of Scotland,
and these youthful pipers were not slow to learn
that it was considerably worse than mere bad
form to play a tune that had evil memories for

certain regiments. Northern units sometimes excited the political antipathies of a South of Ireland regiment by getting the pipers to play "Boyne Water" on the line of march, the Orangemen enjoying the grim looks and muttered imprecations of the Catholic troops; but to the Scots tyro who practised that race - dividing melody on a barrack square came swift protest in the shape of bodily assault, as a few Scots soon discovered.

The Territorial battalions of the London Irish Rifles had had pipe bands since 1906-7, and these were maintained by the officers. Their saffron-hued kilts, however, were not donned until 1914 when the pipers of the 2nd Battalion numbered sixteen and the drummers fourteen.

The pipe bands were very popular with the battalions, the members of which showed their appreciation of the music played by the bands on the march by cheering them repeatedly, astonished that in spite of the heavy kit which the pipers and drummers had to carry, they managed to endure all the discomfort and to keep playing on the longest of their marches. Then, "in the very early hours of morning when the men who had been on duty in the trenches all night were due to return to billets, the band was there to play them back, a service which was extolled by all, an officer remarking that 'the men of the battalion will not easily forget how welcome was their music on these occasions.'"

In action the pipers and drummers were generally employed as stretcher - bearers or as runners, though on one occasion the pipers of the 2nd Battalion were in the front-line trenches, while the battalion were ahead on a raiding expedition in the German lines. The pipers played in order that the battalion might be guided back by the sound of their music.

In 1915 the Tyneside Irish Battalions of the Northumberland Fusiliers could not allow their neighbours of the " Scottish " the glory of having pipers all to themselves; they, too, would have pipes, and Irish ones at that, with the two drones of Ireland. They got them but were compelled by an English brigadier-general to have their pipes with three drones! Before then they had to engage the services of two of the Tyneside Scottish to instruct the willing Irish learners in the rudiments of pipe-playing and in this they were fortunate in having Pipe-Major John Wilson and young Strachan, the latter having to return to his unit on the eve of the battle of the Somme, the pipe-major continuing as pipe-major of the Irish. One could hardly expect that with so little training the Tyneside Irish could compete with the experienced pipers of the Tyneside Scottish.

The Great War had resuscitated the ancient use of the Irish war pipe; it had been allowed to lie dormant except in a few cases till then, but the Irish Free State has continued the practice of having pipers, though they have not as yet sufficient bagpipe makers to keep their bands supplied.

Irishmen were impressed by all that they had heard of the peculiar thrill evoked by the sound of the old Irish airs played by the pipers in the Great War. They were told by Mr Macdonagh,

in his *Irish at the Front,* how their "music
warmed the hearts of the soldiers and fired their
blood whenever they heard the strains of Irish
music. . . . It has magic in it . . . it transforms
the Gael, reawakens in the depths of their being
impressions, moods, feelings, inherited from a wild,
untamed ancestry . . . and thus gives them, more
than strong wine, that strength of arm and that
endurance of soul which makes them invincible."

PIPERS OF THE CANADIAN FORCES

MANY of the Canadian Militia regiments had pipe bands long years before the Great War; they were mostly regiments affiliated to Highland regiments of the Old Country, whose titles they bore and whose traditions they sought to preserve. Oldest of all were the 5th Royal Highlanders of Canada, dating from 1816, affiliated to the Black Watch. There were the Highland Light Infantry of Canada, with headquarters at Galt, Ontario; the Seaforth Highlanders of Canada at Vancouver, and—also allied to the Seaforths—the Pictou Highlanders of Nova Scotia; the 48th Regiment (Highlanders), Toronto, affiliated to the Gordons; the 43rd Queen's Own Cameron Highlanders of Canada at Winnipeg and the Ottawa Highlanders, each affiliated to the Camerons; Princess Louise's (Argyll and Sutherland) Highlanders of Canada, at Hamilton, Ontario, and the Calgary Highlanders, were both representative of the old 91st and 93rd Argyll and Sutherland Highlanders.

Pipers were not only in abundance in these units but also in certain mounted contingents. The 1st and 4th Canadian Mounted Rifles had full pipe bands, which, in times of peace, were also mounted.

In addition to these old established units many regiments raised for service in the Great War adopted pipe bands. There were pipers in

France with all the following regiments: Princess Patricia's Canadian Light Infantry, the 13th, 15th, 16th, 19th, 21st, 25th, 26th, 29th, 42nd, 43rd, 46th, 48th, 67th, and 85th Regiments; the 107th (Pioneers), the 35th (Forestry) Battalion, and the 1st and the 4th Canadian Mounted Rifles.

The Princess Patricia's Light Infantry had the advantage of getting *en masse* the Town Pipe Band of Edmonton, the members of which journeyed to Ottawa in August 1914, and offered to "play the battalion into France and back again." The pipers, who were all good Scots, had volunteered for that distinguished regiment, though only 15 per cent. of its members were Scots, and they learned that the tunes often in request were not always of the type appreciated by true disciples of M'Crimmon. For example, when marching through a village in France occupied by American troops, the pipers played "Marching through Georgia" to the immense delight of the Americans. They had to keep on playing, no matter how long the march; pipers are expected never to tire or allow the men behind them to tire, but a march that requires no fewer than forty-two different tunes to be played seems something in the nature of a record. That, indeed, was the sum totalled one day by the P.P.C.L.I. after an exceptionally long march and was put down to the credit of their pipers!

In action the Canadian pipers were, as in the home regiments, employed as pipers, but oftener as stretcher - bearers, runners, ammunition and ration carriers and transport men. Frequently they were found at the head of their companies, playing them into action, and then resuming their work of stretcher bearing. The pipers of the P.P.C.L.I., two of whom were awarded the D.C.M., played the leading wave of the battalion up the lip of the crater of Vimy Ridge in April 1917, and then went back for their stretcher duties.

The 13th (Royal Highlanders) seem to have been badly handicapped at the outset by lack of pipers, only five having gone out with the original force and of these two were lost in the battle of Ypres in April 1915—H. Robertson, a Muir-of-Ord man, who died of his wounds, and Alexander Singer, who, in consequence of wounds, had to be invalided out. The pipe-corporal, Neil Sinclair, an old piper of the K.O.S.B., who hailed from Islay, was wounded in June 1916, and after recovery was posted pipe-major at Bramshott camp. George Robertson, a Dundee man, was killed in April 1917. Matters were improved in April 1917, by a reinforcement of eight pipers under Pipe-Major A. J. Saunders, an ex-piper of the H.L.I., all the nine being transferred from the 73rd (Reserve) Battalion. They were not as a rule allowed to play their companies into action, but at Amiens, on 8th August 1918, Piper James W. Macdonald played his company and Piper G. B. Macpherson, a Wick man, played his in the action at Arras on 27th September 1918, and returned without casualty.

The 16th (Canadian Scottish) Battalion kept to the old Highland clan system of having the pipers play whenever and wherever possible; no battle seems to have been fought without the strains of one or more of their pipers resounding in the ears of some of the fighters. One colonel had the taste for pipe music so much developed as to have a piper march alongside him whenever he went into action; the music doubtless acted as a tonic for thought as well as action. Casualties in consequence of all these demands on their services were very high among the pipers. Seventeen pipers had set out with the 16th Battalion in 1915 but only three remained in November 1918. The pipe-major, James Groat, was a worthy successor of the pipers of Vimiera and Waterloo. Thrice he had his gallantry recognised in the awards of D.C.M. and M.M. with bar. Groat was severely wounded and had to be invalided out. The other pipers of the 16th were equally gallant; eight of these were awarded the M.M., one of their number, George Firth Paul, causing a sensation at Amiens in 1918 by getting atop a tank as it proceeded into action and there playing his pipes, as though that were the latest development of the complete piper in action.

The crowning award of the Victoria Cross was also reserved for a piper of this battalion, James Richardson, a native of Rutherglen, Glasgow, whose brief, glorious service is summed up in the *London Gazette* recording the deed performed on 8th October 1916, at Regina Trench :—

"This piper performed deeds of the most extraordinary valour. He implored his commanding officer to allow him to play his company over the top. As the company approached the trench they were held up by very strong wire and came under a most terrific fire. The casualties were appalling, and the company was momentarily demoralised. Realising the situation, he strode up and down outside the wire, playing his pipes with the greatest coolness. The effect on the company was instantaneous, and, inspired by his splendid example, they re-formed and sprang at the wire with such fury and determination that they succeeded in cutting their way through and capturing the position. After entering the trench he asked for some bombs from the company sergeant - major, and they together bombed a dugout, capturing two prisoners. He was afterwards detailed to take these prisoners out, together with the company sergeant-major, who had been wounded.

" After proceeding about two hundred yards he remembered that he had left his pipes behind. Although strongly urged to do so, he refused to leave his beloved pipes and, putting the prisoners and company sergeant-major in a shell hole, he returned for them. He has never been seen since. An unrivalled tale of Scottish valour, worthy of the finest traditions of Highland pipers."

Not many pipers were so circumstanced ; those of the 19th (Central Ontario) Battalion acted as stretcher - bearers until 1916, when they were allowed to play their companies to and from the front line, finishing in the advance against Amiens in November 1918. The pipers of the 21st (Eastern Ontario) Battalion also, like their friends of the 19th Battalion, began the campaign as stretcher-bearers, but they all became casualties and were replaced by pipers, of whom two won distinction: Piper W. Currie who, in addition to getting a Military Medal, was promoted lieutenant, in which rank he again was honoured for his "fine work and good leadership during a raid." For that the ex-piper was awarded the Military Cross. The pipe-major, J. K. Mackenzie, had also been appointed a lieutenant; he fell in action on 11th October 1918.

As stretcher-bearers the twenty-five pipers of the 25th Battalion did duty, the pipe-major, J. Carson, a Greenock man, being awarded the Meritorious Service Medal; Pipers W. Brand, and N. J. M'Innis for bravery, getting each the Military Medal. The 26th (New Brunswick) Battalion pipers continued as pipers whenever an opportunity presented itself. There were eighteen of a pipe band, thirteen of whom were emigrants from Scotland; three were natives of St John's, one of Montreal, and the eighteenth was actually an Englishman who belonged to Southend-on-Sea! They all escaped sickness and wounds until the attack against Amiens in 1918, when three were so severely wounded as to be unable for further service. Military decorations did not come to the pipers except the Military Medal, which was awarded Piper Gallacher.

The 29th (British Columbia) Regiment, the pipers and drummers of which were all Scots of Vancouver, suffered severely, losing before the close of 1916 two from wounds and two sick, while four were killed in action on 6th November 1917.

The 46th (Saskatchewan) Battalion pipers

numbered many ex-pipers of pre-war Highland
regiments who, in the Great War, found themselves bearing stretchers instead of playing in
action, as in former times. There was George
Allan, an Edinburgh man, who had been for
twelve years a piper in the Scots Guards, with
the two medals for South Africa; Piper Allan died
of wounds in August 1917. There was also
Peter Baggett who hailed from Leith and who
had piped in the Black Watch for twelve years
before settling in Canada. Baggett was wounded
so severely that he had to be discharged from
service, as had likewise Pipers John Smith,
ex-Seaforths, W. M'Geachin, John Fraser, and
Charles Maclachlan. Another piper who had to
leave was the veteran corporal James Hogg,
whose earlier Army record extended over a
period of twenty-six years, twelve of which were
spent as a piper in the K.O.S.B. and fourteen
years in the Black Watch. Length of years and
increasing infirmities had at last forced him to
retire, just as these disabilities forced his comrade,
Piper William Finlayson, an ex-Seaforth belonging
to Stornoway.

All these departures left but three pipers to
the 46th Battalion, but these three did prodigies
of valour while serving as stretcher - bearers.
Piper Fraser was awarded the Military Medal
and Pipe-Sergeant George M'Intosh, a native
of Forfarshire, after gaining that medal, had a
bar added in 1918.

Into the 67th Battalion—Western Scots of
Canada—went the pre-war pipers of the Gordon
Highlanders of Canada, with the exception of

three, who were transferred to the 16th Battalion. There was a delightful variety about the personnel of these pipers of the 67th. The youngest was a sixteen-years-old boy, and the eldest a veteran of sixty-nine years, and each, curiously, received much military honour. Boy Piper D. Campbell showed himself a brave soldier at Vimy Ridge and was awarded the Military Medal; he was then promoted staff-sergeant and, having attracted the attention of General Ironside, was appointed confidential clerk to that officer, whom he accompanied later to the Russian Front. J. Wallace, the veteran piper, whose soldiering had been learnt several decades back as a piper in The Royal Scots, won the admiration of H.R.H. The Duke of Connaught and of Field-Marshal Haig. These officers, as they watched the massed band performance at Camblain l'Abbé in 1917, made special inquiry into the military history of Piper Wallace, and after the recital, saluted him to the utter embarrassment of that most modest soldier. Another old soldier was Piper George Leslie who, as a Gordon Highlander, had played his pipes in 1897 on the hills of Dargai and carried them over the veldt of South Africa in the war of 1899-1902; he had the good fortune to be promoted pipe-major at the base.

The pipers could not complain of monotony in their duties, for they were at times at the head of their companies playing them into action, at other times they were out with the stretchers bringing in the wounded, or again were back and forth with ammunition for the front line, and when food was required they were sure to be

sent for it.   On the eve of the Armistice the
battalion was disbanded and the pipers were
transferred to the 102nd Battalion.

The pipers of the 85th (Nova Scotia) Battalion
belonged to a province where pipe music was the
favourite form of entertainment, "the people
preferring it to all other kinds of music." So
spoke an officer of the battalion.   The sixteen
pipers therefore who composed the band on the
outbreak of the War were certain of having an
appreciative audience among their comrades who
kept them piping as often as occasion would
permit.   Ten of the pipers were native born—
six Cape Bretoners and four were Ontarians—but
there was room for a much-travelled Scottish
soldier in the person of J. M'Intosh, who, after
his period of service as a piper in the Gordons,
which included the campaigns of Chitral and
South Africa, had emigrated to Massachusetts.
Thence he had journeyed to Nova Scotia to join
the pipe band of the 85th and was appointed
pipe-sergeant.

The sixteen pipers who comprised the pipe band
of the 107th Canadian Pioneers were Scottish
emigrants who had come from various townships
of Manitoba and Saskatchewan.   They were
pipers only when duties allowed.   Making
trenches and wiring occupied much of their time,
but when the Pioneers rested from these labours
the pipers tuned in their pipes for the delectation of all.   Illness and wounds resulted in the
death of one and in the discharge of five others.

The 1st and the 4th Battalions of Canadian
Mounted Rifles resembled the Scottish Horse

P

and the Lovat Scouts in their love of pipe music. The fifteen pipers of the 1st Battalion who mobilised with the troops at Brandon in August 1914 and the ten pipers—all Scots—of the 4th Mounted Rifles found that the conditions of war did not permit of the practice of their art on horseback, nor even of their ordinary routine duties as pipers. They became infantrymen like the rest of the battalion, and were either using the rifle and bayonet or were engaged in the strenuous duty of stretcher-bearers. Two pipers of the 1st were killed in action and four were wounded, while of the 4th one was killed and three were wounded.

THE PIPERS OF THE AUSTRALIAN FORCES

NOTWITHSTANDING the numerous Scots and Scottish Societies throughout the Commonwealth of Australia there was no pipe band attached to any Australian unit—until the outbreak of the Great War.

Then it was the Queensland Battalion—the 42nd—which led the fashion by having a complete band of pipers and drummers. The 8th, 9th, 14th, and 52nd Battalions—the only other units with pipers—did not have these until they had been for some time in the field. The 8th Battalion obtained their pipers from the men of the battalion and one or two from outside battalions. They were not all Scots, four of the eleven being Australians. The Scots in the 9th Battalion were either fewer, or were unable to play the pipes— except the four Scots on whom the battalion depended for the music. The 14th, on the other hand, had twelve pipers and five drummers; and the 42nd Battalion also managed to maintain that number.

None of the pipers had the privilege of being entered on their regimental roll as "piper"; on the other hand they were saved the fate of the bandsmen who were sent to duties behind the line. The pipers were either runners, stretcher-bearers or scouts, according to the battalion and the needs of the moment. It was as scouts that two pipers of the 42nd (which battalion was renumbered the 41st), namely A. Aitken and R. Gillespie, were awarded the Military Medal, a distinction which also was bestowed on Piper Munro Ross of the 8th Battalion.

In 1917 the 41st Battalion had the misfortune to lose all its pipers either by death or wounds—all except the pipe-major, A. R. M'Coll, nephew of the famous Scottish player, John M'Coll of Glasgow. The losses were made good some months later by the transfer of the pipers of the 11th Training Battalion.

The 52nd Battalion had probably the most enthusiastic supporters of pipers and drummers whose programmes, arranged to suit the tastes of men not used to the traditional tunes of the Scottish Highlands, were frequently of the music hall order. Encores were the usual thing, and no mercy was shown to pipers or drummers who could not continue to play as long as these were demanded. When one considers how long some of the marches of the battalion were, for example, the march from Arras to Dernacourt, and how the pipers and drummers had to play all the way and right into action, it will be conceded that theirs was no light task. On that occasion they played under heavy shell and machine-gun fire until their pipes were smashed and two drums were burst by shell splinters. As a rule, however, they did not play in action, but carried out the rigorous duties of stretcher - bearers, ration carriers, and runners; and repaired the barbed wires at front - line trenches. On the disbandment of the battalion in 1917 the pipers were sent to the 49th Battalion, and again, on 20th May 1918, to the 4th Machine Gun Detachment, and there they remained without further mishap until the close of the War.

PIPERS OF NEW ZEALAND

THE various Pipers' Societies in New Zealand that were actively engaged in pre-war years in keeping alive the old martial music of Scotland could never have guessed that their efforts would result in providing two battalions with battle music for the greatest war in modern history. The 2nd Auckland Regiment and the 1st Otago Rifles marched forth to their war zone—the Dardanelles —each equipped with a full pipe band. Several of the pipers had been members of a British regimental pipe band or of one of the old Volunteer pipe bands of Scotland, while others had never heard the sound of the pipes until the New Zealand piper colonists had made them acquainted with the different airs and the method of playing them. One of these was Harry Kennedy, son of a Scottish settler, born in Fiji; another was James Brown, who was born in Temuka, South Canterbury. There was no lack of material. When, as happened, many of the pipers of both regiments were killed or badly wounded on Gallipoli, their places were taken by pipers sent out from New Zealand with the reinforcements. And yet there were in the ranks men who in some instances were accounted better pipers than any in the bands. Jack Cameron was one of these; indeed he was reckoned the best piper in New Zealand. Cameron was with the

battalion of the Otagos when they moved to
France and was badly wounded in the battle of
the Somme, 1916, when Robert M'Kechnie, also
a good piper and Highland dancer, was killed.
More curious yet, there were in the ranks of the
combatants, Charles M'Donald, an ex-pipe-major
of the Black Watch, Archie and Jack MacMillan,
George Moffat and Peter M'Naughton — all
acknowledged pipers.   These pipers evidently
considered that there would not be opportunity
enough for playing at the head of their companies
and in this they were right, though the duties to
which the actual pipers were put were alike
honourable and dangerous.   Running with despatches, carrying ammunition and rations and
stretcher-bearing provided quite enough of excitement—and wounds.

The pipers of the Otago Regiment were
unfortunate.   During the Gallipoli campaign one
piper was killed and nine, including the pipe-
major, were wounded, while three were invalided
home.   When the battalion was moved to France
some of the wounded rejoined and the band was
again restored.   But there Piper N. M'Donald,
who had been one of the wounded of Gallipoli,
and had been promoted pipe-major in place of
Pipe-Major D. Macdonald, who had not recovered
from his wounds, was killed in action.

In the Auckland Regiment the pipe-major,
Hector Cameron, had forsaken both pipes and
regiment for a commission in the Cameron
Highlanders.

It is most gratifying to find that all the pipers
of these two New Zealand battalions whose

interest in pipe-playing is as keen as—if not keener than—any of those in the home country, had that interest shared by the officers and men of their battalions. And it is not surprising that their valour and reliability in action should have been as great as that displayed by the pipers of the crack British regiments.

THE SOUTH AFRICAN SCOTTISH

(INCORPORATING THE DUKE OF CONNAUGHT'S OWN CAPE
TOWN HIGHLANDERS, THE TRANSVAAL SCOTTISH, Etc.)

ONE of the origins of the famous South African contingent which made its name during the Great War in the battle of Delville Wood, is found in the unit which was raised in 1885 by the Scots residents in and about Cape Town. The regiment was destined to take part in many fights, the first and the slightest being concerned with the quelling of the Malay Riots. That, however, does not really count as real warfare; but they had their share in the fighting in Bechuanaland in the Langsberg Expedition of 1897. Two years later the Cape Town Highlanders were plunged into the South African War and fought on till the close in 1902. The pipers were there but did not play—conditions of veldt warfare did not permit of noise of any kind.

The year 1906 marks an era in the annals of the regiment. It was then that H.R.H. the Duke of Connaught inspected the battalion with its eight kilted pipers, and gave officers and men high praise for their smartness on parade. In appreciation of the consideration of the Duke the officers asked whether he would grant the battalion the privilege of styling themselves *his* regiment: "The Duke of Connaught's and

Strathearn's Own Highlanders." The Duke
readily consented and the battalion went on as
a Volunteer unit until 1913, when the Imperial
Defence Act was passed by which the "Highlanders" became a Militia corps with the official
title of 6th Infantry Regiment.

The regiment, which wears the tartan of the
Gordon Highlanders, to which it is affiliated,
has always been popular with Scottish units
stationed at the Cape. The Argyll and Sutherland Highlanders cherish some pleasant recollections of their association together, and are
particularly pleased to recall an occasion when
the pipers of the Cape Town Highlanders played
for the Argylls at one of their important parades
when they marched past the saluting base to the
regimental tune of "The Campbells are Comin',"
played by the Cape Town pipers.

The Great War made imperative certain
combinations of the Scottish units in South
Africa. The Cape Town Highlanders, the
Transvaal Scottish along with Scots in other
corps were merged into one regiment, which
was named "The South African Scottish."

While that strong force marched through
German South Africa in the process of clearing
out all German opposition the pipers were active
as players. When victory was assured they
were embarked for France, where the pipers
took up the rôle of runners or of ammunition
carriers.

Though these duties were exacting in the
extreme, and enabled several of the South
African's pipers to win distinction, they did

not altogether suit the taste of Pipe - Major
Donald Cameron, who knew something of
soldiering. Cameron had been a piper in the
Black Watch and had won the D.C.M. in the
South African War while with his battalion.
The piper's place, said Cameron, was at the
head of his company in action, and if he could
not get that he would go into the ranks.
Cameron thereupon joined his company, was
promoted company sergeant-major and fought
throughout the War. Perhaps, had he remained
with the pipers, he would have shared in the
awards and promotions that fell to some of these.
Pipers E. A. Cumming and W. Durward, for
example, were promoted lieutenants. Charles
Gordon, an ex-Gordon Highlander, who belonged
to Aberdeen, and A. Gray from Glasgow, were
awarded Military Medals, as were some others
whose names have escaped us.

The pipers were mostly experienced soldiers,
able to give an excellent account of their doings.
In addition to those already mentioned there
were Pipe - Sergeant A. Grieve, a Fife man
who had done duty in earlier years with the
Black Watch and the Botha Scouts ; Pipe
Lance-Corporal J. M. Matheson, a Sutherland
man, who had been a piper in The Royal
Scots ; Lance-Corporal Hay, from Ayrshire, who
after the War of 1899-1902 had settled in South
Africa after his service in the Argyll and Sutherland Highlanders. Hay and D. G. Cummings
had also been through the Zululand Campaign
of 1906.

The pipers were thus in some measure prepared for the much more strenuous work which they had to undertake on the Western Front, where the gallantry of all was most justly lauded —especially for their achievement at High Wood.

PIPERS OF THE ROYAL NAVY

ONE is so accustomed to associate kilted pipers with Highland regiments that the spectacle of a party of bluejackets marching smartly along to the music of one or more of their own pipers, is apt to raise a smile on the face of the mere landsman.

Yet the piper in the senior service is not altogether a new departure. Though not officially recognised by the Lords of the Admiralty, he has become an institution on board several ships of His Majesty's Fleet. None can say when the piper was first introduced into the navy; he may have enlivened the crews of those once famous battleships of James the Fourth of Scots —the *Great Michael*, the *Yellow Carvel*, and the *Lion*, but of that there is no record. The earliest hint of his popularity at sea is contained in an advertisement in the *Edinburgh Courant* of 2nd to 5th April 1708, for a "person that plays on the bagpipes willing to engage on board a British man-of-war." When that notice appeared there were in Leith—the port of Edinburgh—thirty-four British and Dutch war vessels. Let us hope that more than one piper was engaged. It is almost certain that wherever a Scots officer was in command there a piper was on board.

Did naval pipers play in battle? Probably not as a rule. There is, however, one instance where an eighteenth century piper did actually play by order of his officer, throughout a three hours' fight against the French. That was in June 1795 when seventy-nine non-commissioned officers and privates of the 97th Inverness-shire Highlanders were "borne as part complement of the *Colossus*—a 74-gun ship—per order of Sir Peter Parker, Bart." Mr H. B. Mackintosh, who, in his account of that regiment, mentions the fact from H. S. Lecky's *A King's Ship*, states that the piper was before the battle ordered to take up his position in the main-topmast staysail netting and there play as long as the engagement lasted. His music was obviously intended for the benefit of his fellow Highlanders, who must have congratulated the piper on accomplishing his mission without mishap.

Those more modern naval officers who em-ployed pipers aboard their ships certainly did not avail themselves of the precedent of 1795. Admirals Lord Beresford, Sinclair, Lord Walter Kerr, Dundas of Dundas, and Duff, and Commodore Wilfred Henderson had the piper for those duties which he performs for officers in the army, particularly playing for the officers at mess. Lord Beresford stated that he "always made a point of having one of Scotland's best pipers on every ship on which he had command; nothing cheers a ship's company so well as the Highland bagpipe." That famous officer, who was better known as Lord Charles Beresford, employed his piper on various offices, but when the appointed hours for piping arrived, he was there dressed in glengarry, kilt, and plaid, the tartan being Royal Stewart.

Not only do the bluejackets cherish the piper, but also that unique corps of Royal Marines— "soldiers and sailors, too." For that the "Jollies" are indebted to their bandmaster, Major Miller, one of the most distinguished bandmasters that the regiment has ever had. The bagpipe, along with the fife and drum, is, according to that authority, superior to all other musical instruments for soldiers on the march. "Without the bagpipe, fife and drum, the musical forces of a foot regiment are incomplete." Major Miller stressed the point in a letter to *The Times* of 5th April 1915, and reminded his readers that "these combinations can touch spots which are beyond the reach of a band; and, moreover, there is no suggestion of effort in their performance, however long a march may be. It is all so easy and enjoyable. Again, a fife and drum band or a pipe band can be split up so as to be useful, not only to a battalion on its march, but also to cheer the companies and platoons on their daily field-training exercises."

Major Miller put his theory into practice by getting some of the Royal Marines' bandsmen and buglers to learn the pipes. When they had attained a certain degree of proficiency they were posted as pipers to various companies. The earliest of these were Musicians Norman and Handford, clarionet players, and Bugler Haynes —all Englishmen; and Corporal Grier, an Irishman from County Kerry; with the sole Scots representative in Bugler M'Laren. Their choice

of a regimental marching tune would not have
satisfied the requirements of a pipe-major of a
Scottish battalion, but the Royal Marines are a
law unto themselves.   Besides, the air of " Joan's
Placket is Torn " is their own regimental tune
and goes well on the pipes—if the supporters of
the " Globe and Laurel " may be reckoned to be
judges of a good tune.   Their example was, at
any rate, followed by naval ratings at Portsmouth,
Chatham, Sheerness, and Granton.

Prior to that the pipes of the Royal Naval
(Howe) Division had been heard all over Gallipoli,
and it is the boast of that Division that their
pipes were the first to resound on that peninsula,
adducing the 8th of April 1915 as the first day
when they were played.   Of their eight pipers
one, Stoker T. Loney, a Belfast lad, was twice
recommended for the Distinguished Conduct
Medal.

The detachment of the Royal Naval Division,
which was sent to relieve Antwerp in August
1915, and found itself cut off from further active
service by being misled into neutral Holland, had
among its officers Commodore Wilfred Henderson,
an enthusiast of pipe music, and two pipers—
Donald Campbell and Malcolm Macdonald—who
were commandeered to play every day for the
entertainment of their fellows in captivity.   The
interest thus created was increased by offers of
more pipes and drums from friends at home.
These, duly sent, were put into the hands of
other interned prisoners willing to learn under
the tuition of the two veteran pipers.   In this
way, by dint of much hard practice, the band of

ten pipers, one bass drummer and three kettle drummers were able to take their place at the head of the battalion of men who had to take their daily route march, and also in the sports where dances — reel and sword — made more tolerable the enforced idleness of men in captivity. The march through the streets of the Hague with pipes and drums resounding, repeated so many times each week, may not have suggested to the Dutch folks the sense of the land of the mountain and the flood, but there is little doubt that it did remind the unfortunate service men of the happy days of home.

Commodore Henderson, who kindly provided these details, expressed his thanks to the Scottish Patriotic Society, The Association of Highland Societies, His Majesty's Consul at Gröningen, some Ross-shire friends, and to other Scots under the care of the Rev. Mr Sime — for sets of bagpipes.

While the Hague Pipers were thus beguiling their tedious days with the music of the bagpipe, the battle cruiser *New Zealand* had got together a full band of pipers and drummers, which delighted not only the ship's company, but various concert parties, fêtes, etc., organised by the Royal Red Cross Society. Their inception had been due to Lieut. A. D. Boyle, R.N., a New Zealander, then serving aboard, and their training to a gunner in the anti-air craft section of the R.G.A., and a pipe-major of the R.S.F.

Of the ten pipers all except the pipe-major, M'Neice, a North of Ireland man, and Durrant, a Londoner, who served as a Royal Marine

Q

artilleryman—were Scots, and all when "otherwise employed" were carrying out their several duties on deck, at the guns, or in the stokehold, and all, with one exception, took part in the battles of Heligoland, Dogger Bank, and Jutland.

H.M.S. *Courageous* had a pipe band of six pipers, of whom two were English—Edwin Short, from Essex, and Oliver Etherington from Cambridge.

On H.M.S. *Barham* there was no pipe band but a Scottish sailor solaced his occasional ennui with a tune on his chanter. Hearing him play an officer inquired whether he had no bagpipe, and learning that he had left it at home the sailor was sent off forthwith to bring back his instrument and with instructions to buy a Highland outfit. Thus equipped the A.B. piper was constituted official accompanist to the ship, playing at the officers' mess and at the physical "jerks" of the Company. Some time later the piper was with others transferred to another ship, though the officers tried hard to have him retained. And so, while the *Barham* lost their piper the *Valorous* found him and welcomed him, much to the piper's astonishment; he had had no idea that his pipe music would ever be appreciated by English and Irish officers and men.

Bluejackets who were stationed at Chatham during the War had their route marches made more interesting by the pipers who accompanied them. These were Scots attached to the R.N.R. and R.F.R. and numbered eighteen in all. That total was diminished in 1917, first, by the death of four in a hostile air raid on 3rd September, and later by the transfer of other four to a battleship.

To Portsmouth Royal Naval Barracks there was attached a band of pipers and drummers of which Chief Writer David Thomson, a native of Uddingston, was pipe-major. Mr Thomson, who is one of the Regular Royal Navy, is an enthusiast on pipe music, as the following interesting account which he kindly wrote will show :—

" In the Navy it is not uncommon to hear the skirl of the pipes reverberating from the surrounding hills of some landlocked harbour after the ships have dropped anchor and the ships' companies have settled down to the evening routine.

" In the days of sail, when steam was quite a luxury in a man-o'-war, the musician of the ship was a recognised fiddler, whose primary duties consisted in encouraging the sailors who were 'manhandling' the capstan bars or manning the falls while hoisting boats, by playing airs on his fiddle to which the men would keep regular rhythm with the tramp, tramp, of their feet ; but with the disappearance of sails and the personality of the fiddler, came the advent of the piper with his strathspeys and reels, and consequently, as necessity claims his services, the piper is quite an event in these evolutions. In addition to this he plays at officers' mess during dinner and he may 'give a turn' at the ship's concert which invariably is warmly appreciated, and it is not unusual on such occasions to witness some Scottish seaman dancing the 'Highland Fling' or the Sword Dance, while the strains of 'Gillie Callum' are heard far over the waters."

Ashore the piper has more varied duties. At the depot or training barracks he leads off the men for drill, fatigues, and church parades. In this way the recruits become accustomed to the music of the pipes before joining their ship.

PART III
SOME WELL-KNOWN ARMY PIPERS

SOME WELL-KNOWN ARMY PIPERS

ALLAN, GEORGE S.—Born in Aberdeenshire, George Allan learned piping while still at school, and having achieved success as a piper he was, in 1909, without any experience of soldiering, appointed Pipe-Major to the 1st Battn. The Royal Scots. He accompanied his battalion to France in 1914, and later went with it to Salonica. Retired in 1920. Winner of many prizes in pipe competitions. His compositions include two which were composed while on active service—" Lothian Lads," and " The Royal Scots' March thro' Salonica."

BALLOCH, JOHN.—The noted composer of " The 25th's Farewell to Meerut" joined the army in 1878 as a piper in the 57th Brigade, which comprised the 42nd and 79th Highlanders, and played his pipes with the leading company of the 79th in the battle of Tel-el-Kebir during the famous charge, and right through the Egyptian Campaign, 1881-84, was conspicuous as a piper. Was transferred as pipe-major to the 1st Battn. K.O.S.B. in 1886, and led the pipers of that battalion on the expedition to Upper Burmah. Retired 1899, and became pipe-major to the 5th Argyll and Sutherland Highlanders (Greenock). In 1914 rejoined his old regiment and was posted Pipe-Major 8th Battn. K.O.S.B., with which he served in France from July 1915-18, when he was invalided home. Even then he was not allowed to be lost to the army, for the 9th Officers' Cadet Battalion at Gailes appropriated the services of the distinguished pipe-major. In addition to his " 25th's Farewell to Meerut,"

Balloch has to his credit a marching tune entitled
"Auchmountain's Bonnie Glen," and a melody for
Retreat which he has named "Sunset in Flanders."

CALDER, ALEXANDER.—Pipe-Major, 72nd Highlanders, 1865-
78, composer of "The 72nd's Farewell to Poona," "Lord
Lawrence's Welcome to India," and other works.

CAMERON, ALEXANDER. — Pipe-Major, 92nd Highlanders.
See chapter on " Gordon Highlanders."

CAMERON, DONALD, D.C.M.—Pipe-Major, and later, Company Sergeant-Major South African Scottish, 1914-18,
gained D.C.M. while serving in the Black Watch as
a piper, for conduct noted in the chapter on that
regiment.

CAMERON, W. KEITH.—Regarded as a " M'Crimmon " by his
brother pipers. Keith Cameron, son of Donald, last
"King of Pipers," made his name at the age of nine
when he competed at the Northern Meeting as a
player of pibroch. Enlisting in the H.L.I. he was
quickly promoted pipe-major, but lost his appointment owing to unsteady habits; but continued to be
regarded as the foremost player of his time and the
favourite performer at Officers' Mess. Died at the
depot of the regiment 18th September 1899.

CAMPBELL, DONALD A.—An excellent piper; winner of the
Highland Society of London's Gold Medal and of
many other prizes, and a composer of some popular
pipe melodies. D. A. Campbell has had a varied and
interesting career as a piper in H.M. Forces. As a
boy of fifteen he enlisted in 1882 as a piper in the
Cameronians, and at the close of seven years' service
transferred to the 3rd Battalion, of which he was
made pipe-major. In 1899 he left because he was
not selected to accompany the battalion to the South
African War, in which he managed to take part by
joining the 3rd Battn. H.L.I. In 1914 he was
appointed Pipe-Major, 5th Battn. Cameron Highlanders,

was posted to 6th Battalion, and was invalided out
in consequence of rheumatism. On recovery joined
the Royal Navy as a piper and served on board
various ships, including mine-sweepers, and at the
naval base. Once more invalided out he left hospital
to join the 2/2nd Lovat Scouts, but left on finding
that there were no pipers but himself.

CAMPBELL, DUNCAN.—Pipe-Major, Queen's Own Cameron
Highlanders, 1877-80, and afterwards piper to the
Marquess of Breadalbane till 1920.   Died 1924.   Com-
posed several pieces, including " Murray's Welcome."

CAMPBELL, JAMES.—Served in 1st Battn. The Black Watch ;
from 1891 to 1901 was piper to H.M. Queen Victoria.

CAMPBELL, JOHN.—Pipe-Major, 2nd Lovat Scouts, 1914-18.
Served with his regiment in Gallipoli.

CLARK, GEORGE.—" The Piper of Vimiera."   A native of
Tongue, Sutherland.   *See* chapter on the H.L.I.

DUFF, JAMES O.—Pipe-Major, 2nd Battn. The Royal Scots,
1903-09.   Enlisted 1891 in the 2nd Battn. Argyll
and Sutherland Highlanders.   Served throughout the
South African War.   In 1914 rejoined the 2nd Battn.
The Royal Scots as pipe-major and accompanied it to
France ; was wounded and captured at Le Cateau.
After internment in Holland in 1917, was appointed
Pipe-Major of the " Hague Caledonian Pipers' Society."
Has the Highland Society's Gold Medal, the Gold
Star of the Scottish Pipers' Society.   He also holds
many prizes for dancing, being one of the finest
Highland dancers of the day.   His compositions
include " Colonel Murray of Giniss " — a reel ;
" Hague Caledonian Society March ";   " Captain
Usher's Wedding "; and " The Buchan Volunteers."

DUNBAR, CHARLES, D.C.M. — 2nd Battn. Gordons, Pipe-
Major, Canadian Regiment, 1914-18.   *See* chapter on
" Gordon Highlanders."

FERGUSON, WILLIAM.—A pupil of the late Farquhar Macrae, Pipe-Major Ferguson began his career as a military piper in the 7th Battn. H.L.I., of which he became pipe-major in 1914. Holder of many important prizes for pipe playing; has composed " Atholl and Breadalbane Gathering," "The Plains of Gaza," and "The 7th Battn. H.L.I.'s Farewell to Dunfermline."

FINDLATER, GEORGE, V.C. — Piper, 2nd Battn. Gordon Highlanders. *See* chapter on " Gordon Highlanders."

FORSYTH, HENRY.—Piper to His Majesty the King. Joined 2nd Battn. Scots Guards in 1887 as a piper. Promoted pipe-major in 1899. Served throughout South African War. In 1905 was appointed piper to H.R.H. the Prince of Wales—later H.M. George V. The office of King's piper fell to Forsyth on the retirement of Pipe-Major James Campbell. Volunteered for active service in 1914 and was appointed Pipe-Major 14th Battn. Argyll and Sutherland Highlanders in 1915. Later was transferred to 40th Division as sergeant-major, and on reorganisation of the base depot he furnished troops to the various battalions in the Division.

GIBSON, JOHN.—Piper, 78th Highlanders. *See* chapter on " Seaforth Highlanders."

GILLIES, JOHN M‘DOUGALL.—For many years manager of the famous bagpipe-making firm of Peter Henderson, Glasgow, Pipe-Major Gillies was known to pipers all over the world. Very successful as player and teacher. Prizes include first for pibroch at Braemar, Gold Medal at Stamford Bridge, medals at Oban, Inverness, and elsewhere. In 1891 he was appointed Pipe-Major of the Volunteer Battalion—later 5th Battn. H.L.I.— the pipers of which he trained to compete for band competitions with such success that they won the Argyll Shield twice along with many other trophies. Died in 1925.

GORDON, JAMES A.—One of the best of Highland dancers, Pipe-Major Gordon is also an excellent piper, particularly of pibroch. His war service was first in the Scottish Horse and latterly as Pipe-Major of the 5/6th Royal Scots. After campaigning in Gallipoli and France, Pipe-Major Gordon ended his active service in the post-Armistice march into Germany. For many years held championship of Highland dancing.

GRANT, JOHN M'GREGOR.—Pipe-Major, Cameron Highlanders, during the Egyptian Campaign, 1882-84, during which he was mentioned in despatches for conspicuous gallantry. Grant, of whom mention has already been made in the chapter on the Cameron Highlanders (q.v.), died of cholera on the Mokattam Heights in 1883.

GRAY, WILLIAM.—Pipe-Major, City of Glasgow Police Band; was Pipe-Major 2nd Battn. Argyll and Sutherland Highlanders throughout the Great War, probably the only instance of a New Army piper being posted to a Regular battalion. One of the leading exponents of pibroch, and winner of Gold Medal for pibroch at the Argyllshire and Northern Meetings, the Pibroch Society Cup presented by Mrs Campbell of Dunstaffnage, and other prizes. The composer of a march, "The City of Glasgow Police Pipe Band," and of two strathspeys, "Pipe-Major M'Dougall Gillies" and "William M'Lean," Pipe-Major Gray has rendered a notable service for all pipe bands by publishing, in collaboration with Drum-Major John Seton, the "Bagpipe and Drum Tutor" and a "Collection of Highland Bagpipe Music and Drum Settings." Has a library of pipe music, which includes many rare MSS.

GROAT, JAMES, D.C.M., M.M.—Pipe-Major, 16th Canadian Scottish. See chapter on "Canadian Forces."

HONYMAN, WILLIAM.—Piper, 42nd Highlanders. See chapter on "The Black Watch."

LAIDLAW, DANIEL, V.C.—Piper, 7th Battn. King's Own Scottish Borderers. *See* p. 81.

LAURIE, WILLIAM.—Pipe-Major, 8th (Territorial) Battn. Argyll and Sutherland Highlanders. Born in 1882 at Ballachulish, where, till 1914, he lived, William Laurie had, by his excellent playing and his notable compositions, made his mark as one of the best pipers of his generation. He had won Gold Medals at the Argyllshire Gathering, the Northern Meeting, and at Crieff; and first prize awards at Inveraray, Portree, Fort William, Cowal, and Bridge of Allan. Of his better-known work mention may be made of the following: "Lament for the late Lord Archibald Campbell"; "Paps of Glencoe"; "Clach Iarick"; "John Macdonald of Glencoe"; and "Inveraray Castle." In France he composed the spirited and tuneful "Battle of the Somme," a favourite marching tune in many battalions. Was invalided home and died in November 1916.

M'COLL, JOHN.—Pipe-Major, 3rd Battn. the Black Watch, and later the Scottish Horse, was for many years an outstanding authority on pipe music and probably the most successful all-round player of his day.

M'DONALD, ANDREW.—Pipe-Major, Scottish Horse, 1908-1918. Accompanied his regiment to Gallipoli where he was wounded in December 1915. A frequent prize-winner at Northern and Argyllshire Meetings, and at Bridge of Allan.

M'DONALD, JAMES. — Pipe - Major, 1st Battn. Seaforth Highlanders, which he had joined as a boy piper, M'Donald, or "The Silver King" as he was nicknamed, had a stirring career in the Indian Mutiny and later in the Afghan Campaign; was one of the Seaforth Highlanders who marched from Kabul to Kandahar. At Lucknow in 1879 he was promoted pipe-major and accompanied his regiment to the Egyptian Campaign, 1881-85. He sounded the time - honoured "Cabar

Feidh " at Tel-el-Kebir. His best-known composition is "The 1st Battalion Seaforths' Farewell to Edinburgh." Retired in 1888.

M‘Donald, John.—Pipe-Major, 42nd Highlanders, The Black Watch, to which he transferred from the Inverness Militia in 1865. Piped his battalion—the 42nd —through the jungle warfare, which ended in Coomassie and Amoaful. At Tel-el-Kebir, El Teb, and Tamai he played the regimental charge. In 1885, while stationed at Cairo, he completed twenty-four years' service and retired. For fifteen years thereafter was pipe-major of a Volunteer battalion, and a constant competitor at the Northern Meetings. The "March to Coomassie" is M‘Donald's outstanding composition.

M‘Donald, John.—Pipe-Major of the Cameron Highlanders from 1840-49. Is best remembered by his delightful "79th's Farewell to Gibraltar."

M‘Donald, John.—Pipe - Major, 72nd Highlanders. A pupil of John Bàn Mackenzie, "King of Pipers." Accompanied his regiment to Crimea and the Indian Mutiny, and on his return had the honour to be presented to Queen Victoria, who spoke to the pipe-major while the battalion was on parade. M‘Donald had evidently impressed Her Majesty either by his appearance or by his address for he received the Royal command to go to London to be photographed in order that a copy might be preserved in Windsor. A reproduction of this photo appeared in the *Illustrated London News* of 31st January 1857. After retiring from the army in 1865 he was appointed pipe-major of the Stirlingshire Militia, and still later became piper to the Governor-General of Canada, the Marquess of Lorne.

M‘Donald, John.—Pipe-Major of the 1/4th Queen's Own Cameron Highlanders (Inverness Territorials), this distinguished exponent of pipe music who has been described as " the great artist of the piping world," was

mobilised in August 1914 along with his unit and
proceeded to training at Bedford where, in consequence
of severe illness, he was forced to resign. On recovery
was appointed instructor of the Army School of Piping,
a post which he resigned in 1920. Winner of all the
most important cups and medals during the last twenty
years, he is looked upon as one of the three greatest
players of pibroch.

M‘DONALD, J. D.—Pipe-Major, 2nd Battn. Scots Guards,
1921-27, is one of the younger school of pipers; has
won several prizes at the principal Gatherings and has
written a pipe melody for Retreat called "Tamline
Bay."

MACDONALD, JOHN.—A young Glasgow police officer, a
native of South Uist, who leapt into the first rank of
pipers in 1926 by winning the Oban Gold Medal for
pibrochs, reels, and strathspeys, and the 1st at the
Northern Meeting for pibrochs and 1st for marches.
A pupil of John M‘Donald of Inverness, young
Macdonald joined the special reserve of the Camerons
at the age of fifteen, in 1913, and in 1917 was in
France with the 6th and 7th Battalions of that
regiment.

MACDONALD, WILLIAM.—Pipe-Major, Queen's Own Cameron
Highlanders, 1880-89, when he became colour-sergeant
of a company. Macdonald was an excellent all-
round soldier of fine physique and with a high
reputation for tossing the caber. With war service
ranging from the Nile Expedition of 1884-85, and the
Soudan Frontier Field Force operations in 1885-86, to
the South African War in 1901 when he served as one
of the permanent staff of the Volunteer Battalion,
Colour-Sergeant Macdonald retired to civil life in 1908.

M‘KAY, ANGUS.—Pipe-Major, Stirlingshire Militia, and
piper to H.M. Queen Victoria 1839-54. Composed
several pipe melodies of high standard, including "The
Stirlingshire Militia" and Mrs "M‘Leod of Raasay's

Reel." Is credited with having introduced the present system of fingering in march playing.

M'KAY, DONALD.—Piper to H.R.H. Edward, Prince of Wales, afterwards H.M. King Edward VII. Won Gold Medal of Northern Meeting in 1872. Died 1893.

M'KAY, HUGH.—Piper, 71st Highlanders, in 1840; was later Pipe-Major, Stirlingshire Militia. Composed ".Stirlingshire Militia Quickstep" and "Prince of Wales' Welcome to Holyrood Palace."

M'KAY, HUGH.—Piper, 73rd Regiment. Retired in 1840.

MACKAY, JOHN.—A son of Pipe-Major Mackay, K.O.S.B., John Mackay was born in India in 1860; joined the Argyll and Sutherland Highlanders and in 1881 became pipe-major; transferred to 4th Battalion in 1885. In 1903 became pipe-major of the Liverpool Scottish. Died 1925. A very fine player, Mackay won the Army Piping Championship in 1888 and the Scottish Open Championship on two occasions. Of his many well-known pipe compositions mention may be made of "The Heir of Lunga," "The Renfrewshire Militia," "The Heir of Cloncaild," and "The Badge of Scotland."

M'KAY, KENNETH.—Piper of the 79th Cameron Highlanders 1802-16. Son of Donald M'Kay, Tongue, Sutherland. Transferred from the Caithness Fencibles to the 79th in 1802. He is remembered for his intrepidity at the battle of Waterloo (for which see the chapter on the "Queen's Own Cameron Highlanders").

M'KELLAR, ALEXANDER. — Pipe-Major, 78th (Ross-shire Buffs), during Indian Mutiny. Famous by reason of one pipe melody known to everyone, "The Barren Rocks of Aden," one of the most melodious of pipe marches.

MACKENZIE, ALEXANDER, D.C.M.—Joined in 1889 the 2nd Seaforths, of which his father Ronald Mackenzie was pipe-major, but for several years declined the offer made by the colonel of taking the pipe-majorship, electing instead to remain a sergeant. In 1897, however, he acceded to the request and served with his battalion through the campaigns of Hazara (1891), Chitral (1895), and South Africa (1899-1902). Retired in 1907. In 1914 rejoined his regiment and was posted pipe-major of the 8th Battalion. Took part in the battles of Loos and the Somme, and was awarded the D.C.M. for conspicuous gallantry. Was later posted to the 3rd Battalion, and in 1918 was gazetted 2nd lieutenant.

MACKENZIE, RONALD.—Father of Alexander, noted above. Was indebted for much of his training to his uncle, John Bàn Mackenzie, "King of Pipers." A native of Fodderty, Ross-shire, he joined the 78th Highlanders in 1860 as a piper and in less than four years was appointed pipe-major, which rank he held until 1879, when he was posted to the Ross-shire Militia. Long regarded as the best piper of his day, Mackenzie's fame began at the age of seventeen when he won at the Northern Meeting the Dirk, Gold Medal, and Set of Pipes in open competition. After the conclusion of his army career he became piper to the Duke of Richmond and Gordon. "The Portree Men" is Ronald's most notable work.

MACKENZIE, DONALD.—Son of John Bàn Mackenzie, and cousin of Ronald Mackenzie, mentioned above. Served in the Crimean War in the Transport Department and later was appointed Pipe-Major of the King's Own Scottish Borderers. After leaving the army became piper to the Duke of Sutherland.

MACKINNON, WILLIAM.—Of high reputation as a piper, Mackinnon rose to the rank of major, and made his mark in more than one field. A Lanarkshire man, he joined the 74th Highlanders in 1863 as a piper, and was almost immediately afterwards promoted pipe-major. Quitting that post eleven years later for the post of paymaster-sergeant, he was quickly promoted regimental quartermaster sergeant, and was commissioned Quartermaster of the 4th Battalion. On retiring was given the rank of Major. Died in Glasgow in 1918. Major Mackinnon's piping successes date from 1864 when he was awarded 1st prize for pibroch and 1st for reels at the Northern Meeting. Of his compositions the most popular are the " 71st's Quickstep" and the " 74th's Farewell to Edinburgh."

M'LELLAN, JOHN, D.C.M.—Poet and piper. M'Lellan won distinction as a soldier piper of the H.L.I. in the South African War, where he was awarded the D.C.M. In the Great War he was again at the Front as a piper in the 8th Argyll and Sutherland Highlanders, and used to occasion considerable surprise to his comrades by composing and writing light verse 100 yards from the German lines. Most of these productions found a place in the newspapers of the West of Scotland. Better known are his pipe melodies the "Clachan Fiddler," a strathspey, "The Taking of Beaumont Hamel," a march, both in the Cowall book ; and "The Battle of the Sands"—said to be the original air of "The Road to the Isles."

M'LENNAN, DONALD.—The youngest son of the late Lieut. John M'Lennan, Edinburgh Police, an outstanding authority on pipe music. Donald M'Lennan joined the Scots Guards as a piper in 1919, was promoted pipe-corporal shortly afterwards, and in 1922 was transferred as Pipe-Major of the 3rd Battn. Seaforth Highlanders, getting his rank and place as Pipe-Major of the 1st Battalion in 1925.

Has won many important prizes at all the important meetings.

M'LENNAN, Lieut. JOHN. — One of the most notable authorities on pipe music, this descendant of generations of pipers, pupils of the school of the Mackays of Gairloch, had decided opinions on the manner in which pibrochs should be played, opinions which he expressed in two books published in 1907 and

R

(posthumously) in 1925.   The earlier, *The Piobaireachd
as M'Crimmon played it*, created much controversy
among pibroch enthusiasts who did not share the
ideas formulated by this able and life-long student
of the bagpipe and its lore.   A teacher of ability, his
most distinguished pupils were his two sons, George
S. M'Lennan, late Pipe-Major, Gordon Highlanders,
and Donald M'Lennan, Pipe-Major, 1st Seaforth
Highlanders, and his nephew, the late Donald G.
M'Lennan.   Though over seventy years old when the
Great War broke out, Mr M'Lennan offered his services
in any capacity, was appointed Recruiting Officer in
Falkirk, and was rewarded for his zeal and efficiency
with the honorary rank of Lieutenant in H.M. Army.
He died in 1923.

M'Lennan, George S.—A son of Lieut. John M'Lennan,
George began his eventful career at the age of ten
by playing by royal command before H.M. Queen
Victoria; a year later he won the Juvenile National
Championship for marches, strathspeys and reels; he
won at Edinburgh in 1894 and 1895 the Scottish
Amateur Championship.   In 1896 and 1897 he won
in London the Amateur Championship at the Scottish
Gathering there.   Joined the Gordon Highlanders in
1899 as a boy piper, and three years later was promoted pipe-major, the youngest in the army with
that rank.   Since that time Pipe-Major M'Lennan
has been acknowledged as one of the three greatest
pipers of the century, with all the gold medals and
cups of the principal competitions to his credit.   He is
also a composer and has two exceptionally fine tunes in
the Cowall book: " Inverlochy Castle," and " Conon
Bridge," both marches.   The pipe-major served with
his regiment throughout the Great War.   Debonair
and kindly, Pipe-Major M'Lennan, quite unspoiled by
his many successes, is a deservedly popular personality.

M'Leod, Alexander. — Pipe-Major, 26th Cameronian
Regiment, was a well-known composer, his best tunes

being "The 26th Cameronians"; "The Drucken
Piper"; "Weel Dune, my Hielan' Lads"; "The Wee
Sergeant's March"; "March to Pretoria"; "Relief of
Mafeking"; and the "Sirdar's Welcome to Edinburgh."

M'LEOD, JOHN. — Pipe-Major, 93rd Sutherland Highlanders during the Crimean War and Indian Mutiny
periods. Introduced the tune "Green Hills of Tyrol"
in 1854 after hearing Sardinian Band play Rossini's
William Tell, in which the Tyrolean air occurs. *See*
chapter on the "Argyll and Sutherland Highlanders."

M'LEOD, KENNETH, D.C.M.—A stalwart piper of Stornoway
who joined the Gordon Highlanders and distinguished
himself in the South African War, gaining the D.C.M.
for conspicuous gallantry. Rejoined for the Great
War and was appointed Pipe-Major, 11th Bn. Gordons
—later 51st (Young Soldiers') Battalion.

M'LEOD, NORMAN.—Pipe-Major, 78th Seaforth Highlanders,
and afterwards of the Argyll and Bute Militia. Served
throughout the Indian Mutiny and played on the
historic march to the relief of Lucknow. Composed
many excellent tunes, the best known of which is
probably "Dunolly Castle," a march.

M'MILLAN, DONALD.—Pipe-Major, 1st Lovat Scouts, 1914-
1918. A first-class piper whose emigration to Detroit
is regarded as a loss to Scottish pipe playing.

M'PHEDRAN, ARCHIBALD.—Pipe-Major, 7th Battn. H.L.I.,
pupil of and successor to J. M'Dougall Gillies, Manager,
Peter Henderson & Co., Glasgow.

MACRAE, ANGUS.—Blair-Atholl. Piper, Scottish Horse.
A successful competitor at all Highland Gatherings.
Was for many years piper to Lord Charles Beresford in
the Royal Navy. Served throughout the Great War.

MACRAE, DONALD.—Pipe-Major, 72nd, from 1784-89, of 78th,
1793-1801. Won 1st prize for piping in Edinburgh in
1791. In 1835 at age of 80 again competed and was
awarded a special silver medal.

M'Sporran, Duncan.—Pipe-Major, 10th Battn. Argyll and Sutherland Highlanders. Served throughout the Great War and played his battalion into action at Longueval and other engagements. A fine pibroch player.

Matheson, Alexander.—A Golspie man who at the age of seventeen accompanied the Duke of Sutherland as piper on yachting voyage round the world. Played before the King of Siam and the Sultan of Johore. In 1889 was appointed Pipe-Major, 1st Royal Scots. Served in South African War and after that was posted Pipe-Major to 3rd Battalion. Retired to pension in 1912. Winner of many prizes.

Matheson, Dugald.—Pipe-Major, 2nd Battn. Cameron Highlanders, 1913-19. Born at Kyle of Lochalsh. Served with his battalion in Salonica as sergeant in charge of snipers. Severely wounded, he was on recovery posted to the 3rd Battalion and later was selected for training for commission. Holds four Gold Medals for pipe playing in South Africa. His pipe melody "The Battle of the Struma" is descriptive of the Camerons' part in that action.

Mathieson, D. B., D.C.M.—Pipe-Major, 1st Battn. Seaforth Highlanders throughout the Great War. *See* chapter on "Seaforth Highlanders."

Mauchline, James.—78th Seaforth Highlanders. Composer of the "Skye Crofters"; "Here's to him that's ower the Water"; "Ada Crawford," a strathspey; and the "Barren Rocks of Aden" which Alex. M'Kellar improved. Was instructor to Scottish Pipers' Society.

Meldrum, Robert.—Born at Fearn, Ross-shire; enlisted when sixteen years old as a piper in the 78th. Four years later was transferred as Pipe-Major to the 93rd Sutherland Highlanders with which he served for nineteen years. From 1887-92 was Pipe-Major 3rd Battn. Cameron Highlanders which he rejoined in 1914, continuing with it until 1918 when he was

appointed Instructor of the Boy Pipers of Queen
Victoria School, Dunblane. Pipe-Major Meldrum has
always been one of the most popular figures in the
piping world. In the painting of the colonel, the
major, and the adjutant made on the occasion of
the amalgamation of the 93rd with the 91st as the
2nd Battn. Argyll and Sutherland Highlanders Pipe-
Major Meldrum has his place along with the regimental
sergeant-major. One of the best players of pibroch,
Pipe-Major Meldrum can point to his Championship
Medal won in 1884, and to another won in 1890.
His compositions include "The 93rd's Farewell to
Edinburgh"; "The Doune of Rothiemurchus"; and
"The Bridge of Bogie."

MILNE, JAMES, D.C.M.—*See* chapter on "Gordon Highlanders."

PATON, JAMES.—Pipe-Major, 79th Cameron Highlanders,
which he joined in 1855. Promoted pipe-major 1868.
Served in the Indian Mutiny. Retired in 1877.

REID, ROBERT.—Pipe-Major, 7th Battn. H.L.I. One of the
foremost of the younger pipers, Reid, a pupil of
M'Dougall Gillies, and a member of the pipe band
of the 5th H.L.I., of which Gillies was pipe-major,
served from 1912 to 1918 as a piper, his active
service being spent in Palestine and France, 1915-18.
Among his prizes are: Gold Medal, with three clasps,
for pibroch, at Northern Meeting; Gold Medal for
pibroch at Argyllshire Meeting and the Dunstaffnage
Cup; Crieff Gold Medal for pibroch, 1923; first prize
"American Clansmen's Medal" for pibroch, 1926;
Brymay Challenge Trophy (Cowal), 1921 and 1926;
the Glen Caladh Challenge Trophy (Cowal) 1925 and
1926, besides being one of the leading prize-winners
at the Gatherings held at Bridge of Allan, Callander,
Luss, Strathendrick, Lochaber, Aboyne, and Braemar.

RICHARDSON, JAMES, V.C.—Piper, 16th Canadian Scottish.
See chapter on "Pipers of Canadian Forces."

Ross, George.—Pipe-Major, 2nd Battn. the Black Watch, 1887-1905. An excellent, "all-round" player and a composer of several popular pipe melodies, with prizes won at the Dublin, Oban, and Northern Meetings, including the Gold Medals of the two last-named places; and the Scottish Pipers' Society Badge. After taking part in the South African War, Ross was one of the British Army representatives at the Australian Commonwealth Inauguration Ceremony, 1902.

Ross, William.—Piper, 42nd Royal Highlanders, 1839-54. Took part in Crimean War. Composer of "The Alma." In 1855 was appointed piper to H.M. Queen Victoria. Published in 1876 a collection of pipe music to which was prefixed an essay on "The Bagpipe and its Music" by the Rev. Dr Norman MacLeod. Ross died in 1891 deplored by the Queen in her "Journal."

Ross, William (Ross-shire). — Pipe-Major, 42nd Royal Highlanders. Brother of George, mentioned above. Left the 2nd Battn. the Black Watch in 1894 for the pipe-majorship of the 1st Battn. Seaforth Highlanders. Served in the Egyptian and Sudan Campaigns 1898, and was wounded at Atbara while playing "Cabar Feidh" to his battalion in action. Was appointed Pipe-Major, Permanent Staff, Highland Light Infantry, in 1900. Was chosen to accompany the Scottish Curlers to Canada, 1911-12. Retired from the army in 1912 but soon after rejoined the Territorial Service—4th Battn. Royal Scots (Queen's Edinburgh)—with which he continued till 1916 (Home Service). Though not fond of competition, Pipe-Major Ross is regarded as an excellent piper, in token of which his Gold Medal won in 1903 at Oban is testimony.

Ross, William.—Pipe-Major, 2nd Scots Guards. Born at Glenstrathfarrar in 1879. Learned to play from his father and mother, both skilful pipers. In 1896 enlisted in the Scots Guards. Took part in the South African War, for which he holds the Queen Victoria

and King Edward VII. Medals, the former with six
clasps, the latter with two.   In the Great War Pipe-
Major Ross served with his battalion from the
commencement till June 1918, when owing to acute
rheumatism, he was invalided out of the Service.   Is
now Instructor of School for Army Pipers, Edinburgh
Castle.

In four successive years he held the title of Champion
All-Round Piper of Scotland, a record entitling him
to the Macdonald Shield.   Seven times winner of the
Championship Gold Clasp at Inverness; and eight times
winner of the Lochaber Gold Medal with six clasps.
To Ross has also been awarded the following much
coveted distinctions: Dunmore Gold Star, Scottish
Pipers' Society's Badge, Crieff's Gold Medal for " All-
Round Championship," Highland Society's Gold Medal,
Argyllshire Gathering's Silver Medal, Newcastle
Champion's Gold Medal, Pibroch Society's Gold Medal
and Clasp, Dunstaffnage Silver Cup, Lindsay Trophy,
Culter Trophy, twice winner of Lawrie Trophy and
thrice winner of Braemar Championship.   Has published
book of pipe tunes.   Ross's handsome figure in Scotland's premier regiment, his prominence in all musical
events before H.M. the King—who honoured the piper
with the Medal of the Royal Victorian Order—have
made Ross known to most Londoners.   To a still wider
circle he is, thanks to his gramophone records, equally
well known.   Such widely different periodicals as the
British *Boy's Own Paper* and the French *Nos Loisirs*
have extolled the genius and portrayed the person of
the genial piper.

SMITH, JOHN.—Pipe-Major, 93rd Highlanders.   *See* chapter
on " Gordon Highlanders."

STEWART, JAMES. — Piper, Cameron Highlanders.   *See*
chapter on " Cameron Highlanders."

SUTHERLAND, JAMES.—Pipe-Major, 1st Battn. Seaforth Highlanders 1893-95.   Saw service in Egypt.   Pipe-Major
Edinburgh O.T.C. 1908.   Was in 1912 appointed

Pipe-Major of 5th Royal Scots (T.F.) Queen's Edinburgh. In 1915, on the eve of the battalion's departure for Gallipoli was rejected for active service and transferred to the Reserve, becoming Pipe-Major of the 1st Volunteer Battn. Royal Scots. Composed "3rd Seaforth's Farewell to Cairo." Is regarded as an excellent piper and Highland dancer. Winner of medals at Oban, Inverness, and elsewhere.

TAYLOR, GEORGE DOUGLAS.—Well-known in London as a teacher of Highland dancing, Pipe-Major Taylor was Pipe-Major of the 4th Royal Scots (Queen's Edinburgh Rifles) from 1902-4, and Pipe Instructor to the Royal Caledonian School at Bushey from 1904-8. In August 1914 was appointed Pipe-Major of the 7th Battn. King's Own Scottish Borderers. At the battle of Loos he was severely wounded while acting as stretcher-bearer and was discharged in consequence of these wounds.

TAYLOR, JAMES.—Son of Henderson Taylor, a well-known piper of Reay, Caithness. Entered the 1st Battn. Seaforth Highlanders as a piper in 1895 and took part in the Crete Expedition, 1897, and in the Soudan Campaign. In 1904 was transferred to the 1st Battn. Highland Light Infantry as Pipe-Major. Posted to 3rd Highland Light Infantry in 1910; demobilised 1919. Pipe-Major Taylor is one of the finest of pibroch players and is much in demand as a judge in piping competitions. Pipe-Major Taylor has several tuneful compositions to his credit, two of which, "The Medium Spree" and "Dreghorn Castle," are in the Cowal Collection.

TAYLOR, WILLIAM.—A brother of James Taylor noted above. Joined 1st Battn. Seaforth Highlanders in 1894 and saw service in Malta, Crete, and the Soudan. In 1900 was promoted pipe-major, and in 1909 was posted to 3rd Battalion. In 1914 was appointed Pipe-Major to the 7th Battalion. Was mentioned in despatches for his work as a stretcher-bearer, and awarded the Meritorious Service Medal and the Croix de Guerre. Since 1919 has been instructor of piping and dancing to the Queen Victoria School, Dunblane. Won the Gold Medal at Oban 1920.

THOMSON, COLIN.—Pipe - Major, 1st Battn. Argyll and Sutherland Highlanders, 1894-1904; of 3rd Battn. Seaforth Highlanders, 1904-8, when he transferred to the 5th (Territorial) Battalion, with which he remained until the close of the Great War. A pupil of Ranald Mackenzie and of "Sandy" Cameron, Thomson quickly proved his abilities by winning most of the prizes in the North between 1890 and 1894; in 1894 he won the Gold Medal at the Northern Meeting for marches, was 2nd in 1892 and 1st in 1893; at Stamford Bridge in 1895 he won 2nd prize for pibroch, and 1st for marches, strathspeys, and reels in 1896. Marches, schottisches, and jigs are favourite subjects, and of these he has composed and published a collection.

WEATHERSPOON, JAMES, D.C.M.—Piper, 42nd Highlanders. *See* chapter on " The Black Watch."

NOTE BY THE EARL OF DARTMOUTH, K.C.B., ON THE PICTURE AT PATSHULL HOUSE REPRESENTING PARADE OF TROOPS AT TANGIER IN 1683

THE picture represents an incident described in the *History of the Grenadier Guards*, vol. i., p. 259, and is referred to in the Dartmouth Papers (*Hist. MSS. Commission*), vol. i., p. 94.

It took place on 26th September 1683, or on the following day.

"Lord Dartmouth was requested by the Alcade (the leader of the Moors) to grant him a personal interview, whereupon the new governor took the opportunity of drawing out all the available troops of the garrison, and in order to make a still greater impression upon the Moor, he took advantage of the recent arrival of new clothing for the Scots and Trelawny's regiments to dress up his seamen in red coats, and paraded upwards of 4000 men in line in addition to leaving strong guards at other posts. The line of troops extended from Pole's Fort on the right to Fountain's Fort on the left, while the seamen—about 1000 strong—drew up from thence along the sands by the seaside."

In the picture Lord Dartmouth's own battalion of seamen—200 strong—"clothed in white and blue striped linen, and with four Union flags," are on the right of the line on the sands (Dartmouth Papers).

Next to them stand "two other battalions of 200 men each," clothed with such clothes as the Scots shall furnish, with eight colours of Colonel Trelawny's Regiment (Dartmouth Papers).

On the left of the line Sir John Berry's battalion "clothed with the colours Mr Hewers shall give, with four Irish colours" (Dartmouth Papers).

THE MOLE OF TANGIER IN 1684.

From a picture by Stoop in the possession of the Earl of Dartmouth.

These Irish colours are St George's Cross "fimbriated" with a white edging on a blue ground, and appear to be exactly similar to the colours of the Coldstream Guards at that date.

The whole of the seamen were under the command of Sir John Berry.

Lord Dartmouth himself seems to be viewing the Alcade—behind him is an escort of the Tangier Horse, now the 1st Royal Dragoons. Their guidon is crimson charged with the Royal Crown. On their return home the Royal cipher was added below the Crown to the Colonel's colour.

On the left of the picture is the garrison of Tangier. First comes a composite regiment of five companies called "the King's Battalion." It was originally composed of two companies of the King's Regiment of Guards, and one company of the Coldstream Regiment with two companies from Portsmouth, Plymouth, the Tower, and the Isle of Wight. Two colours were issued to the two companies of the 1st Guards, the Red Cross of St George on a white ground, with a royal badge on each colour and one blue colour with St George's Cross fimbriated white to the Coldstream company, in June 1680, when they left England.

In the picture there appears to be only one colour of the 1st Guards and four of the Coldstream ones. Renewals may have taken place in the interval.

The battalion next in line has eight colours (or four?): St George's Cross fimbriated white, with three white rays issuing from each corner of the Cross, on a dark green field, and is, therefore, Colonel Kirke's Regiment (now the Queen's), as these colours correspond to the description given of them by one, Nathan Brooks, who published an account of a review held at Putney Heath the following year, when this regiment and the others in the picture were present.

Next to them, coming down the hill, are the Royal Scots, with eight colours, the Colonel's colour white, the other seven St Andrew's Cross, white on a blue ground. Each of these colours had a golden thistle and crown, with the motto " Nemo me impune lacessit " in gold letters round the thistle,

on the centre of the Cross; but the picture is on too small a
scale to show this.   It does look, however, as if the Colonel's
white colour had gold splotches on it.

In the fort is the third battalion—which is Trelawny's
(now the King's Own).   There are eight colours, one plain
red, the Colonel's, the others of the same character as the
others.

The Dartmouth Papers describe the seamen as carrying
the colours of Trelawny's Regiment, so probably new colours
were sent out to replace the old ones, and the ones so carried
answer to Nathan Brook's description of the colours of the
regiment in 1684 when it became H.R.H. the Duchess of
York and Albany's Regiment of Foot, viz., St George's
Cross fimbriated on a yellow ground, with rays issuing from
the centre of the Cross.   Perhaps it was on account of the
change of name that new colours were sent out, but they
look much the same as those in the fort, except for the red
Colonel's colour.

It is noticeable that the battalions of soldiers have the
pike men in the centre and musketeers on the flanks, while
the seamen's battalions have no pike men.

The details of the picture seem amazingly accurate.

The King's battalion on its return was made into
additional Grenadier companies for the Guards at Lord
Dartmouth's suggestion—one to each regiment.

INDEX

S

M'Lennan, Pipe-Major Donald, Seaforths, 97; record of, 257

M'Lennan, Donald G., 258

M'Lennan, Pipe-Major George S., Gordons, 97; record of, 258

M'Lennan, Lieut. John, 257, 258

M'Lennan, Piper Kenneth, D.C.M., H.L.I., 120

MacLeod, Lord (John Mackenzie), H.L.I., 111

M'Leod, Pipe-Major Alexander, 26th Cameronians, 259

M'Leod, Pipe-Major Dan, Black Watch, 107, 109

M'Leod, Pipe-Major John, Argyll and Sutherland Highlanders, regiment proud of, 179-181; record of, 259

M'Leod, Piper Kenneth, D.C.M., Gordons, 152; record of, 259

M'Leod, Pipe-Major Norman, Seaforths, 130; record of, 259

M'Leod, Rev. Dr, 262

M'Leod of Dunvegan, 30

MacMaster, Pipe-Corporal D., Black Watch, 109; awarded Panama Medal, 110

Macmillan, Pipe-Major, D.C.M., Gordons, with the "Royals" in France, 63

MacMillan, Piper, Otago Rifles, 231

Macmillan, Pipe-Major Donald, Lovat Scouts, 191, 259

MacMillan, Piper Jack, Otago Rifles, 231

M'Minn, Piper, M.M., K.O.S.B., 82

M'Nab, Pipe-Major, R.S.F., 66

MacNaughton, Alexander, raises 200 Highland bowmen, 24

M'Naughton, Piper Peter, Otago Rifles, 231

M'Nee, Piper Peter, Black Watch, 105; killed, 106

M'Neice, Pipe-Major, with battle cruiser *New Zealand*, 241

M'Neill, Major, 78th Highlanders, 171

M'Neill, Col. Malcolm, Argyll and Sutherland Highlanders, 188

M'Niven, Piper James, 188

M'Phail, Pipe-Major, Gordons, 145

M'Phedran, Pipe-Major Archibald, H.L.I., 259

M'Phedran, Piper Archie, Scots Guards, recommended for and accepts Commission in a Yorks Battalion, 59

Macpherson, Gen. Duncan, Gordons, 148

MacPherson, Cluny, Chief of his Clan, 23

Macpherson, Piper G. B., 13th (Royal Highlanders) Canadians, 219

Macpherson, Corporal Malcolm, Black Watch, 93, 94

Macpherson, Pipe-Corporal Murdoch, Scots Guards, 55

Macpherson, Corporal Samuel, Black Watch, 93, 94

MacRae, Clan, 123

M'Rae, Piper Andrew, Camerons, 161

Macrae, Angus, Blair-Atholl, 259

Macrae, Pipe-Major Donald, 72nd and 78th Highlanders, 259

M'Sporran, Pipe-Major Duncan, Argyll and Sutherland Highlanders, 187, 260

M'Tavish, Pipe-Major Alexander, Black Watch, 99, 100

MacWilliam, H. D., 94

Mahdi, the, 150

Maitland, Piper John, K.O.S.B., 79

Malcolm, Peter, xii

Mar, Earl of, 46

Martin, Pipe-Sergeant Alexander, D.C.M., 57, 58; death of, 59

Mary, H.R.H. Princess, 67

Mathias, Colonel, Gordons, 150

Mathieson, Pipe-Major D. B., D.C.M., Seaforths, 135, 260

Mathieson, Pipe Lance-Corpl. J. M., South African Scottish, late Royal Scots, 234

Matheson, Pipe-Major, Royal Scots, 260

Matheson, Pipe-Major Dugald, Camerons, 165, 260

the 78th, 130, 132; of Camerons, 157, 158, 160; "Badge of Scotland," 200; of Irish pipers, 209, 210

Piper, the, memorial to Roman, xi; uniform and duty of, 3; earliest record of Pipe-Major, 5; status of army piper, 4-16; and the H.Q. Staff, 6; sanction for, 7, 61; kilted, 9, 10; the present day, 11; Scot *versus* English, 12; in barracks and camp, 16; regimental customs, 17; and the Scots Guards, 19; big demand for, 23, 24; clan pipers, 23; pay, 26; mischief-loving, 29; Irish *v.* Scottish, 30; and the Great War, 43; Greek, Serb, and Bulgar, 65; edict against, 89; Irish, 208; promoted to commissioned ranks of the Scots Guards, 59; K.O.S.B., 82; Black Watch, 107; Seaforths, 135; Argyll and Sutherland Highlanders, 185; London Scottish, 197; Liverpool Scottish, 201; Canadian Forces, 222; Camerons, 231; South African Scottish, 235

Planner, Piper Leonard A., Argyll and Sutherland Highlanders, 185

Playford, John, 27

Pondicherry, the Siege of, 38, 125

Porteous twins, the, pipers of London Scottish, 197

Porto Novo, 32, 112

Portsmouth, Royal Naval Barracks, 243

Pratt, Piper, London Scottish, 198

Princess Patricia's Canadian Light Infantry, 218, 219, 220

Princess Louise's (Argyll and Sutherland) Highlanders of Canada, 217

Purgavie, Sergeant-Piper, K.O.S.B. at the Dardanelles, 44, 79, 80

Queen's Own Cameron Highlanders, pipers as marksmen, 3; first to use green doublet, 9; regimental tunes of, 16, 43, 48; at Waterloo, 42, 43; customs of, 157, 158; pipers of, 160; grant of title, 161; at Atbara, 163; in the Great War, 164, 165; heavy loss of pipers, 166

Queen's Own Cameron Highlanders of Canada, 217

Queensland Battalion, 42nd (Australian), 227

Quhele, Clan, 23

Rae, Piper, Liverpool Scottish, 201

Raglan, General Lord, 160

Redmond, John, 211

Reed, Colonel John, 204

Rees, L. E. L., a survivor of Lucknow, 130

Regimental customs, 16-21

Reid, Piper James, executed, 31

Reid, Pipe-Major Robert, 261

Richardson, Piper James, V.C., 16th Canadian Scottish, 220, 221, 261

Richmond, Duchess of, ball at Brussels, 141

Robb, Piper, Argyll and Sutherland Highlanders, 177

Roberts, F.M. Earl, 146

Robertson, Sergeant-Piper, D.C.M., Royal Scots, 63

Robertson, Piper, M.M., Cameronians, 89

Robertson, Piper George, 13th (Royal Highlanders), Canadians, 219

Robertson, Piper H., 13th (Royal Highlanders), Canadians, 219

Ross, Pipe-Major, H.L.I., 117

Ross, Pipe-Major Alexander, Scots Guards, 57

Ross, Mr Andrew, 53

Ross, Captain Edouard, 108

Ross, Pipe-Major George, Black Watch, in South Africa, 59, 262

Ross, Piper Munro, 42nd Battalion, Australians, 228

Ross, Pte. Roderick, Scots Guards, 55, 56, 59

Ross, Pipe-Major William (Rossshire), 42nd Royal Highlanders, in Great War, 59; record of, 262

Ross, Piper William, 42nd Royal Highlanders, composition of, 42; piper to Queen Victoria, 100

Appendix

The following is a short historical note on the eleven regular Scottish regiments serving in the British Army at the time *The Piper in Peace and War* was written. This brief summary lists the tartan worn by pipers; the regimental marches for pipes only; and affiliations to each unit.

The Scots Guards

TARTAN WORN BY PIPERS: Royal Stewart

REGIMENTAL MARCHES: Quick time: *Highland Laddie*

Slow time: *Garb of Old Gaul*

AFFILIATED REGIMENTS:

Canada: The Winnipeg Grenadiers

Australia: 3rd Bn., The Royal Australian Regiment

PRESENT STATUS: Part of the Guards Division

The Royal Scots

TARTAN WORN BY PIPERS: Royal Stewart

REGIMENTAL MARCHES: Quick time: *Dumbartons Drums*

Slow time: *Garb of Old Gaul*

AFFILIATED REGIMENTS:

The Canadian Scottish Regiment (Princess Mary's)

The 10th, Princess Mary's Own Gurkha Rifles

PRESENT STATUS: Part of the Scottish Division.

The Black Watch

TARTAN WORN BY PIPERS: Royal Stewart
REGIMENTAL MARCH: *Highland Laddie*
AFFILIATED REGIMENTS:
The Tyneside Scottish (T.A.)
Canada: The Black Watch (The Royal Highland Regt.) of Canada
       59th A.A. Regt., R.C.A. (The Lanark and Renfrew Scottish)
Australia: 30th Bn. (The New South Wales Scottish Regiment)
       42nd Bn. (The Capricornia Regiment)
New Zealand: The 1st Armoured Car Regt. (New Zealand Scottish)
South Africa: The Transvaal Scottish

PRESENT STATUS: Part of the Scottish Division.

The Highland Light Infantry

TARTAN WORN BY PIPERS: Mackenzie
REGIMENTAL MARCHES:
In column: *Blue Bonnets O'er the Border*
Close column: *Highland Laddie*
Marching into Barracks: *Scotland the Brave*
AFFILIATED REGIMENTS:
Canada: The Highland Light Infantry of Canada

PRESENT STATUS: Amalgamated in 1959 with the Royal Scots
                   Fusiliers to form the Royal Highland Fusiliers,
                   which is now part of the Scottish Division.

The Seaforth Highlanders

TARTAN WORN BY PIPERS: Mackenzie
REGIMENTAL MARCH: *Pibroch 'O Donuil Dhu*
AFFILIATED REGIMENTS:

Canada:	The Seaforth Highlanders of Canada
	The Pictou Highlanders
Australia:	27th Bn. (South Australian Scottish Regiment)
New Zealand:	The Wellington Regt. (City of Wellington's Own)

PRESENT STATUS: Amalgamated in 1961 with the Queen's Own Cameron Highlanders to form the Queen's Own Highlanders, now part of the Scottish Division.

The Royal Scots Fusiliers

TARTAN WORN BY PIPERS: Erskine
REGIMENTAL MARCH: *Highland Laddie*
AFFILIATED REGIMENTS:

Canada:	The 54th Light A.A. Regiment, R.C.A. (Scots Fusiliers of Canada)
Australia:	The 23/21 Battalion (The City of Geelong Regt. and the Victorian Rangers)
South Africa:	Prince Alfred's Guard

PRESENT STATUS: Amalgamated in 1959 with the Highland Light Infantry to form the Royal Highland Fusiliers, which is now part of the Scottish Division.

The King's Own Scottish Borderers

TARTAN WORN BY PIPERS: Royal Stewart
REGIMENTAL MARCH: *Blue Bonnets O'er the Border*
AFFILIATED REGIMENTS:
Canada: The New Brunswick Scottish Regiment
Australia: 25th Bn. (The Darling Downs Regiment)
                  34th Bn. (The Illawarra Regiment)

PRESENT STATUS: Part of the Scottish Division.

The Cameronians (Scottish Rifles)

TARTAN WORN BY PIPERS: Douglas
REGIMENTAL MARCHES: 1st Bn. *Kenmuir's On An' Awa'*
                      2nd Bn. *The Gathering of the Grahams*

AFFILIATED REGIMENTS:
Canada: The Perth Regiment
Australia: 26th Bn. (The Logan and Albert Regiment)
New Zealand: The Otago and Southland Regiment
South Africa: The Witwatersrand Rifles
                  The 7th Gurkha Rifles

PRESENT STATUS: Disbanded in 1968.

The Gordon Highlanders

TARTAN WORN BY PIPERS: Gordon
REGIMENTAL MARCH: *Cock o' the North*
                    (Until 1932, *Highland Laddie*)
AFFILIATED REGIMENTS:
Canada: 48th Highlanders of Canada
Australia: 5th Bn. (The Victoria Scottish Regiment)
South Africa: The Queen's Own Cape Town Highlanders

PRESENT STATUS: Part of the Scottish Division.

The Queen's Own Cameron Highlanders

TARTAN WORN BY PIPERS: Cameron of Erracht
              (In 1934 permission to wear Royal Stewart)
REGIMENTAL MARCH: *Pibroch 'O Donuil Dhu*
AFFILIATED REGIMENTS:
Canada: The Cameron Highlanders of Ottawa (M.G.)
                The Queen's Own Cameron Highlanders
                of Canada
Australia: 16th Bn. (The Cameron Highlanders
                of Western Australia)
                37/39 Battalion (The Henty Regiment)
                52nd Battalion (The Gippsland Regiment)
New Zealand: The Otago and Southland Regiment

PRESENT STATUS: Amalgamated in 1961 with the Seaforth Highland-
                 ers to form the Queen's Own Highlanders, now
                 part of the Scottish Division.

Argyll and Sutherland Highlanders

TARTAN WORN BY PIPERS: Government, or 42nd tartan.
REGIMENTAL MARCHES: 1st Bn. *The Campbells are Coming*
                       2nd Bn. *Highland Laddie*
AFFILIATED REGIMENTS:
Canada: The Argyll and Sutherland Highlanders of Canada
                The Calgary Highlanders
Australia: 41st Battalion (The Byron Regiment)

PRESENT STATUS: Part of the Scottish Division.